1956 AND ALL THAT

Is it possible to look back beyond anger?

It is said that British drama was shockingly lifted out of the doldrums by the 'revolutionary' appearance of John Osborne's *Look Back in Anger* at the Royal Court in May 1956. But had the theatre been as ephemeral and effeminate as the Angry Young Men claimed? Was the era of Terence Rattigan and 'Binkie' Beaumont as repressed and closeted as it seems?

In this bold and fascinating challenge to the received wisdom of the last forty years of theatrical history, Dan Rebellato uncovers a different story altogether. It is one where Britain's declining Empire and increasing panic over the 'problem' of homosexuality played a crucial role in the construction of an enduring myth of the theatre. By going back to primary sources and rigorously questioning all assumptions, Rebellato has rewritten the history of the making of modern British drama.

Plays discussed include: *Look Back in Anger, The Entertainer, Personal Enemy, Epitaph for George Dillon* – John Osborne; *The Kitchen, Chicken Soup With Barley, Roots, I'm Talking About Jerusalem* – Arnold Wesker; *Johnson Over Jordan* – J.B. Priestly; *Each His Own Wilderness* – Doris Lessing; *Serjeant Musgrave's Dance* – John Arden; *Cockpit* – Bridget Boland; *The Shadow Factory* – Anne Ridler; *A Taste of Honey* – Shelagh Delaney; *Salad Days* – Julian Slade; and *Valmouth* – Sandy Wilson.

Dan Rebellato lectures in Drama and Theatre at Royal Holloway, University of London.

1956 AND ALL THAT

The making of
modern British drama

Dan Rebellato

London and New York

First published 1999
by Routledge
11 New Fetter Lane, London EC4P 4EE

Simultaneously published in the USA and Canada
by Routledge
29 West 35th Street, New York, NY 10001

Typeset in Sabon by Routledge
Printed and bound in Great Britain by Biddles Ltd, Guildford and
King's Lynn

British Library Cataloguing in Publication Data
A catalogue record for this book is available from the British Library

Library of Congress Cataloging in Publication Data
A catalogue record for this book has been requested

ISBN 0–415–18938–1 (hbk)
ISBN 0–415–18939–X (pbk)

CONTENTS

ILLUSTRATIONS

Figures

ACKNOWLEDGEMENTS

I would like to express my warm thanks to the Society for Theatre Research for a research award which made it possible to include photographs in the book. Suzanne Collins at Routledge was immensely helpful in tracking down illustrations. Special thanks must go to Richard Mangan at The Raymond Mander and Joe Mitchenson Theatre Collection for his kindness and patience in answering queries and providing several photographs; other help in the location of photographic material came from Lian at Advertising Archives, Lydia Cresswell-Jones at Sotheby's, Janet Birkett at the Theatre Museum, Norma Campbell-Vickers at the John Vickers Theatre Collection, and Frederick Bentham who kindly located a photograph of his Light Console from his personal collection.

For their help in the development of the ideas in this book I want to thank Lucie Wright, Adam Mills, Jackie Clune, Stella Bruzzi, Alison Barker, Ben Payne and Kirstie Macdonald for their great and varied contributions; Peter Coulson for starting everything off; the British Academy for funding the research; Royal Holloway for giving me a sabbatical to complete the book; Ellie Roper 'without whom..."'; the various readers, especially Neil Bartlett, Richard Cave, Alan Sinfield and Clive Barker, whose encouragement and criticisms were stimulating and generous; Peter Burton and Adrian Wright for wickedly useful information; Talia Rodgers, my editor at Routledge, for enthusiastic, helpful and patient emails – her clear-sighted advice always precise and welcome; David Bradby's enthusiasm was infectious and his comments on individual chapters serenely illuminating; most of all, I want to thank Jacky Bratton, whose lucid and acute judgements (however painful) have always been for the immeasurable good of this book, and who has been simply an inspiration.

INTRODUCTION

'Come with us, Larry and me, to the National,' [Tynan]
had said to me earlier. 'And make history.' 'Thank you,' I
replied. 'I've already made it.'

(John Osborne, *Damn You, England*, 155)

By 1956, British theatre was in a terrible state. The West End was
dominated by a few philistine theatre managers, cranking out
emotionally repressed, middle-class plays, all set in drawing rooms
with French windows, as vehicles for stars whose only talent was
to wield a cigarette holder and a cocktail glass while wearing a
dinner jacket. While war and suffering raged around it, the theatre
continued to reflect a tiny segment of society, and ignored the rest.
Reluctant Debutantes held Cocktail Parties in Pink Rooms and
Confidential Clerks spent Saints Days in Living Rooms at Separate
Tables, all of them talking Dry Rot. Post-war hopes for a Poetic
Drama revival, boosted by the fashionable success of Fry and
Eliot, soon foundered on the plays' lack of dramatic substance.
Led by Kenneth Tynan, theatregoers bayed for a vigorous contem-
porary theatre, but despaired; where could anything better be
found?

Then, on 8 May 1956, came the breakthrough. At the Royal
Court, *Look Back in Anger*, John Osborne's fiery blast against the
establishment burst onto the stage, radicalising British theatre
overnight. And who would have thought it would happen at this
crumbling little theatre in Sloane Square? In the hands of the
English Stage Company with its eccentric council of management?
But on 8 May 1956, everything changed. New, youthful audiences
flocked to the Royal Court to hear Jimmy Porter express their
own hopes and fears. At a stroke, the old well-made dramatists
were shown up as stale and cobwebbed, and most of them left to

1

ply their trade in films. A new wave of dramatists sprang up in Osborne's wake; planting their colours on British stages, speaking for a generation who had for so long been silent, they forged a living, adult, vital theatre.

A good thing

This trite little account of the impact of the Royal Court dominates virtually everything written on modern British theatre. Even if not always adhered to in detail the broader outlines are there, and all accounts use some of its figures, its images, its tone and its metaphors. From the briefest encyclopaedia entry to book-length study, in A-level notes and autobiography, we read that British theatre was flimsy and artificial, that serious-minded people yearned for something new, that *Look Back in Anger* ushered in a renaissance of British theatre, and that the people were grateful. In short, for the theatre 1956 was 'A Good Thing'.

This book offers a counter-reading of this period. I am not trying to suggest that nothing of note or value happened in the mid-fifties, nor do I want to shift the turning point, to find such and such a premiere or event and proclaim it the decade's pivotal moment. On the contrary, I think the events usually cited were decisive; I want to argue that this change has been badly misunderstood, but change there certainly was.

In fact there seems to have been so decisive a change that commentators trying to look back beyond anger encounter a curious phenomenon. In the mid sixties, J.C. Trewin writes,

> it is not easy now to look back over a gulf that seems as deep as that between the Swaying Stone and the Trembling Spur, to a London that had not heard of the point of deviation or Beckett or Osborne, and where the Royal Court was an unfashionable address on the fringe.
>
> (1965, 57)

He also calls pre-Osborne theatre 'the primeval world' (11). In 1963, John Russell Taylor – only half-jokingly – takes us 'as far back into the mists of antiquity as 1951' (16).

Why should it be so hard to remember British theatre before 1956? Perhaps one reason is that so many books start with *Look Back in Anger* and ignore what came before. The books are titled things like Taylor's *Anger and After*, Lloyd Evans's *Plays in*

Review: 1956–1980, and Hayman's *British Theatre Since 1955*. The subtitle of Marowitz, Milne and Hale's selection from *Encore* announces the coverage '1956–1963', even though *Encore* started in 1954. Michelene Wandor's *Look Back in Gender* claims to cover 'post-war British drama', but the war seems to have ended in 1956, since the first British play she considers is *Look Back in Anger*.

The result, as John Elsom has said, is to consign everything that went before to a 'pre-Osborne dark age' (1979, 74). *Look Back in Anger* marks an impermeable boundary, behind which no one can go. It is a boundary marked '8 May 1956'. Virtually everyone writing on the era mentions this date.[1] But why? There are, after all, many decisive moments in theatre history, but very few come so obsessively datestamped.

The '8 May 1956' is not just an inert historical marker; it is animated, made to play a role by the discourses that throng around it. Its precision supports the image of the revival of serious theatre as 'sudden' (Kernodle and Kernodle 1978, 176; Hinchliffe 1974, 46), as happening 'overnight' (Wellwarth 1965, 222; Rusinko 1989, 1). Although we know that the play crawled through the summer and only picked up after a televised excerpt in mid-October, we read that the play was an 'explosion' (Taylor 1963, 16; Harwood 1984, 305). This is a complicated and polyvalent image, but an immediate effect of calling *Look Back in Anger* an explosion is to emphasise by contrast the supposed silence which preceded it. As one writer puts it, *Look Back in Anger* 'was not so much produced as detonated in the quietness of Sloane Square' (Vargas 1960, 210).

This quietness is constituted in and reinforced by an unctuously *faux-naïf* quality adopted by many commentators trying to imagine life before Osborne. This is John Russell Taylor:

> the outlook for the young dramatist must have looked fairly grim around the beginning of 1956. There was hardly a straw in the wind, since it would have been an optimist indeed who relied too strongly on the English Stage Company or Theatre Workshop to save the day. Anyway, managers and critics would ask each other periodically, where was the new dramatic talent to be found? And what sort of reception would the public give it if and when it did emerge? – none too enthusiastic if the experience of Whiting and Cannan was

anything to go by. Then, on 8 May 1956 came the revolution.

(1963, 28)

The style constitutes the alleged silence through a kind of verbally bated breath, before unleashing the pay-off of *Look Back in Anger*. Tynan writes 'we begin in the dust-bowl of Shaftesbury Avenue, a wasteland owing its aridity to improvident speculators. Famine seems imminent, when suddenly, to everyone's amazement, life blossoms in the virgin lands of Sloane Square and the East End' (1964, 16).

What both that explosion in the silence and those flowers in the desert have in common is an image of a repressed force bursting out. The phrase 'breakthrough' is common (Williams 1964, 304; Hinchliffe 1974, 59); one critic says the play 'breached the dam' (Tynan 1967, 13), another that it 'breached the barrier' (Watt 1957, 59); more prosaically, Tynan compares *Look Back in Anger* to a burp in public (1964, 55). Hobson calls a chapter on the period 'The Great Uprising' (1984); Elsom calls his 'Breaking Out' (1979). According to Kitchin, 'something was banking up under the stodgy surface of life in mid-century England' (1962, 99).

These repressive images suggest an underlying continuity, that the spirit of Anger was always there, repressed until 8 May 1956. Consequently, the old era becomes exclusively characterised by the absence of Anger, and the new era by its presence. 1956 becomes year zero, and time seems to flow both forward and backwards from it. Tynan describes the first part of his collection of reviews as covering 'the events *leading up to and away from* that memorable upheaval' (1964, 16, my emphasis). Before discussing the New Wave, Taylor announces his intention to look at 'one or two forerunners' (1963, 16), as if the previous fifty years of drama were just vamping till ready. Between them, silence and repression throw a pall of irony over the prior generation, as if modern British theatre divides into two eras, 'Before the Court' and 'After Devine'.

This has had startling effects on the reputations of those luckless enough to have been writing in the 1940s. Critics have written of Terence Rattigan with a kind of amused, patronising tolerance, complimenting his plays as they might compliment a child's drawing: Taylor, for example, heartily calls him a 'conscientious and intelligent craftsman who specialised in solid emotional dramas with good meaty acting roles' (1968, 15). Since after

1956, none of these qualities were considered terribly valuable, this was to damn him with faint praise. Rattigan seems to exist on borrowed time; *The Deep Blue Sea* is routinely judged against the standard of *Look Back in Anger* (Kitchin 1962, 102; Hewison 1988, 83–84; Innes 1992, 90–91; Sierz 1996, 138), as if Rattigan were *trying* to write an Osborne play. (It is more likely that Osborne was trying *not* to write *Separate Tables* (1954), the first part of which his play vaguely resembles. As Rattigan remarked at the premiere of *Look Back in Anger*, Osborne could have titled his play 'Look, Ma, I'm not Terence Rattigan' (Wansell 1995, 270).

The verse dramatists of the 1940s suffer particularly badly; it sometimes seems as if you can say anything you like about Christopher Fry. But then he, as Lumley put it, had 'slipped into the theatrical past; he belongs to the period immediately preceding the Royal Court Revolution of 1956' (1972, 288). Largely, it seems, because these writers happened to produce their work in the 1940s, the interest and excitement they generated can be dismissed as epiphenomenal: 'more a hangover from wartime romanticism than a new development', sniffs Hewison (1988, xiii); Tynan calls it a 'vogue' (1967, 12); Arden says it was 'at the top of *fashion*' (1960, 15, my emphasis), and Taylor describes the 1946 West End success of Ronald Duncan's *This Way To The Tomb* as 'modish' (1963, 20). They may have 'met the post-war desire for colour, fancy and escape' (Hinchliffe 1974, 33), but really their work catered only to 'academically elite audiences' (Rusinko 1989, 4), and 'remained obstinately on the margin of public taste' (Kitchin 1962, 59). (Note that the combined runs of *The Lady's Not For Burning* (1948), *The Cocktail Party* (1949), *Venus Observed* (1950), *Ring Around the Moon* (1950) and *The Dark is Light Enough* (1954) would have filled the Royal Court for a decade). Hewison suggests that *The Dark is Light Enough*'s 'more frugal use of verse exposed the underlying weakness of characterization and plot' (1988, 81), and then adds, 'Fry later moved to Hollywood,' as if he slunk away convinced of the paucity of his own talents.[2]

The scorn heaped on the period can sometimes make it puzzling that anyone ever went to a theatre that was 'constricted' (Elsom 1979, 7), 'stagnant' (Handley 1990, 63), and wreathed in 'cobwebs of despair'.[3] It also makes one wonder how anyone could possibly defend such a theatre. Unsurprisingly, few people have tried. Charles Duff's *The Lost Summer* argues that in the early fifties 'the standard of individual acting was very high, and that its playwrights knew more about the human heart and wrote with greater literacy than many of their successors of the late 1950s and 1960s' (1995, xii). Stephen Lacey suggests that one could rethink the history of the period, by seeing *Godot* as the turning point 'and, perhaps, revalue the work of John Whiting' (1995, 2). Reassessing writers from the forties and fifties like this is valuable and necessary, but it can fall into the same pattern as the denunciations. By whose standards does one judge these playwrights? We have already seen the unbreachability of 8 May 1956, and dragging a play across that date to reconsider it in the present may reveal a play of surprising interest, but it will be on the basis of its relation (precursor, forerunner, antecedent) to what came after it. Duff's judgement of Whiting bears this out: 'He was a precursor: his work shaped others. He was a considerable influence on major theatrical figures – but not, I think, one himself' (181–182). In other words, rather than amplify the theatre of the early fifties, such practices may further deepen the silence that hangs over it.

The repressive hypothesis

The general picture, then, describes a movement which had been silenced until it finally burst out at the Royal Court Theatre. Michel Foucault, in *The History of Sexuality*, names this historiographical figure 'the repressive hypothesis'. Opposing the popular view that the Victorians were repressed about sex, he argues that calling sexuality a secret, claiming that it was hidden, is actually part of the contemporary mechanism inciting us to talk ceaselessly about sex, and misrepresents a very different attitude to, and understanding of, sexual behaviour. What Foucault asks us to consider is whether the image of repression may legitimise not the breakthrough of an idea, but the production of a new one.

Key to this repression thesis is the assertion that audiences had without response been crying out for something better. Certain critics even suggest that they longed for something like the English Stage Company (e.g. Browne 1975, 1). If Lumley's description of theatre in the early fifties as 'dull', 'safety-first', 'stale', 'apathetic', 'a drawing-room museum' (1972, 256) is right, then it would not be surprising. There were, of course, complaints made about theatrical standards, but then we can *always* find voices raised in criticism. As John Whiting wryly observed, 'Every present time is always a bad time for the theatre' (1956, 6).

Far commoner than scorning the standard of new plays was a belief that naturalism was on its way out; Allardyce Nicoll judged before the war that 'the prose drama [...] is dying or dead' (1938, 61). Similar sentiments were voiced by George Devine (see p. 95), Ashley Dukes (1942, 246), and Raymond Williams, who described Eliot as pointing the 'solution' to the limitations of naturalist drama (1952, 246). J. C. Trewin confidently cites John Harrison of the Nottingham Playhouse to declare that 'The future lies with the Theatre Theatrical' (1953, 215). None of these proclamations came to pass, though I don't note this in any spirit of derision. Hindsight can be cruel, and there is a curious pathos to find this recognised by Trewin alongside a spectacularly faulty prediction, in an article looking back at 1956:

> posterity has a trick of looking down its nose, giving a patronising sigh. Even so, I find it hard to believe that it will reject three plays that rise from the cloud-wrack of the last twelve months: *The Chalk Garden, Under Milk Wood* and *Romanoff and Juliet.*
>
> (1957, 6)

The impression that Osborne was the unknown answer to the theatregoer's prayer can only be given by selective quotation. The same is true of those farsighted individuals who appear unerringly to have discerned the true way forward. But who is this writing in 1950 prescribing for the theatre that 'we recover a few more social standards, a little more respect for neo-classicism, and a little more concern about rules and traditions' (5)? Step forward, Kenneth Peacock Tynan. While many books quote his famous attack on the theatre of 'Loamshire', far fewer remember the less accurate lines that end the article: 'the theatre must widen its scope, broaden its horizon so that Loamshire appears merely as the play-pen, not as the whole palace of drama. We need plays about cabmen and demigods, plays about warriors, politicians, and grocers' (1964, 32).

To promote the idea that the theatrical establishment repressed anger it is claimed that Tynan saved *Look Back in Anger* from 'an almost unanimous verdict of disapproval from the press' (Wickham 1962, 76; also Osborne 1991a, 21–22). Tony Richardson takes up this theme, remembering reviews which were 'almost universally disastrous' (1993, 78). By way of illustration, he cites the *Guardian*'s description of the play as 'frenzied preaching in an empty conventicle [...] numbness sets in', which indeed is thoroughly damning, though less so placed alongside the same review's 'it has enough tension, feeling and originality to make the choice understandable [...] must have awoken echoes in anyone who has not forgotten the frustrations of youth...I believe they have got a potential playwright at last' (Elsom 1981, 78). He also quotes *The Times* saying 'its total gesture is altogether inadequate' which is very bad, and rather worse than the full sentence which begins 'This first play has passages of good violent writing, but [...]' (Lloyd Evans and Lloyd Evans 1985, 51). Conversely, historians rarely recall that Tynan's review condemned the play as twenty minutes too long and deplored the 'painful whimsy of the final reconciliation scene' (1964, 42). Even the ringing final sentence ('It is the best young play of its decade') is qualified by that adjective 'young', a hesitation that led Osborne to call it 'the most hedging rave ever written' (quoted, Tynan 1988, 125).

The effect of all this is to cast a long shadow over the period before it. If we are to avoid the condescension of history, it is critical that we attend to its crucial differences from the styles and practices that succeeded it. It is this kind of historical revisioning that Foucault calls 'genealogy'. Rather than presume an essential continuity, genealogy 'finds that there is "something altogether different" behind things' (1977b, 142). Rather than read eras in the shadow of their demise, 'it must record the singularity of events outside of any monotonous finality' (139). And where these events present themselves as inevitable, it stresses their contingency (146).

This book will argue that the theatre of the forties and early fifties was quite unlike the theatre we have been told it was, that the theatrical revolution was motivated by different concerns from those conventionally proposed, and that the manner of its unfolding involved far-reaching transformations of the modes of theatrical production and reception. This is, then, not a celebration of country house, cocktail glass, or cigarette holder, which are metonyms used to suture a particular construction of mid-century British theatre. Instead, I hope to describe an unfamiliar theatre, with resonant and telling differences from our own.

The symbolic explosion of 8 May 1956 contains further clues to the concerns and anxieties of the New Wave. It has been shown how metaphors of war and revolution appear through the literature on this period (Lacey 1995, 1; Sierz 1996, 141). It is also striking how often the picture slips between suggesting that the theatre was changed by *Look Back in Anger*, and that it was destroyed by it. Alan Sillitoe writes, 'John Osborne didn't contribute to the British theatre: he set off a land-mine called *Look Back in Anger* and blew most of it up' (quoted, Taylor 1968, 185). Findlater describes the Court as keeping their 'explosive discovery [...] in reserve', suggesting that they saw Osborne more as ammunition than a playwright (1981, 18). Sandy Craig, using an image with a Foucaultian ambivalence between enlightenment and destruction, writes that *Look Back in Anger* was 'the torch that set the theatre alight' (1980, 13).

Indeed, a hostility to theatricality underpins everything marked by 8 May 1956. If Foucault has provided the historiography, it is Jacques Derrida whose textual theory places theatre in a chain of cultural concerns. In the controversy over Derrida's discussion of J.L. Austin's work one of the cruxes was the function of communication in theatre, and, crucially, vice versa. A concern over the hazards that theatricality can set for the theatre underpins the political stance and theatrical practice of the New Wave, and reveals a very different set of cultural affiliations than those ordinarily presumed, touching on the sense of cultural and imperial decline, the structures of arts funding, and the 'problem' of homosexuality.

As Foucault remarks, writing a history *in terms of* the present may simply reinforce conditions that obtain in the present. Many of the institutions shaped by the New Wave persist: the English Stage Company, the National Theatre, the Royal Shakespeare Company, and (just) the Arts Council. Generally, the moment of *Look Back in Anger* remains subliminally an example to aspire to. In this sense, writing an account of theatre in the fifties is also what Foucault calls a 'history of the present' (1977a, 31); writing a history of the present that shows, as genealogy at its best can, that things could have been different, may also be an *intervention* in the present. This may be thought a surprisingly critical account of the glorious revival of British drama; perhaps it is, but it's time we had one.

1

'WHY SHOULD I CARE?'

The politics of vital theatre

Vitality! / It matters more than personality!
Originality, or topicality! / For it's vitality!
That made all those top-liners tops!

Vitality! / They each had individuality!
But in reality, their speciality / Was a vitality!
Enough to make hits out of flops!
(from *Gay's the Word!*, 1951, Ivor Novello
and Alan Melville)[1]

The politics of *Look Back in Anger*, have generally been characterised as, if not explicitly aligned to one movement or other,
defiantly resistant. What it was resistant to, or where that resistance sprung from, has been far less easy to pin down.

The attitude of opposition was struck in Tynan's first review,
which praised the play's 'drift towards anarchy, the instinctive leftishness, the automatic rejection of "official" attitudes' (1964, 42).
There is already some confusion here in the uncomfortable yoking of
three rather different statements. Since then, this confusion has, if
anything, deepened. Some commentators fastened more on the sense
of 'instinctive leftishness', as we shall see. Others praised the anar-
chically oppositional character of the new movement. Some, like
Lindsay Anderson, felt the key interest of the new generation was
simply in relating 'directly to the political and social experience of its
audience' (*Serjeant Musgrave at the Court* 1990). Early on, a few
figures believed the new movement to be marking the emergence of a
specifically working-class British theatre. Raymond Williams criticised such claims (1968, 319), and Chambers and Prior insist that if
Look Back in Anger tells us anything, it is that 'Osborne had not the
slightest knowledge of working-class life' (1987, 36).

Several members of the New Wave claimed to be socialists and tried to define what it meant to them. Osborne wrote in *Reynold's News* that 'socialism is about people living together' (1994, 190). In his essay in the manifesto of the angry young men, *Declaration*, he suggested that 'socialism is an experimental idea, not a dogma; an attitude to truth and liberty, the way people should live and treat each other' (1957a, 83). Wesker announced that for him socialism meant 'a definite and humane attitude to the world and people around me' (Burton 1959, 24). Joan Littlewood declared herself in favour of 'that dull working class quality, optimism' (1959, 289). Osborne's grand-father once defined a socialist as 'a man who doesn't believe in raising his hat' (1957a, 83); Tynan commented approvingly, 'Osborne has never found a better definition of his own Socialism' (1964, 58). While these definitions are no doubt compatible with socialism, they hardly distinguish it from most other forms of political belief; but then, as Sinfield dryly observes, 'the new drama was not characterized by coherent political thought' (1983, 178).

Some were not clear that the New Wave was even broadly left-wing. Some believed, like John Whiting, that in *Roots*, Wesker was 'speaking up good and clear against the working class' (1960, 34). Whiting was no friend of the Court's work, but it is not enough to dismiss his remarks, as David Hare has recently done, as 'cheesy phrase-making' (1997, 10); several others believed Wesker to be hostile to his working-class characters; in a preface to *Roots* published in 1959 Bernard Levin wrote, 'Mr Wesker, I take it, is a Socialist, not because he thinks working-class people are the best in the land, but because he does not' (9–10). Here the same claim is repeated in milder form, and note the uncertainty that has prompted Levin's hesitant 'I take it' (see also Garforth 1963, 229). Christopher Hollis insisted that from reading Osborne's work, he had assumed him to be 'a man of conservative opinions' (1957, 504), a point of view which would hardly be modified by the next thirty years of Osborne's invective.

The politics of anger

The title of Osborne's play seems key to all this. Hence the much-repeated question, 'what is he angry *about?*'. Hollis, again, writing with deliberate facetiousness, remarked,

> I wish that I could understand who the angry young men are, how many of them there are and what they are angry about. [...] Mr Colin Wilson had spent a weekend in my

house and gone away again before I ever suspected that
he was supposed to be angry, and then I only suspected it
because I read it in a newspaper.

(1957, 504)

The play offers no clear answer to this question, since Jimmy
Porter seems to be angry about everything, and arguably political
targets (say, the H-Bomb, the prime minister and the middle
classes) are intertwined with his attacks on friends and lovers. As
Stephen Lacey has persuasively argued, Porter's opinions are not
'directed out to the audience, or even naturalised as "political
opinions", but are part of Jimmy's psychological warfare with
Alison (and occasionally Cliff)' (1995, 30).

Osborne has himself claimed that wondering what Porter is
actually angry about is to miss the point. In *Déjàvu* (1993), his
sequel to *Look Back in Anger*, the middle-aged Porter reflects on
his famous emotional state: ' "What's he angry *about?*" they used
to ask. Anger is not *about* [...] It is mourning the unknown, the
loss of what went before without you, it's the love another time
but not this might have sprung on you' (1993, 372).

Whether or not Osborne is within his rights to mount a
personal redefinition of this everyday word, his persuasion that
there is something 'intransitive' about his anger was shared by
many of his first commentators. David Marquand, writing in
Universities and Left Review, holds that 'what these angry young
men are most angry about is that they have nothing on which to
focus their anger' (1957, 57). This opinion receives its most decisive support in perhaps the most famous speech in Osborne's play.
Porter is in full flood:

I suppose people of our generation aren't able to die for
good causes any longer. We had all that done for us, in the
thirties and the forties, when we were still kids [...] There
aren't any good, brave causes left. If the big bang does
come, and we all get killed off, it won't be in aid of the
old-fashioned, grand design. It'll just be for the Brave
New-nothing-very-much-thank-you.

(1993, 83)

Two things are curious about this passage; firstly, as with
Marquand's argument, it is hard to understand why someone
should be angry about having nothing to be angry about. This

12

would seem to situate the anger entirely in a prepolitical psychological realm, and remove it from political consideration at all. And secondly, looking back at the fifties, one can see a whole range of brave causes which could furnish material for any angry young man: the increasing brutality of Britain's attachment to Empire, the H-bomb, and the Cold War are just three. Given all this, it is tempting to agree with John Mander's comment that 'the play simply does not add up to a significant statement about anything' (1961, 22).

But it would be smugly retrospective to dismiss the New Wave's politics on this basis, for the reason that this sense of frustrated apathy reflected a more general feeling of paralysis experienced by many on the left. The 1930s and early 1940s saw a high watermark for the confidence of the left. After the disillusionment of the 1931 sterling crisis, and Ramsay MacDonald's acquiescence in a Tory-led National Government, the socialist analysis seemed more relevant than ever. The government's failure to support anti-fascist action, both at home and abroad, encouraged the development of a powerful extraparliamentary network of activists. The high unemployment and widespread poverty of the thirties was widely felt to be a product of Tory policies which lent legitimacy to the Soviet Union's model of collective planning. After Germany unexpectedly attacked the USSR in 1941, support for the Soviet Union became government policy. Growing support for Keynes's and Beveridge's redistributive, interventionist policies, coupled with the evident success of wartime's virtually command economy, was first shown in the two by-election victories for the collectivist Common Wealth party in 1943. This all culminated in the 1945 election, which saw enormous support for Labour's socialist policies, and, indeed, the election of two Communist MPs to parliament.

Much of the radicalism which had been directed towards the Labour Party during the war began to evaporate as the new government seemed blighted and compromised. Economically tied to the United States by the conversion of wartime Lend-Lease agreements into a loan, and by the provisions of the Marshall plan, Labour in office conducted a strongly anti-communist policy. New rules prevented communist organisations affiliating to the Labour Party, and in March 1947, communists were banned from public service. Furthermore, by refusing to repeal the wartime labour control orders, those strikes which took place between 1945 and 1951 were illegal 'and many took place in an atmosphere of "red-baiting"' (Chambers 1989, 301). In Unity's 1946 revue, an item called 'Oklahokum', a long parody of *Oklahoma!*, included the lines, 'Cryptos and their friends'd better look out, / Morgan Phillips's got his little black book out' (305). Morgan Phillips was general secretary of the Labour Party.

The freezing over of Anglo-Soviet relations partly worked to remove the legitimacy of the Soviet model that had proved so compelling in the thirties. But this change in attitude was not simply government-led. Reports about show-trials and mass purges, which had begun leaking out in the late thirties, now came in a flood. In 1950, *The God That Failed* gathered six prominent communists to recant their faith, a book that Wesker has described as giving rise to a shattering moment of political disillusionment (1994, 287). The indefensible interventions in East Germany, Yugoslavia and Hungary only confirmed this discomfort. As Perry Anderson wrote, by the mid fifties the Soviet Union's image had created 'an ideological barrier which blocked the Labour movement's outward political advance and dried up its every inner impulse' (1965, 4).

The economic policies of the new government have passed into socialist folklore, but it is not obvious that these represented an unambiguously decisive moment of socialist economic management. Despite fighting talk of bringing the 'commanding heights' of the economy under its control, nationalisation was piecemeal; the decision was made simply to create public corporations out of industries, which were already hugely loss-making, retaining their existing management structures and personnel. And as for what were by then the *real* commanding heights, apart from the mainly technical measure of nationalising the Bank of England, the City financial institutions were left pretty much alone (Hennessy 1993, 203).

The fifties broke the remembered link between Conservative administration and poverty. In 1951, despite gaining more votes, Labour lost a General Election, due to the familiar anomalies of Britain's boundary divisions. The opportunity to rethink and the exhaustion of figures on the left of the party like Nye Bevan allowed a group of revisionists to seize the agenda, urging the abandonment of socialist policy. Anthony Crosland in *The Future of Socialism* (1956) argued that Marx's ideas 'relate to conditions that have long since passed away' (21). Private monopolies of the means of production, the old unequal distribution of wealth, and with it class antagonism had all, he declared, been consigned to history (62–66). Thirty-five years before Tony Blair, Gaitskell attempted to abandon Labour's commitment to the common ownership of the means of production, enshrined in Clause IV of the party's constitution.

Meanwhile, the Conservative governments of the fifties were able to preside over a fairly momentous upturn in the economy. While Labour, struggling to control an economy shattered by the costs of prosecuting a world war, had been forced to introduce further rationing of bread, eggs, meat, travel and clothing, the Tories were able to abolish rationing within three years of office. Average earnings doubled between 1951 and 1961 (Marwick 1990, 114) and throughout the decade consumption increased by 20 per cent (Bogdanor 1970, 95–96). William Hickey, writing in the *Daily Express* in 1955, declared: 'this is an essentially satisfied country. The basic problems of sharing wealth in an industrial community have been solved' (quoted, Laing 1986, 10).

Given the atrophied state of socialist activity in the mid fifties, it is not surprising that Jimmy Porter's generation see a lack of brave causes in the contemporary world. At the end of *I'm Talking about Jerusalem* (1960), Ronnie Kahn picks up a stone, throws it high in the air, and watches it fall back to the ground. The arc described by Ronnie's stone is emblematic of the political shape of the period covered by Wesker's trilogy, from the rising exhilaration of collective action at the beginning of *Chicken Soup With Barley* (1958), resisting the blackshirt rally on Cable Street, to 1959 and the gloom of a third successive Conservative victory in *Jerusalem*.

The same pattern informs the individual plays. Ronnie Kahn in *Chicken Soup* moves from being inspired and dazzled by the possibilities of communism to disillusionment. In *Roots* (1959) Beatie Bryant takes up some of his enthusiasm, but even her final elated outpouring plays out against the pessimistic contrast of her family ignoring her: 'The murmur of the family sitting down to eat grows as Beatie's last cry is heard. Whatever she will do they will continue to live as before' (1964, 148). Even this retreat from collective action into passionate individualism is dashed in *I'm Talking about Jerusalem*, as Ada and Dave Simmonds begin their experiment in rural nostalgia, setting up home in the countryside, trying to escape the 'brutality' of factory work in a rural Owenite utopia. The political naivety of their position is indicated clearly in the ironic section where Ronnie returns from exploring the land:

Ronnie: [...] Hey Addie – you know what I discovered by the well? You can shout! It's marvellous. You can shout and no one can hear you.

Ada: (*triumphantly*) Of course!
Sarah: (*derisively*) Of course.
Ronnie: Of course – listen. (*Goes into garden and stands on a tea-chest and shouts*). *Down with capitalism! Long live the workers' revolution!* You see? *And long live Ronnie Kahn too!* (*Waits for a reply*.) No one argues with you. No one says anything. Freedom!

(1964, 160)

And yet even this retreat fails; they are defeated by the need to engage economically in the society they are not challenging, and, listening to the report of the 1959 Tory election victory, they pack up and move back to a basement in London, like the one in which we first met the Kahns. As Stuart Hall worried in 1961, the end of the trilogy left Wesker in a 'dramatic and intellectual [...] impasse' (216).

Many of these plays pour scorn on the potentiality of collective action in favour of a retreat into the self. In *The Entertainer* (1957), Archie Rice's son, Frank, makes this deterioration seem inevitable:

You'd better start thinking about number one, Jeannie, because nobody else is going to do it for you. Nobody else is going to do it for you because nobody believes in that stuff anymore. Oh, they may say they do, and may take a few bob out of your pay packet every week and stick some stamps on your card to prove it, but don't believe it – nobody will give you a second look.

(1998, 62)

For Frank, it seems, the collectivist ethos of the Welfare State is spitting in the wind. Jean's final speech explains,

Here we are, we're alone in the universe, there's no God, it just seems that it all began by something as simple as sunlight striking on a piece of rock. And here we are. We've only got ourselves. Somehow, we've just got to make a go of it. *We've only ourselves.*

(79–80)

The same move is found in Doris Lessing's *Each His Own Wilderness* (1958). Tony returns home after National Service and

16

ridicules his mother for her continued faith in 'old-style' socialist campaigning. In an echo of Jimmy Porter, he tells her, 'You're so delightfully old-fashioned. Getting killed for something you believe in is surely a bit of a luxury these days? Something your generation enjoyed' (1959, 15). Instead he advocates 'inner emigration [...] to escape the corruptions of modern life' (28, 33). He eventually forms an attachment with a young woman, equally disillusioned, and in the final moments, they are left sitting together, pleading, 'Leave us alone, we'll say. Leave us alone to live. Just leave us alone...' (95).

It is interesting to observe how these plays use theatrical devices to evade making a direct political case. They characteristically resort to rhetorical questions to express their points, which raise questions that the plays seem unable to answer. Archie Rice's 'Why should I care?' (1998, 19), is an obvious example; but in the final moments of Wesker's *The Kitchen* (1959), we see the proprietor ask his mutinous staff, 'I give work, I pay well, yes? They eat what they want, don't they? I don't know what more to give a man' before intoning repeatedly, 'what is there more? What *is* there more?' (1960, 61). Wesker's stage direction that 'we have seen that there must be something more' only defers the proper answer.

Despite Arden's reputation as one of the more politically astute dramatists of the period (Hunt 1974, 21; Lacey 1995, 37), *Serjeant Musgrave's Dance* (premiere 1959), for all its evident theatrical power, displays the same sense of political stagnation. Musgrave and his fellow-soldiers have all deserted from a colonial war, and have brought the body of a dead comrade back to his home town; they intend to impress upon the townsfolk the evils and horrors of war by killing twenty-five of them. The play was inspired by a similar revenge killing in Cyprus. The revulsion from war is unmistakable, but the play equivocates dramatically. The theatrical force of the troopers' pacifist case is made through moments of violence and intimidation: Hurst's accidental murder of Sparky, the Gatling gun trained on the market square, and Hurst's murder by the cavalry. Despite Arden's own professed pacifism, the play can only offer a sense that such an ideal is impossible to sustain. Certainly, it is hard to see the play's final image, comparing Attercliffe and Musgrave's hanged bodies with the growth of an orchard, as much more than a powerful but ultimately stultifying theatrical metaphor.

It is clear that these plays were, as Lindsay Anderson claimed, responding very sharply to the political and social experiences of their audiences. But Tom Milne's defence of Osborne's habit of failing to say what he is *for* – 'it is almost as if Osborne feels the positive side of his work – the affirmation – to be so self-evident that it does not occur to him to define it' (1961, 57) – is generous, but unsatisfactory. As E.P. Thompson wrote,

> what is peculiar to the apathetic decade is that people have, increasingly, looked to *private* solutions to *public* evils. Private ambitions have replaced social aspirations [...] people tend to feel – in the prevailing apathy – that they are impotent to effect any change.
>
> (1960, 5)

In that sense, it is surprising that these plays should have been so applauded by the left, since they would seem, on this account, part of the problem, not part of the solution.

Nonetheless, despite the plays' dramatisation of a despairing retreat into the self, they still became a rallying point for opposition. As Stuart Hall wrote, '*Look Back in Anger* was painful in its accuracy and immediacy, even for those people who would *not* ever have agreed that "there were no brave causes left" [*sic*]' (1959, 114). To appreciate fully what *Look Back in Anger* meant politically we need to look at those people.

A sense of life

Nineteen fifty-six was not only a decisive point for British theatre. It was a also a crucial year for the British left. Two events catalysed the final collapse of the Soviet Union as a model for British socialism. In February, Khrushchev's acknowledgement of Stalin's butchery followed hard on previous revelations. What was decisive was not so much the revelations themselves as the response of the Communist Party of Great Britain (CPGB). Three delegates, Harry Pollitt, George Matthews and Palme Dutt, went to the conference where these admissions were made; while they may not have been present at the secret session in which Khrushchev delivered his speech, they knew the contents of it within two months, yet they initially suppressed the information and then played it down in the name of workers' unity. After failing to get the matter aired through the normal channels, two party workers, E.P. Thompson and John Saville, decided to set up a new journal, *The*

Reasoner, in the early summer, in which they discussed Jewish persecution in the USSR, Khrushchev's speech and the CPGB's attitude. Such a move was strictly contrary to party discipline and the two men were told to cease publication, under threat of expulsion (Saville 1976).

They persisted and in October as they were going to press, two further decisive events unfolded. In Hungary, a student demonstration was fired on by Soviet-backed troops; as the situation became revolutionary, Soviet tanks entered Budapest and the uprising was brutally suppressed. As Mervyn Jones, a journalist on the *Daily Worker*, recalls, this brought to a head 'all the political and moral questions that had presented themselves so unavoidably since the death of Stalin' (1976, 70). And Eden's simultaneous military intervention in Egypt over Nasser's nationalisation of the Suez Canal Company was a double blow. In *The Reasoner*, Saville and Thompson condemned the Hungarian invasion, noting that, over and above its savage and oppressive character, it had deprived the communist left of the moral authority to criticise the British and French action (Saville 1976, 14). The CPGB's response was, as usual, to offer unequivocal support for the Soviet Union, and to suspend Saville and Thompson from the party. The two editors resigned, and they were not alone. In all, 7,000 left the party in 1956, almost one-fifth of the total membership (Heinemann 1976, 50).

This mass exodus forced these activists to define a space which had barely existed before; a place for the independent communist left. In Thompson's article for the first issue of *Universities and Left Review*, he argued that circumstances had happily conspired to open this new space, in which resignation from the CPGB was no longer disreputably to be associated with voluntarism and retreat, and which could offer a forum for a new kind of left politics, drawing together forces which had been stifled for too long (1957b, 31).

This grouping was soon dubbed the 'New Left'. Its landmarks were books like Richard Hoggart's *The Uses of Literacy* (1957), Williams's *Culture and Society* (1958) and *The Long Revolution* (1961), and journals like *The New Reasoner* and *Universities and Left Review* (ULR), which merged in 1960 under the title of *New Left Review*; its activism manifested in the emergence of the Campaign for Nuclear Disarmament, and the Aldermaston marches. It was also marked by the rise of what Alan Sinfield has called a new-left subculture (1989, 259). It held meetings, discussions, forums for debate. The journals carried reviews of theatre, film and music. In his poem, 'To My Fellow Artists', Christopher Logue invoked this scene with the lines, 'the Film Institute, the Royal Court / Better Books, and the ICA' (1958, 21).

Relations between the Court and the New Left were mutual and intimate. Raymond Williams had edited a journal, *Politics and Letters*, with Wolf Mankowitz in the late forties. Tynan, Logue, Bill Gaskill, Bernard Kops, Wesker and Anderson spoke at *ULR* meetings alongside Williams, Hoggart and Hall. Doris Lessing was on the editorial board of the *New Reasoner*, which shared contributors with *Encore*, *ULR* and *New Left Review*. The Royal Court organised block bookings through the *ULR* clubs and Hall and Williams were regular commentators on the new generation of playwrights. Devine, Anderson, Logue, Wesker and Osborne carried the Royal Court banner at the Aldermaston marches. Thompson, otherwise more distant from the theatrical aspects of the New Left, praised the 'rebellious humanism' to be found in 'the work of the younger writers and dramatists' (1960, 190). Hoggart himself was occasionally included amongst the angry young men (Ritchie 1988, 35), and once commented, somewhat gnomically, that 'what has become known as the angry young man movement, has, in fact, some very positive aspects at bottom' (1958, 137). Wesker returned the compliment years later remembering the scene as 'a meeting point where old dogmas were challenged and young intellectuals were fashioning dazzling aspirations' (1994, 464).

It should be said that the New Left shared with the New Wave that frustrating vagueness as they groped towards new definitions of socialism. *Declaration*'s New Left sequel, *Conviction* (1958), contains a vision of socialism from Norman Mackenzie: 'memory and hope' (7) and Peter Townsend's fuller, but no more persuasive, 'an attitude of trust, tolerance, generosity, goodwill – call it what you like – towards others: a pervasive faith in human nature' (95).

The New Left's abstention from questions of economy and the state has been much criticised, not least by themselves (Thompson 1961, 38; Williams 1979, 364–365). A great part of their attention was directed towards culture, which was in itself a novelty for the British left. Introducing the *New Reasoner*, Thompson excoriated mechanistic forms of Marxism for their reduction of art to questions of content and its treatment of form as 'a kind of salad-dressing to make political theory more palatable, or else as forms of entertainment, amusement, relaxation' (1957a, 122). This is partly reflected in the design of *Universities and Left Review* which broke with the austerity of previous Marxist journals (including *The New Reasoner*), in favour of a magazine format, owing more to *Picture Post* than *Our Time*. More fundamentally, there was a recognition amongst the members of the New Left that while the working class may be more affluent, as Hoggart put it in *The Uses of Literacy*, 'the accompanying cultural changes are not always an improvement but in some of the more important instances are a worsening' (1957, 318).

Throughout their writings, certain phrases recur: 'common culture', 'the means of life', 'structure of feeling'. These can seem nebulous. Roger Scruton, in *Thinkers of the New Left*, claims, as one might expect, little of substance for Williams's work. Rather than understand him as a thinker, he argues that we should see his 'breathless prose' as 'iconographic' (1985, 62), and concludes that 'his appeal is sentimental' (60). But Scruton has not followed up on his own insight; the iconography of Williams's prose relies on the way he has intensified and given particular force to certain words, creating a structure of association and meaning which goes far beyond sentiment.

'Life' is the crucial word. It is part of a cluster of terms that are distributed equally through the works of the New Left and the New Wave: the variant forms, 'live', 'living', 'alive', the antonyms, 'dead', 'death', the synonyms, 'vital' and 'vitality', and the related term 'feeling'. In 1956, *Encore* changed its subtitle to *The Voice of Vital Theatre*, and promoted the term in articles like 'Vital Theatre?' and 'Vital Theatre: A Discussion'.[2] Tynan's review of *Look Back in Anger* saw it offering 'evident and blazing vitality' and found Porter 'simply and abundantly alive' (1964, 41). Williams praised the new movement for its vitality (1961, 26, 33). Osborne identified 'vitality' as *Look Back in Anger*'s 'principal ingredient' (1993, viii), and prefaced *The Entertainer* with the hope that using the music hall device has helped make his play 'immediate, vital and direct' (1998, 3). Devine, announcing plans for the English Stage Company, anticipated a 'vital, living, popular theatre' (quoted, Browne 1975, 12).

The plays themselves are full of such references. Recall the end of *Each His Own Wilderness*, with the young couple begging to be left alone to 'live'. Wesker's trilogy conducts its argument through this term; in *Chicken Soup With Barley*, Harry proclaims, 'Show a young person what socialism means and he [*sic*] recognizes life' (1964, 32). Beatie Bryant in *Roots* says that Ronnie is teaching her 'how to live' (115), which seems to be working because Mrs Bryant thrills Beatie by remarking that she has brought 'a little life' with her (116). In this play, the virtues of Life are characterised by the roguish Stan Mann, who grumbles about young people because 'None on 'em like livin'' (107), and then obligingly symbolises the decline of life by dying; 'Blust!' confirms Beatie, 'That man liked livin'' (128). Beatie, on her chair, develops this theme: 'we're so mentally lazy we might as well be dead. Blust, we are dead!' (147). In *I'm Talking about Jerusalem*, David and Ada insist that they are not running away from socialism: 'we want to live it – not talk about it' (164), and hope that one day people will look to them for inspiration because '*we* do the living' (215).

In *The Entertainer*, Archie's failure is described by the way he walks onto the stage: 'his face held open by a grin, and dead behind the eyes' (1998, 53). Jimmy Porter, ranging around his Midlands attic for a reaction, bursts out,

> Oh heavens, how I long for a little ordinary human enthusiasm. Just enthusiasm – that's all. I want to hear a warm, thrilling voice cry out Hallelujah! (*He bangs his breast theatrically.*) Hallelujah! I'm alive! I've an idea. Why don't we have a little game? Let's pretend that we're human beings, and that we're actually alive.
>
> (1993, 11)

It was this aspect of the plays that seems to have excited the New Left most strongly. Stuart Hall admired Wesker's 'sense of life' (1959, 110), and Tom Milne claimed that some people rejected *Chicken Soup With Barley* because for them 'Wesker came too close to life' (1958, 81). Hall's review of *Serjeant Musgrave's Dance* is strewn with these phrases, as it praises Arden's 'crude but direct feel for life' (1960, 50). W.I. Carr in *Universities and Left Review* finds that 'Mr Osborne (and one or two others) are a salutary reminder to the effect that we are, after all, alive' (1958, 33).

The defence of 'life' against the creeping possibility of 'death' is a motif which unites a great deal of New Left thinking. Williams described the 'culture and civilization' tradition that he traced in *Culture and Society* as asserting 'the claim to life' (1965, 23). For him, the cynicism and denial of contemporary society were 'deposits of practical failures to live' (1993, 334). Hoggart characterises the society which he sees as under threat as being 'the "dense and concrete life" ' (1957, 104). Conversely, Hall saw all the elements of the New Left as evidence of a people beginning to 'choose to "live" ' (1959, 113).

It would be easy to see these terms as being roughly approximate to 'healthy' or 'vigorous', or to see their place in the theatrical criticism of the time as something close to 'realistic'. But when Michael Kaye writes in *New Left Review* that in the new drama 'Life has hit the London stage at last' (1960, 64), he is not concerning himself with representation. To trace the source of this term we need to look back at a theorist from a previous generation, F.R. Leavis.

To see the force Leavis gives to the term 'life', we need only look at the first few pages of *The Great Tradition* (1948). Discussing Jane Austen, he affirms her 'awareness of the possibilities of life' (1962, 10), 'her interest in life', the 'intense moral interest of her own in life' (16), her 'peculiar' and 'unusually developed interest in life' (18). He engages polemically with Lord David Cecil's judgement that Austen 'fully satisfied the rival claims of life and art' (quoted, 15). This inflames Leavis, for whom there is no such rival claim; literature, if it is great, *embodies* life. For Leavis, Austen's greatness is precisely in that the moral concerns of her life insist themselves upon her as intensely personal ones; thus, 'aesthetic value' is inseparable from 'moral significance' (16). This is given full force in his famous and ringing declaration of the great novelists' 'vital capacity for experience, a kind of reverent openness before life, and a marked moral intensity' (18).

Leavis's stamp upon the word 'life' is carried straight over into the New Left. In an article for *Encore* by Stuart Hall, Leavis's notion of 'reverent openness before life' is plainly visible: 'many young people [...] recognized what Arnold Wesker called "being alive", and turned to it with an act of unashamed reverence' (1959, 111), an act which will be completed by 'a permanent *openness*' (112). In the second part of *The Uses of Literacy*, Hoggart's tone often recalls Leavis: what, for example, he finds lacking in pulp fiction compared to 'great literature' is 'the moral tone, the differences in the approach to life and to relationships which lie between each passage' (1957, 236). And when Williams discusses the working class in 'Culture is Ordinary', he is virtually praising their instinctive grasp of Leavisite criticism: they have, he says, 'as much natural fineness of feeling, as much quick discrimination, as much clear grasp of ideas within the range of experience as I have found anywhere' (85–86).

This debt was widely acknowledged. Hoggart was, and still is, avowedly Leavisite. Williams, returning from the war, was inspired by Leavis's attempt to turn the tools of practical criticism on the products of contemporary mass society (1979, 66). *Politics and Letters* was an attempt to combine radical left politics with Leavisite literary criticism (particularly tricky, given Leavis's life-long hostility to Marxism). In *Culture and Society* Williams is more critical of Marxist cultural theory than he is of Leavis (in fact more than he is of almost everyone else), and he later wrote that 'Leavis [...] knows more than any Marxist I have met about the real relations between art and experience' (1979, 81). For the New Wave, John Wain and Lindsay Anderson both praised Leavis (1957, 104; 1958b, 51).

The attractions of Leavis were manifold. Leavis's alliance of moral concern and textual analysis provided one model for reshaping a Marxist approach to literature. And at a time when socialist thought seemed helpless in the crossfire between affluence and totalitarianism, Leavis's celebrated certainty was deeply attractive. Williams cites him in *Culture and Society*, briskly insisting that a proper concern for culture 'is not so much a matter of announcing some political allegiance. It is a matter [...] of declaring that "this is worth more than that, this rather than that is the direction in which to go"' (1993, 262). This certainty was complemented by a humanism, which, as Sinfield suggests, was intuitively counter to the terrors of Stalinism (1989, 244).

One further source which fed into Leavis's thinking and remains visible in the work of the New Left is that of T.S. Eliot. In 1921, Eliot used the occasion of a new anthology to discuss the Metaphysical Poets, who had been commonly thought in the history of poetry to be a curious 'digression from the main current' (1951, 281). Eliot's argument breathtakingly inverts this history by claiming that the Metaphysicals are the true representatives of poetry and that everything since the English Revolution has been the digression. Famously, the cause of this historical error is what he calls a 'dissociation of sensibility' (288). The Metaphysical Poets, he argues, were engaged in bringing into harmony all aspects of human experience. Notably this meant thought and feeling, since poetry for them was 'a direct sensuous apprehension of thought, or a recreation of thought into feeling' (286). The proper role of poetry, for Eliot, lay in this integration of human faculties; but in the mid seventeenth century, he argues, words and feelings went their separate ways: 'the language became more refined, the feeling became more crude' (288). Here Eliot overlaps with Leavis's critique of Milton, who, Leavis argues, 'exhibits a feeling *for* words rather than a capacity for feeling *through* words' (1936, 50), his verse displaying a 'certain hollowness' (46) and 'a certain sensuous poverty' (47).

What Leavis and Eliot share is a certain historical view, a belief that at one point thought and word, feeling and expression, style and sensuousness were unified, before being torn asunder. Leavis's vision of life before this fall was of an 'organic society'. In *Culture and Environment* (1933) he and Denys Thompson imagine a life where culture was the expression of 'an art of life, a way of living, ordered and patterned, involving social arts, codes of intercourse and a responsive adjustment, growing out of immemorial experience, to the natural environment and the rhythm of the year' (1–2). Fantasising a historical sociology around Eliot's thesis, Leavis and Thompson imagine a time when word, thought, feeling and the body worked in harmony with each other and with their environment (86–91).

For Leavis, this organic society is an ideal state, now lost, the only present traces of which may be found in literature (82). As Anne Samson puts it, 'literature is not so much *evidence* of a past culture as a part of that culture itself, embodying its values and a whole way of life' (1992, 40). It is not content, or the isolated quality of a poet's insight, that is to be treasured. It is the very striving to unify that 'post-seventeenth-century insulation of feeling from intellect' (114) that is of value. But our decline is now such that only the tiny minority of readers 'capable of unprompted, first-hand judgement' may appreciate the fact (Leavis 1930, 4).

This conception animates Leavis's vocabulary; the language of 'embodiment', 'muscularity', and so on, is an attempt to bring bodily values back into literature, to reunify the mind and body. His belief that poetry could only properly be appreciated when read aloud suggests this too, as well as a momentary reproduction of the lost oral culture of organic society. Underlying the Leavisite notion of life, then, is the physical, sensuous, thinking presence of the individual in the text. 'Life', in other words, is life in the organic community.

Culture can save us

It is hardly necessary to point out that Leavis's vision of the organic community is damaged by its never having existed; several

critics have done so already (e.g. Wright 1979, 52). Raymond
Williams himself had little time for this vision of a pre-industrial
golden age, deprecating its 'surrender to a characteristically indus-
trialist, or urban, nostalgia – a late version of mediaevalism, with
its attachments to an "adjusted" feudal society. If there is one
thing certain about "the organic community", it is that it has
always gone' (1993, 259).

Nonetheless, Williams argues that there is much to learn from
these thinkers. In *Culture and Society* he praises Leavis for
opening the institutions of mass society to the techniques of practical criticism. And while he denounces Eliot's persuasion that the
effects of a few fine minds engaged in scrupulous reading and
discrimination will trickle down to the rest of us, he sees his work
as offering a profound breakthrough in our thinking about
culture. This breakthrough is characterised by seeing culture as 'a
whole way of life'. Eliot had worried that as society levels out, and
splits into small fragmented groups, the ability of the best to
handle the spiritual life of the rest will become impossible, since
the common culture which ordinarily allowed for this transmis-
sion will have disappeared. Williams argues that in this very
admission, Eliot has acknowledged that there is more to culture
than his group of fine minds (1993, 233–243).

It is here that Williams makes a decisive break with Leavis and
Eliot's work. He argues that there are two visions of culture. There
is the literary culture, the great tradition, that Leavis and Eliot
discuss. But then there is the anthropological notion of 'a whole
way of life', a network of experiences and practices that bind us
together. It is important to note that while Williams is, of course,
too much of a Marxist to imagine that society can be improved by
turning the clock back, he does preserve some of the spirit of the
organic society in his theory; many of those *values* which Leavis
had exiled to some remote pre-industrial dawn, Williams sees as
still visible in the working-class attitude to life.[3]

Williams has no interest in the romantic fantasy of a group
working in harmony with the soil. Instead, his vision of unity is
entirely social; embodied in the characteristic institutions created
by the working class is a vision of life as common, of society 'as
the positive means for all kinds of development, including individual development [...] The human fund is regarded as in all
respects common, and freedom of access to it as a right constituted by one's humanity; yet such access, in whatever kind, is
common or it is nothing. Not the individual, but the whole

society, will move' (326). So rather than root the common culture, upon which our individual and social health depends, in literature, Williams, in characteristically Marxist style, turns this on its head; the health of our literary culture is, in fact, dependent on the health of our common culture.

In practical terms, this image of working-class collectivity may be seen in the metonym of neighbourliness. Hoggart writes warmly of the neighbourhood, where 'the front door opens out of the living-room on to the street' so that 'when you go down the one step or use it as a seat on a warm evening you become part of the life of the neighbourhood' (1957, 58), generating a 'group life, but one which has started from the home and worked outwards in response to the common needs and amusements of a densely packed neighbourhood' (68). Williams describes the maintenance of collective feeling as a 'positive practice of neighbourhood' (1993, 334).

Precisely this concern for neighbourliness shapes *Chicken Soup with Barley*; friends and relatives pass through the Kahn home, eating, planning the demonstration, keeping in touch, gossiping and arguing. But in the second half of the play, set after 1945, they have moved into an LCC council house, and things have changed. The deterioration in their ideals is charted in the deterioration of their neighbourliness. Cissie explains: 'These flats are a world on their own. You live a whole lifetime here and not know your next-door neighbour' (1964, 68). The central image of *Each His Own Wilderness* is explained by Tony who blames affluence for the destruction of neighbourhood:

> Everybody a kind of wilderness surrounded by barbed wire shouting across the defences into the other wilder-nesses and never getting an answer back. That's socialism. I suppose it's progress. Why not? To every man his wife and two children and a chicken in the pot on Sundays. A beautiful picture – I'd die for it. To every man his front door and his front door key. To each his own wilderness.
>
> (Lessing 1959, 50–51)

That image, the front door fearfully locked against the outside world, is found in *The Entertainer*, where the decline of the halls has thrown Archie into perpetual debt, and Phoebe admits 'whenever there's a ring at the door, I daren't answer it, in case it's a policeman standing there with another summons' (1998, 40).

Williams and Hoggart are not merely sentimental about the decline of this life; it's much more serious than that. Hence the ominous tone Williams employs to imagine its complete demise: 'we live in almost overwhelming danger, at a peak of our apparent control', he writes; 'we need a common culture, not for the sake of an abstraction, but because we shall not survive without it' (1993, 336, 317). It is not just literary culture that is dependent on the preservation of a common culture; it is communication itself. In *The Entertainer*, Osborne links this with the decline of neighbourliness, as Jean asks:

> Have you ever got on a railway train here, got on a train from Birmingham to West Hartlepool? Or gone from Manchester to Warrington or Widnes. And you get out, you go down the street, and on one side maybe is a chemical works, and on the other side is the railway goods yard. Some kids are playing in the street, and you walk up to some woman standing on her doorstep. It isn't a doorstep really because you can walk straight from the street into her front room. What can you say to her? What real piece of information, what message can you give to her?
>
> (1998, 79)

Here we see Eliot's 'dissociation of sensibility' filtered through Leavis's and Williams's more sociologically inclined positions. Just as Eliot saw a rift between word and feeling, Archie Rice's language has deteriorated into patter: 'apparently absent-minded, it is a comedian's technique, it absolves him seeming committed to anyone or anything' (29). This breaks down at the end of Act One, when Archie has been playing down the news of Mick's capture in Suez. He is in mid-routine:

> Well, there I was walking along the front, to meet what I think we used to call a piece of crackling. Or perhaps it was a bit of fluff. No that was earlier. Anyway, I know I enjoyed it afterwards. But the point is I was walking along the front, all on my own, minding my own business, (*Pause*) and two nuns came towards me – (*Pause*) two nuns –

*He trails off, looking very tired and old. He looks across
at* JEAN *and pushes the bottle at her.*
Talk to me.

(37)

The momentary resurrection of feeling arrests his performance
and he makes a desperate plea for communication.

Even more directly, Wesker shows Ada and Dave in *I'm Talking
about Jerusalem*, trying to mend this estrangement between words
and things, in a game they play with their son, Danny. Dave plays
'Mr Life', and acts out creating a new human being, Danny. The
boy is to have another go at life, and begin describing the world
without using *names* for things. He sees a hedge and is coaxed
into describing it as 'thin pieces of wood. Going all over the place.
With bumps on them, and thin slips of green like paper, and some
funny soft stuff on them' (1964, 196). Having repeated this exercise with other features of the landscape, he is rewarded by Ada:
'Now you are a real human being Daniel who can look and think
and talk' (197).

This explains Williams's apocalyptic tone. The collapse of a
common culture does not only threaten the literary culture, but
our very means of communication, our humanity, indeed life itself.
This is what underlies Sarah's warning in *Chicken Soup*: 'Ronnie,
if you don't care you'll die' (76). And it is striking how this death
is imagined as a physical reality, how the decay of society is
mapped intensely onto the body. In Act Three of *Chicken Soup*,
Harry has an attack of incontinence and shuffles apologetically to
the bathroom. 'Poor Sarah and Harry,' cries Monty, 'Jesus! It's all
come to this?' (64). The question's rhetoric seems to take in a
broader panorama of dysfunction. This is even clearer in
Jerusalem when Ada reports back from visiting Harry, whose
second stroke has now affected his brain: 'He kept shouting in
Yiddish, calling for his mother and his sister Cissie. Mummy told
me he was talking about Russia' (193).

In *Roots*, we find the collapse of Life in Norfolk manifesting in
an outbreak of gut-ache (116), more incontinence (102), and Stan
Mann's death (119). Beatie's vitality leads her to steer clear of the
ills that may beset the body; she hates death (119), can't bear sick
men because they smell (103) and approves Ronnie's dislike of fat
people (97). Obesity is seen as a sign of idealism gone sour in
Jerusalem, as Libby Dobson, Dave's wartime friend, describes a
growing disillusionment through his wife's changing body: 'and

she became so gross, so indelicate, so unfeeling about everything. All the grace she had was going, and instead there was flesh growing all around her' (183–184).

Against this, Wesker shows us examples of a wholesome unity of feeling and physical expression. The trilogy is full of moments staging people's sensuous enjoyment of their bodies: Dave stripped to the waist and washing in the outdoors (178), the family doing the washing up together and singing a Yiddish folk-song (173), Beatie's bath (124), and, more ludicrously, her sensuous love of housework: she is described as 'making an attack' on some discarded clothes (97), she just has to organise their cupboard space and 'energy sparks from her' (98); when she gets a broom in her hands she is irrepressible, 'now gurgling with sort of animal noises signifying excitement. Her joy is childlike' (100). Whenever Ronnie wants to communicate properly, he physically augments it by standing on a chair (41, 89), contrasting with the opposite move at a point of disillusionment: 'Can you understand what it is suddenly not to know? (*Collapses into armchair.*) And the terrifying thing is – I don't care either' (72). And Ronnie, ventriloquising through Beatie, claims that full physical expression is the hope for the future: 'Socialism isn't talking all the time, it's living, it's singing, it's dancing' (129).

This metaphor weaves through one of *Look Back in Anger*'s main narrative threads. Jimmy, trying to goad a response out of Alison, tells her,

> If only something – something would happen to you, and wake you out of your beauty sleep! (*Coming in close to her.*) If you could have a child, and it would die. Let it grow, let a recognizable human face emerge from that little mass of indiarubber and wrinkles.

He cruelly predicts that this might even make her into 'a recognizable human being' (1993, 34). Porter's curse comes to pass, and Alison's response is to release the 'feeling' she has been holding back: 'This is what he's been longing for me to feel. This is what he wants to splash about in! I'm in the fire, and I'm burning, and all I want is to die!' (94). Alison realises, albeit through a crudely literal analogy, the full force of her own 'inner death'.

This is why many of these plays are characterised by a call for a retreat into the self. The individual is the site that marks the opposing tensions of public affluence and private cultural decline.

Tony, in *Each His Own Wilderness*, says 'the whole world is getting mass-produced and organized. But inside everybody's varnished and painted skin is a tramp [...] Every morning in front of the bathroom mirror we polish our teeth and our hair and our skin [...] But inside, we've emigrated. We're tramps' (1959, 68). The most famous expression of this is in Archie Rice's fleeting analysis of his own emptiness:

> You see this face, this face can split open with warmth and humanity. It can sing, and tell the worst, unfunniest stories in the world to a great mob of dead, drab erks and it doesn't matter, it doesn't matter. It doesn't matter because – look at my eyes. I'm dead behind these eyes.
>
> (1998, 66)

We can see the avoidance of explicit politicizing in this light; tending to the withering 'inner self' is, for many, more urgent than any public political cause. Ada, in *Chicken Soup*, cries out, 'Care! Care! What right have we to care? How can we care for a world outside ourselves when the world inside is in disorder?' (1964, 43).

For many, the importance of the New Wave lay precisely in attending to this personal crisis, and reunifying the inner with the outer. Stuart Hall praises Osborne for:

> trying to burn his way into that tangled subliminal area where the issues of politics and the issues of love and sex merge, mingle and collide [...] Jimmy Porter is like a destructive element, blasting away at some indistinct target, trying to shift layer after layer of cant and cynicism, until he reaches that inner core where people either 'feel' or are irretrievably 'dead'. The dead thing which drives Jimmy to distraction within Alison, and the 'death' which looks out from Archie Rice's eyes, is also the dead heart of England, the bloody unfeeling core.
>
> (1961, 217)

This is what Osborne means by saying that 'anger' is not *about* anything. The political force of *Look Back in Anger* lay not in the targets of Porter's anger, *but in the anger itself*: the experience and spectacle of someone, caring, feeling, living. When Archie asks 'Why should I care?', we do not answer him by listing world crises, but by an affirmation of the humanising, unifying quality of caring itself. This is why Williams felt that looking for 'social content' in these plays was misplaced (1961, 35), because they represent 'not so much a new area of life [...] as a new wave of feeling'. *Look Back in Anger*'s political value is precisely *because* 'it is primarily emotional protest, barely articulate, with an intensity beyond its nominal causes' (34).

As Osborne announced, in his essay for *Declaration*, 'I want to make people feel, to give them lessons in feeling' (1957a, 65). The politics of anger are to be found here, in the profound conviction that society was flourishing at the expense of human feeling, and in a blazing determination to bring human emotion back into the centre of cultural life.

Vitality and iterability

It is this analysis that came to play a major part in what certain people felt was wrong with British theatre before 1956; many of the Royal Court's initiatives may be seen as a drive to remedy a theatre culture which had encouraged (and luxuriated in) the effects of this cultural malaise. It seems to me that there is much more to be said about (and for) the theatre before Osborne and, before we assume the sheer rightness of the Royal Court's action, it is important to assess the theoretical dimensions of this drive for cultural rebirth.

The New Left and the New Wave shared predominantly a cultural analysis. I have remarked that the New Left placed culture at the centre of their thinking, but there are veiled references to common ownership in *Culture and Society*, and on the pages of *Universities and Left Review* cultural critique sits side by side with economic debate. Their particularly critical focus on *mass* culture could be seen as informed by a tradition of Marxist analysis stretching back at least as far as the first Frankfurt School writings of the 1920s. Still, this has largely to be supplemented by the reader since their critique is conducted more at the level of cultural form than its economic basis.

Ronald Duncan, a poetic dramatist, and co-founder of the English Stage Company, launched a bizarre attack on the new generation's plays for being obsessed with 'questions of wages, working conditions, and so on' (1968, 385; 1960, 17), which they obviously are not. Indeed, the playwrights of the new generation hardly concerned themselves with economic questions, almost exclusively addressing the critique at mass culture. Wesker's *Roots* has harsh things to say about football, rock 'n' roll and comics (1964, 89), dance music on the radio (108) and pop songs (114–115). Beatie's great final speech – which Michael Kaye in *New Left Review* described as 'a *ULR* Editorial to end all *ULR* Editorials' (66) – invokes another inventory of mass cultural forms, deriding the patronising bad faith of 'the slop singers and the pop writers and the film makers and women's magazines and the Sunday papers and the picture strip love stories' (147–148). Billy Rice, in *The Entertainer*, bemoans the presence of a television in his local pub (1998, 17). Archie makes asides about crooners (26) and television adverts (31) and Jean scorns the tabloids (38–39). In both *Look Back in Anger* and *The Long and the Short and the Tall* (1959), the angry young protagonists read satirically from the problem pages (Osborne 1993, 8; Hall 1961, 24). In the film of *A Taste of Honey*, Helen's moral laxity is suggested, as Lacey argues, by the trip to Blackpool, with its candy-floss and pop music soundtrack (1995, 174). At the end of Osborne's 1960 television play, *A Subject of Scandal and Concern*, the narrator signs off sardonically suggesting that the audience may all be waiting for the adverts: 'That's all. You may retire now. And if a mini-car is your particular mini-dream, then dream it' (1972, 47). (Presumably the sports car Osborne bought with the first profits of *Look Back in Anger* was a maxi-dream.)

At the root of these complaints was the *mechanical* quality of mass culture. John Wain attacked 'this worship of the machine' and felt that the only defence was 'to humanise [...] society' (1957, 87; see also Groombridge and Whannel 1960, 52; Cooper 1970, 264). In *The Entertainer*, Billy Rice's criticism of modern entertainers focuses on the mechanical element of their performance: 'these new five-minute wonders with a microphone' (1998, 75). In the film, this is given particular emphasis in a sequence which begins with Billy being called up to sing some of his old songs in the pub; brusquely he refuses the offer of a microphone. After one song we cut to Archie's 'Thank God I'm Normal' routine, performed in front of a tatty curtain with what appear to be tin-foil stars attached to it, and, damningly, sung through a microphone.

The image of the machine repeats the same concern which we have already met; machines have no feelings, no 'inner' life. And this whole critique hinges on a debate which is very familiar to literary theory: intentionality. Williams addresses this concern directly in the final section of *Culture and Society*. He dismisses suggestions that mass production is to be criticised for distancing the audience from the author, since this is true of all printed media, including the novel (1993, 301). Since it is largely a product of expanding education and suffrage, we can hardly object to the expansion of the reading public (302). He says instead that we need to discriminate good and bad uses of mass communication.

The basis on which he founds this distinction is 'the intention of the speaker or writer' (303). He distinguishes two kinds of speakers within mass communication, the 'source' – who is immediately responsible for the matter being communicated (303) – and the 'agent', 'whose characteristic is that his [*sic*] expression is subordinated to an undeclared intention' (304), as in the case of a journalist whose editorial stance has been urged on him or her by a newspaper proprietor. In the former case intention and expression are unified, in the latter they are separate. The definition of good communication is, then, a unity of intention and expression in the cultural object, with disunity defining the bad.

This argument seems clear enough, and would have some radically democratising effects on parts of mass media, if somehow converted into a general policy. The problem arises when you try to fit it with the rest of Williams's analysis. Remember that Williams's audacious reworking of Eliot involved an inversion of Eliot's presumed relations between literary and general culture. Williams argued, against Eliot, that the health of the literary culture was dependent on the health of the common culture. And, as we have seen, he expanded this to suggest that the decline of community feeling will have damaging consequences for communication, humanity, our very existence. A healthy common culture may sustain the holism of the literary tradition, but contemporary culture threatens to tear it apart.

This is hard to square with his emphasis on intention. In a fragmented culture, *all* utterance, sincere or not, appears soulless and divided. It is, according to this other portion of his argument, structures of reception, not structures of production, that determine the fate of utterance. Ironically, it was Eliot who wrote,

> When there is so much to be known, when there are so many fields of knowledge in which the same words are used with different meanings, when every one knows a little about a great many things, it becomes increasingly

difficult for anyone to know whether he [*sic*] knows what
he is talking about or not.

(quoted, Leavis 1930, 19)

If a fragmented culture can divide utterance against itself like
this, the presence or absence of intention seems only of marginal
importance.

These theoretical concerns are ones which Jacques Derrida has
addressed in his essay 'Signature Event Context', in which he
engages with the work of British language philosopher, J.L.
Austin. Derrida notes that all linguistic signs ('marks') have to be
able to be quoted to be of any use; we must be able to use a word
in a variety of instances, and have that sign recognised by
someone else for communication to take place; 'what would a
mark be,' asks Derrida, 'that could not be cited?' (1988, 12). To
insist on the presence of some inner act of 'intending' every time a
word is spoken is to rely on a Cartesian division between mind
and body, which matches our actual behaviour so badly as to be
untenable. Derrida calls this function of language 'iterability' and
thus far he is entirely in accord with Austin.

The force of Derrida's deconstructive reading begins to emerge
when he observes that this has some curious knock-on effects for
another part of Austin's argument. Austin states that he is going to
exclude from his concerns insincere, non-serious speech acts, since
he regards this use of language as '*parasitic* upon its usual use'
(1980, 22). He gives as examples of non-serious use words spoken
in a poem, and, interestingly, on stage. However, the distinction
between serious and non-serious use, like Williams's between the
source and the agent, hangs on the intention of the utterance.
Words spoken on stage are not really *meant* by the actor, and are,
hence, not *seriously* uttered.

But, as Austin has already established, words do not require the
presence of some private set of intentions to function. As Derrida
reminds us, this is part of their 'positive and internal condition of
possibility' (1988, 17). Words are necessarily detachable from
their authors or speakers; and this operates within successful and
unsuccessful utterance alike. While this is certainly how misunder-
standing, reinterpretation and rereading is made possible, it is also
what makes it possible to understand, interpret and read in the
first place.

The result of this is the vision of an ideally reunified intention
and expression disappears over the horizon. The image of the

'organic society' is revealed, once again, as a fantasy, but Williams's division between source and agent is also untenable, since intention and expression are always internally divided against themselves. Furthermore, the New Wave project of trying to revitalise British drama by removing those forces which had compromised expression must be considered very doubtful, as to do so would be to exile all signification, and with it all meaning and communication, from the theatre. And note Austin's acknowledgement that these problems seem particularly prominent in the theatre, which is practised almost exclusively by – in Williams's terms – agents rather than sources. The theatre characteristically exists on the borderlines of seriousness; lines spoken, event enacted in a play are both meant and not meant, serious and not serious, real and unreal.

In many ways, of course, this is rather truistic. Joan Plowright did not have to intend personally every line she spoke in *Roots* for the play to be meaningful, and no one but the most ardent Method actor would claim that she did. But, given that, it becomes necessary to ask some new questions. We need to ask why this otherwise unexceptionable feature of theatrical performance (and indeed all communication) became a call to arms for a whole generation of British theatre, why this became such an urgent, brave cause. What compulsions were at work giving it particular force in the mid-fifties? And given the fundamental incoherence of the project, how could it become the subject of a critical consensus that it actually succeeded?

The inconsistencies in his theorising aside, one of the many lasting values of Williams's work lies in his insistence that a concern for literary and theatrical culture is incomplete without attention to the structures and institutions in which they issue. Before considering why mid-century British theatre might have exacerbated concerns about the instability of theatrical communication, it is therefore crucial to look at one of the most decisive forces shaping theatre practice in the 1950s: the development of the Arts Council.

2

THE NEW ELIZABETHANS
The docile bodies of arts funding

He [*sic*] who is subjected to a field of visibility, and who
knows it, assumes responsibility for the constraints of
power; he makes them play spontaneously upon himself;
he inscribes in himself the power relation in which he
simultaneously plays both roles; he becomes the principle
of his own subjection.
(Michel Foucault, *Discipline and Punish*, 1977a, 202–203)

Tynan's characterisation of the New Wave as instinctively oppositional is nowhere better illustrated than in their attitude to the
West End. They treated the Court as an adversary, and the engagement as a none-too-civil war. John Whiting neatly parodied the
rhetoric in 1959:

The main engagement took place in Sloane Square. There
was a complementary action in the far east, at Stratford.
These separate forces were never coordinated. The east
relied very much on mercenaries recruited from another
country. The west, although at one time there was an
uneasy and short-lived alliance with France, employed the
natives. The west once occupied the Palace and the
Comedy, but these were not held […] The situation is now
confused.

(105–106)

He does not exaggerate. Tynan described the new drama as a
'three-pronged suburban assault that has lately been launched on
the central citadel' (1964, 85). Marowitz saw Osborne's 1959
musical, *The World of Paul Slickey*, as a 'revolutionary […]
weapon' (1959, 103), and brushes aside its critics, insisting that

'the revolution has begun and nothing in the world can stop it!' (105).

Royal Court to the West End is as David to Goliath; the integrity and ambition of the Court puny weapons against the giant accumulation of bricks-and-mortar, capital and conservative loyalty that Hugh 'Binkie' Beaumont and 'the Group' had amassed. This is history as fairy-tale; the smooth villainy of 'Binkie' Beaumont, the self-evident wickedness of the West End, and the Court's fresh-faced triumph against all the odds are there in every history. In the final showdown integrity triumphs against glitter, artistry against decoration and passion against repression.

I want to argue here that the picture routinely offered to us is false in three ways: that the Royal Court should not be simply opposed to the West End, that the criticisms of the West End were misplaced, and that the Court's success was not out of the blue, but was shaped by wider forces organising the cultural life of the nation.

The key figure that links the two sides is the Arts Council. As Sinfield writes, '*Look Back in Anger* signalled a change in English theatre in 1956 in great part because it coincided with and helped to stimulate a new institutional arrangement: subsidized theatre' (1989, 27). Understanding the changes in British theatre that took place in the fifties is impossible without analysing the developing agenda of the Arts Council.

Art for the people

Before 1939, British governments had resisted offering subsidy to support the arts. There had been some indirect subventions to Covent Garden through the BBC in the early thirties, and at various points certain artefacts had been 'acquired for the nation'. J.B. Priestley noted ruefully in 1939, Britain had 'the one government in the world that does nothing for the theatre except tax it' (135).

The situation changed very quickly after the outbreak of war. Within a month, the Treasury and the Board of Education had met to discuss how to maintain cultural activities during the conflict. They almost certainly had in mind the memory of the 1914–18 war, in which the arts had suffered a collapse from which they had still not fully recovered. Basil Dean, who had organised concert parties during the first war, had approached the NAAFI (Navy, Army and Air Force Institutes). With their support and facilities,

Dean had managed to obtain use of the Theatre Royal, Drury Lane as the headquarters for his organisation, the Entertainments National Services Association (ENSA). The Board of Education, however, feared that the jovial entertainment which was soon issuing from ENSA would simply replicate the cruder shows of the earlier period and cast around for a complementary organisation.

For a couple of months energies circulated around two bodies: the Art and Entertainment Emergency Council, which was lobbying the government to find work for professionals in the arts, and Kenneth Clark's War Artists' Advisory Committee, which was seeking private sponsorship. As the policies of these organisations were ill-matched to the government's plans, they both proved abortive (Leventhal 1990, 290). But Clark had approached Thomas Jones, the secretary of the Pilgrim Trust, founded in 1930 by American millionaire and Anglophile Edward Harkness. Thomas Jones responded positively to the suggestion that the Pilgrim Trust make endowments to support cultural activities. He was himself very taken with the model of 'Art for the People', established in 1935 by W.E. Williams of the British Institute of Adult Education to organise educational tours of paintings loaned by private collectors and galleries to towns and villages which had little access to fine art and art education (Williams 1971, 20). Jones decided that what was needed was an organisation which could do the same thing for music and drama.

Lord De La Warr, President of the Board of Education, and Lord Macmillan, Chair of the Pilgrim Trust and Minister of Information, met on 14 December 1939 and agreed that, to avoid an artistic blackout and sustain morale, money should be made available to support cultural activities throughout the country. A week later, the Treasury indicated that it would match any subvention from the Pilgrim Trust up to £50,000. With the agreement of the Pilgrim Trustees and the Treasury, all that was left was to formally constitute the body. And on 19 January, the Council for the Encouragement of Music and Art (CEMA)[1] was convened. In doing so, as Janet Minihan points out, 'the British Government did more to commit itself to supporting the arts than it had in the previous century and a half' (1977, 215).

The 'Art for the People' model captures two important early emphases: firstly, CEMA was to run tours, not just to major cities, but to areas which were not served by galleries, theatres or concert halls. The first initiative was to establish a group of 'Music Travellers': professional musicians who would tour rural areas and factory canteens, in collaboration with the Rural Music Schools, promoting musical appreciation and practice. In the first five months of 1940, they claimed to have started 34 orchestras, 235 choirs, and 184 concerts, playing to over 38,000 people.[2] This illustrates the second emphasis, which was on amateur work: De La Warr in a letter to Jones in December laid great emphasis on this as a means of maintaining morale (Leventhal 1990, 291–292). The expert in amateur theatre, L. du Garde Peach, was brought onto the committee as Honorary Director of Amateur Drama, with four regional advisers under him. By April, money had been made available to women's institutes, townswomen's guilds, the Scottish Community Drama Association, the YWCA and the English Folk Dance and Song Society, amongst others (White 1975, 26). The principles of maintaining regional tours and promoting amateur work were enshrined in March 1940 in a Memorandum to the Treasury, setting out its aims, which was rewarded by official Government agreement to co-fund these activities.

Within three months of the Treasury's first awards, discontent surfaced. In mid June, *The Times* ran an editorial deeply critical of CEMA.[3] Apparently surprised that government money was going to 'stimulate the interests and energies of the people' it asked, tendentiously, 'what has such musical propaganda got to do with the war?' In patrician tones it advised the Council to turn its attentions elsewhere; 'Is Sadler's Wells to receive no encouragement while it alone is providing opera and ballet on a generous scale and of high artistic excellence to a not ungrateful public?' Its antipathy, even incomprehension, towards amateur work is evident: at one point it formulates a straight opposition between 'musicians' and 'the people', as if an overlap were just unthinkable. As John Pick writes, it surely 'summarised a discussion which had occurred among the great and the good, rather than stimulated one' (1985, 9).

A month later, John Christie, perhaps irked by Glyndebourne's exclusion from subsidy, complained that money was being wasted with ' "nothing to show for it". As a result standards were "lagging far behind in a sea of mediocrity" ' (Leventhal 1990, 301). An even more eminent complainant was John Maynard Keynes. Mary Glasgow, CEMA's secretary, seconded from the Board of Education, was summoned to his London home:

40

He wanted to know why the council was spending so
much money on amateur effort. Why was it missing this
obvious opportunity to support artistic ventures of
standing? [...] It was standards that mattered, and the
preservation of serious professional enterprise, not
obscure concerts in village halls.

(Glasgow 1975, 262)

None of these complainants feels the need to explain what they
mean by 'standards', yet it seems to come back to visibility; it is
there in *The Times*'s 'large scale' and 'conspicuous courage',
Christie's 'nothing to show' and Keynes's 'obscure concerts'. These
phrases are adverting to a vision of art grounded in conspicuous
prestige. Suffice it to say that for a certain influential body of
opinion prestige, and therefore art, was incompatible with helping
amateurs in the West Midlands and sending tours around the
industrial villages of the North-East.

Over the next ten years, the three emphases of CEMA –
amateur activity, touring and regionalism – were successively
abandoned, and turned towards their precise opposites: professionalism, buildings and London.

From amateur to professional

Amateur work was by no means the exclusive focus of the early
Council. Alongside du Garde Peach, Lewis Casson was the
director of professional drama. The Old Vic, the Pilgrim Players,
Perth Repertory Company, and Barry Jackson's company were all
professional groups and early beneficiaries of CEMA grants.
Nonetheless, CEMA's association with these companies was to
facilitate touring. Initially, CEMA had organised tours of the
London Symphony Orchestra (LSO) and London Philharmonic
Orchestra (LPO) to 'smaller towns and industrial areas' (White
1975, 26), but, by the end of the year, responsibility for funding
these tours had been hived off to the Carnegie Trust.

In the initial submission to the Treasury setting out CEMA's
function, mention is made of raising standards and of indirectly
providing wartime employment for professionals. Leventhal has
argued that these aims are incompatible with those of helping
amateurs and spreading cultural provision (1990, 295). But is this
true? The example of the Music Travellers indicates that it need
not be: professionals can be employed to help amateurs. He also

argues that spreading professionals around the country might prohibit the production of large-scale works (296), the implication being that this may defeat the aim of raising standards. But there is no necessary reason to suppose that only large-scale works can inspire the best efforts of theatre or music workers. What *is* certain is that large-scale works require large-scale venues, and therefore are more likely to attract large-scale attention. Like *The Times*'s leader-writer, Leventhal seems to be presuming the greater merit of conspicuous, prestigious cultural activity.

ENSA suffered from the same slights. It became notorious for its amateurism; a contemporary cartoon shows a busker arriving home, opening a letter and delighting to his wife, 'Oh look dear! It's a contract from ENSA!' (Fawkes 1978, 17). In fact, of 50,000 applications from amateurs, only 800 were employed. But the first tour turned to farce in December when a pontoon bridge bearing Billy Cotton's Band collapsed. The government gave ENSA relatively little support, compared with the enormous public relations effort underpinning CEMA; while the War Office toured certain stars under its own steam, it apparently believed ENSA performers to be security risks, often refusing to give specific directions to camps, thus rendering many expeditions abortive. Contrast this with the memories of the Pilgrim Players that arrangements were made with the Ministries of Labour, War Transport and Customs and Excise to facilitate their activities (Browne and Browne 1945, 63–64; *The Arts in Wartime*, 1944, 14).

The impetus behind the subsequent change in CEMA's direction came straight from Keynes. I have already described his antipathy to the endowments to amateurs. As Kenneth Clark recalled, 'He was not the man for wandering minstrels and amateur theatricals. He believed in excellence' (quoted, Baldry 1981, 15). Excellence, like standards, is a weasel word, which can mean many things, depending who uses it. Charles Landstone, the Assistant Drama Director for CEMA from November 1942, argues that Keynes 'loved glamour, he loved success' (1953, 67), and that his priorities for the theatre were not therefore with amateur work, nor indeed with tours to industrial towns.

The withdrawal of the Pilgrim Trust was a nail in the amateurs' coffin. It soon became clear that CEMA was likely to grow, and that its work might even continue after the war. The scale of the undertaking would soon be beyond the Trust's resources, and they would have to back out of the deal. This meant the departure of Thomas Jones and Lord Macmillan, who were both on the

Council as Pilgrim Trust representatives. A new Chair needed to be found and Rab Butler, at the Board of Education, favoured Keynes. But in a letter to Butler in December 1941, Keynes admitted himself 'in only limited sympathy with the [Council's] principles' (quoted, Leventhal 1990, 305).

However, he was reassured by the exit of the Pilgrim Trust and by the presence of Mary Glasgow, who by this point was firmly in Keynes's camp. Furthermore, the ambiguity of CEMA's constitutional position (both a government body and independent) meant that he actually had considerable freedom to impose his stamp on its operation and, in particular, exploit the ambiguity of its early statement of aims. Finally, the amateur side of CEMA's work was jettisoned at the end of December, almost certainly as an extra enticement to attract Keynes. He accepted the job and at his first Council meeting in April 1942 he proposed bringing into association professional opera and ballet companies, which thus far had been deliberately excluded (Leventhal 1990, 306). In January 1943, the Council retrieved the responsibility for the LSO and LPO tours from the Carnegie Trust. National professional companies were now at the heart of its policy.

So amateurs were now no longer directly funded by CEMA. Yet the original impetus for supporting them – the desire to encourage people to experience art through practice, not just consumption – was slower dying. When the Arts Council's charter was being written, it was only at the last minute that Charles Landstone was able to have the words 'and practice' added to 'knowledge and understanding of the arts' as a description of its principle aims (Leventhal 1990, 315).[4] Despite this addition, in 1950, an Arts Council pamphlet designed to publicise its activities asks itself the question, 'Are Drama Societies associated with the Council?' and answers firmly, 'No. These are almost invariably amateur societies; and the Council, being unable to cover all the ground, has adopted a deliberate policy of directing its financial help towards the professional aspect of the arts' (*The Arts Council* 1950, 8). Six years later, the Arts Council reminiscing on its first ten years, surmised that while there may be some vigour to be found in amateur work, 'the achievement and preservation of standards in the arts is, primarily, then, the rôle of the professional' (1956, 13).

From tours to buildings

Many commentators remarked on the success of the tours (e.g. Hudd 1943, 16; Browne and Browne 1945, 54; Landstone 1953, 54–55) and CEMA was proud to trumpet its achievements; the 1943 report describes touring as 'so encouraging that the Council regards this branch of its work as perhaps the most important of all and the most far reaching in its results' (*The Arts in Wartime*, 1944, 17). The tours to workers' hostels which began in the summer of 1942 were particularly praised.

However, not everyone was so impressed. Mary Glasgow recollects that of the 'factory concerts, performances in small halls and touring exhibitions of paintings [...] Keynes was appreciative, but this was not where his sympathies lay' (1975, 263). Landstone thinks that he barely knew the tours were happening (1953, 58). Soon after assuming the Chair, Keynes began redirecting CEMA's attention towards buildings and building-based companies. In September 1942, CEMA acquired the Bristol Old Vic's lease, which opened, refurbished, the following May. In September 1943, the Glasgow Citizens company opened its theatre. In February 1946, the Sadler's Wells Ballet company occupied its new home in the Royal Opera House, Covent Garden. Keynes made funds available, but in doing so reduced funding for touring activities. Williams remembers him negotiating down an 'Art for the People' request for money, and ascribes it to his new passion for 'acquiring historic buildings or homes for the arts' (1971, 22).

Amateur work was the link between 'standards' and 'distribution'. Once CEMA had stopped trying to encourage people to practice the arts themselves, tours simply meant moving professionals around the country. And since there will only be a finite number of professionals, this resurrects the claim that CEMA is spreading the arts too thinly. Michael Macowan, the first Drama Director of the Arts Council, argued that 'if we think too much about distribution, and concentrate too much on something for everybody, we shall probably end by lowering standards so much that there is nothing worth having for anybody' (1950, 16).

I have indicated that the word 'standards' remains mysterious in their accounts, yet perhaps that is part of its force. The work of the Music Travellers involved taking some of the mystery out of creating music. 'Art for the People' invited people to examine paintings free of a gallery's hushed mystique, by placing them in non-traditional environments, and once even toured an exhibition of 'Art *by* the People'.

In 'The Work of Art in the Age of Mechanical Reproduction', Walter Benjamin argues that the 'aura' surrounding traditional artworks derives from their unique placement at the heart of cult and ritual processes. With the increasing availability of contemporary culture, through wider distribution and greater reproducibility, art may not be materially altered, 'yet the quality of its presence is always depreciated [...] That which withers in the age of mechanical reproduction is the aura of the work of art' (1992, 215). This Benjamin sees as positive, 'a revolutionary criticism of traditional concepts of art' (224). The 'Art for the People' project could usefully be seen like this. On occasion, when a particular painting was unavailable, or needed in two places at once, good-quality lithographs were toured in place of the original.

The change in CEMA's operation was an attempt to reverse this drift, to restore an 'aura' to the artwork, by reducing the availability and reproducibility of the art they encouraged. The authors of the *Eighth Annual Report* write, 'Plays should be performed in playhouses if the mystique of the theatre is to be fully communicated, and a Town Hall or a Village Institute seldom offers a hope of that revelation which a good play aims to disclose' (Arts Council 1953, 9). This is perhaps what is implied by Macowan's otherwise bewildering set of precepts when he upbraids small touring venues: 'Hard chairs, echoing rafters, inferior coffee and stodgy buns, with perhaps school maps, charts and pictures around the walls, hardly creates the right atmosphere for an evening's pleasure' (1950, 40).

So as to reinstate an auratic mystery to the culture, touring is slowly abandoned. The Music Travellers were cut drastically in 1943 and were disbanded a year later, to the fury of Sybil Eaton, their coordinator: 'Now, having created the demand, mobilized the enthusiasts and built up audiences, the cut has come, without warning...it will strain all our loyalty to CEMA to explain the sudden change without causing bitter resentment' (quoted, Leventhal 1990, 310). The *Sixth Annual Report* of the Arts Council ruminates:

> In reconsidering the exhortation of its Charter to 'Raise and Spread' the Council may decide for the time being, to emphasise the first more than the second word, and to

devote itself to the support of two or three exemplary theatres which might re-affirm the supremacy of standards in our national theatre.

(1951, 34)

The touring relationship between producer and consumer is entirely inverted through the fifties. The same report that announced the abandonment of touring introduces a combined ticket-and-bus scheme to encourage audiences to travel to the theatre, rather than the other way round (1951, 25). The next year's report develops this idea (1952, 36). In 1953, the report affirms the priority of raising over spreading even more strongly than it did two years previously (12). And by the time of the *Ninth Annual Report*, the Arts Council has fixed on making the audience circulate between a small number of prestigious venues: 'the first thing to be done is to provide a concentration of high quality at a limited number of centres' (1954, 25).

The retreat from touring was clearly part of the same process as the ending of involvement with amateur groups. It was a move away from encouraging cultural practice and towards cultural reverie. And the intertwining of tradition and heritage reveal the contours of a policy of prestige. The early decentralising, regionally sensitive work gave way to a new hierarchical integration of activities. E. Martin Browne recalled the progress of his group, The Pilgrim Players, through the war: 'We had been, so to speak, the spearhead of CEMA's dramatic work, and at first were left to carry on our own life and book our own tours, while other organisations were being built up. But gradually a larger framework began to appear' (Browne and Browne 1945, 63).

From the regions to London

This 'larger framework' was the organisation of these different areas of cultural practice in relation to one another, and then to the Council itself. Describing the Arts Council's projected policy, Keynes cooed, 'The artist walks where the breath of the spirit blows him [*sic*]. He cannot be told his direction; he does not know it himself' (1945, 31–32). In fact, Keynes resented the free wanderings of the artist. Notoriously unwilling to devolve responsibility, he began to be concerned that theatre workers on tour in rural districts were hard to keep tabs on (Glasgow 1975, 260). Companies based in buildings were easier to regulate and, with the desire for prestige increasingly becoming his focus, London came ever more to be seen as the natural focus of endeavour.

He was not alone. J.B. Priestley's *Theatre Outlook* (1947), supports the establishment of a network of regional repertory theatres, but placed in a structured relation to the metropolis: no one should feel 'that, here in their playhouse, they are making an isolated effort [...] They should know that their playhouse has its own place in the whole wide scheme of the British Theatre, that there are stout ladders to higher levels of their art' (52–53). Charles Landstone called the major repertory theatres 'the last rung of the ladder up which artists climb to the height of London or Stratford-upon-Avon' (1954, 84). These altitudinal metaphors were to become commonplace throughout the forties. Priestley imagines 'at the apex of this pyramid' a small number of large, directly state-funded national companies which would provide a 'shining example and inspiration to the whole Theatre of the nation [...] Men and women working in little theatres in remote small towns would work better because they knew about these national companies'. And where would these theatres be sited? London – 'of course' (1947a, 54, 55).

These images, and the policies they supported, were responding to a widespread anxiety about the use of leisure. The inter-war period saw a general and dramatic increase in leisure time (Urry 1990, 26–27). By the thirties, 'leisure was [...] regarded as a right of all the people – irrespective of economic circumstances' (Walvin 1978, 135). The increase in leisure time did not see a proportionate increase in the pursuit of fine art, music and drama. The major beneficiaries were, instead, holidays to coastal resorts, football, dancing and the cinema (133–143). The governments of the thirties were not immediately concerned, but did little to encourage this trend. It was only after considerable public pressure and a Royal Commission that it passed the *Holidays with Pay Act* in 1938. The war deferred the full enactment of this legislation, but as the end of the conflict came into view, concern began to be expressed about how people would use the increasing freedom available to them.[5]

In 1944, *The Author* asked a number of contributors for their thoughts on the future of state funding for the Arts. One observes that 'it is recognised that the difficulty of the post-war years will be fruitfully to fill the leisure hours rather than to provide them' (Bridie *et al.* 1944, 52). Basil Dean gave his views in a lecture looking ahead to the role of the arts in the post-war reconstruction. The people need, he declared,

> education in the right use of leisure. It would be a political error of the first magnitude if the great mass of the people were to find themselves with an unusual amount of spare time on their hands and no guidance nor help in the wise spending of it.
>
> (1945, 1; also 1948, 60)

Charles Landstone agreed that 'the theatre can, if it cares to, achieve a decisive rôle in the employment of leisure' (1952, 3). This anxiety about leisure became firmly entwined with planning for the post-war theatre.

Michel Foucault's *Discipline and Punish* is an account of the birth of the modern prison system, and also of the birth of the modern individual. It describes how eighteenth-century punishment, exercised through threats and displays of physical pain, gave way to a new method of control, not focused on punishment but on surveillance. Jeremy Bentham's designs for a new kind of prison, the Panopticon, was the model. The Panopticon has a large number of cells arranged in a circle around a central viewing tower. This ensures that the prisoners are constantly aware of their ability to be seen, but are unable to see one another. The principal effect of this arrangement is 'to induce in the inmate a state of conscious and permanent visibility' which functions even if the guard is not actually in the viewing tower. In this way, 'the inmates should be caught up in a power situation of which they are themselves the bearers' (1977a, 201). As Foucault describes it, this model begins reappearing in other buildings, hospitals, schools, orphanages, factory-convents. Everywhere the principle is the same, 'to establish presences and absences, to know where and how to locate individuals [...] to be able at each moment to supervise the conduct of each individual' (143). The law is internalised, and its maintenance taken on by each individual. Foucault describes these new beings as 'subjected and practised bodies, "docile" bodies' (138).

This system can be seen operating through the Panoptical pyramid, in the first place in relations between the Council and its associated companies. As CEMA became the Arts Council, a number of changes took place. It moved from being directly run by the Board of Education to being an independent body; at the same time the size of the advisory panels increased from six to sixteen, one immediate effect of which was to make unanimity much less likely and effectively to transfer power upwards. New regulations meant that assessors from the Treasury, the Board of Education or the Scottish Office could sit in on any meeting. Each company was required to appoint a figure to represent it to the Council which could then go into 'very minute detail indeed. Every one of its associated organisations, large or small, submits its budgets, balance-sheets and trading returns to the Council, and is called upon to justify its figures and forecasts' (Arts Council 1956, 16). This was not merely a matter of profitability; after all, they were happy to imagine a projected National Theatre being 'economically "unprofitable"' (1952, 4) – this in the same report that criticises touring for not covering its costs (36).

The control continues down the system. During the war the lively response of the largely captive audiences in subways, barracks, and hostels seemed to augur well for attendances after it. But after VE day the audience seemed to evaporate. 'It was as if these newcomers were saying "Theatre? That's something we went to during the war. We want to forget all about the war"' (Landstone 1953, 60). By 1947, Robert Speaight is referring to the 'artificial prosperity' of the war (8). Perhaps as a way of trying to regain this audience, the Arts Council hit upon the idea of arts centres. Throughout 1945, they toured a model of a potential centre, produced a document promoting it (*Plans for an Arts Centre*), and organised an exhibition at the Royal Academy (British Drama League 1945).

The key to this innovation lies in the statistic that Landstone cites in his *Notes on Civic Theatres*: although an average of three percent of the population regularly visited the theatre, as much as ten percent went to see some sort of performance (1950, 4–5). The proposed Civic Theatre was 'designed for the presentation of plays, opera, ballet, concerts, and films. The auditorium can be cleared for ballroom dancing and will be suitable for exhibiting travelling art collections. Restaurant facilities will also be a feature of these institutions' (Kelsall 1945, 27; see also Leacroft 1949, 36). The idea is that the same venue can gain their audiences and keep them; once there, the audience can be guided towards more 'healthy' ways of occupying its leisure time. An article on the audience in *Civic Entertainment* uses the unflattering, but telling metaphor: 'you must first catch your goose before you can cook it'.[6]

The pyramid structure is a mechanism to inscribe everyone into the values embodied at the peak by the prestigious national companies. Keynes declared in 1945, 'We look forward to a time when the theatre and the concert-hall and the gallery will be a living element in everyone's upbringing, and regular attendance at the theatre and at concerts a part of organised education' (32). Lord Jowett, during the debate on the *National Theatre Bill*, even hoped that it would stimulate the British people culturally to emulate the aristocracy (Shepherd and Womack 1996, 307–308).

The repertories were to be kept firmly in their place: a rung on the ladder, not a venture in themselves. The Arts Council took over direct management of the Salisbury Arts Theatre in 1945. But the next five years had seen a greater streamlining of operations, geared ever more tightly towards metropolitan prestige. They backed out in 1951. Charles Landstone recalls, 'I could not convince them that the scheme at Salisbury was exactly the scheme designed by the Charter; they craved, as always, for the spectacular, and Wessex was in too much of a backwater for their taste' (1953, 143). Trying to persuade him of the real achievements of the repertories, Landstone took Bronson Albery, a theatre manager and member of the drama panel, to see *To-night at 8.30* at the Salisbury Playhouse: 'I was prepared for the best. I was not prepared, however, to hear within two minutes, a whisper from Sir Bronson: "This is magnificent. But it's much too good for Salisbury"' (110).

The Shadow Factory

The Pilgrim Players disbanded after the war. Armed with an unshakeable faith in the necessity of verse theatre, E. Martin Browne established himself at Ashley Dukes's Mercury Theatre, Notting Hill, to plan the Poetic Drama revival. His first season in 1945–46 brought Christopher Fry to prominence with *A Phoenix too Frequent*, saw a brief West End transfer of Ronald Duncan's *This Way to the Tomb*, and included well-received productions of Norman Nicholson's *The Old Man of the Mountains*, and Peter Yates's *The Assassin*. One play sticks out from the others. Anne Ridler's *The Shadow Factory* (1945), while being on one level a meditation on the contemporary power of the Nativity story, can be seen as engaging with debates about the role of the state cultural policy. (The title of the play is perhaps a kind of Platonic joke about the Arts Council).

The play concerns a factory. The Director is keen to make his factory the centre of his workers' lives: 'The factory must manage its workers lives, / Leisure hours like labouring hours. / The factory must give them recreation; / The factory must give them satisfying art' (Ridler 1946, 10). His current schemes are not having the right effect. His education officer's protest that 'You can't grow trees on the seashore' receives the Director's rebuke, 'we may be obliged / To use compulsion' (3). He hires an artist to paint a series of murals in the factory canteen as a means of tying the workers ever more closely to their workplace.

The Director's scheme recalls the advice of one *CEMA Bulletin* to add artistic decoration to civic restaurants:

> eating being a necessary, and sometimes enjoyable, occu-
> pation, and being also in this case a social matter, it is
> especially desirable that it should be carried out in
> premises which are relieved from dullness or gloom, and
> show that 'taste' is not a word limited to victuals merely.[7]

The familiar pattern of the arts centre is already here, arranging the activities in structured relations so as to 'elevate' taste and appreciation.

The Director has no interest in art except as a means of social control, a way of maintaining production. The factory is itself a Panoptical means of surveillance and control: 'I planned this building of ours myself' he declares, 'My office, you see, is a focal point; / You get from here a bird's-eye-view / Of the whole process' (Ridler 1946, 9).

The artist agrees to take the job on, with the condition that no one can see his work until the unveiling ceremony. When the mural is revealed, the Director is appalled; it shows him as a semi-bestial figure moving his workers around like pawns on a chess board: 'it has the vigour of the crude cartoons / Drawn on the flap of a tent at the fair' (46–47). The danger for the state is that the recipients of subsidy might bite the handouts that feed them.

This story would be remarkable enough, but after the workers have been ushered out, the parson advises the Director not to have the designs removed:

> accept them. Don't you see?
> Your position would then be stronger than ever.
> Finding the courage to leave them there –

Showing the factory rich enough to afford it –
Sturdy enough to contain such satire
Right at its heart.

(44)

The Director admits the efficacy of the idea:

>   All may be well.
> All is in order – discipline kept,
> Position safe, all
> Sensible yet. Prestige – some little loss,
> Quickly retrievable.

(49)

Panoptical power operates by letting things be seen, by opening
everything to scrutiny. As Foucault writes,

> a fear haunted the latter half of the eighteenth century: the
> fear of darkened spaces, of the pall of gloom which
> prevents the full visibility of things, men [*sic*] and truths.
> It sought to break up the patches of darkness that blocked
> the light, eliminate the shadowy areas of society, demolish
> the unlit chambers where [...] plots, epidemics and the
> illusions of ignorance were fomented.

(1980, 153)

The Arts Council's Panoptical gaze spread through the system,
articulating a diverse number of elements for its own purposes.
Shortly after the war, Unity Theatre, which had prided itself on its
amateur status, founded a professional company. This new Unity,
as Colin Chambers puts it, was 'London-based and London-
biased' (1989, 265); Ted Willis even proposed a 'nationwide
network of democratically run professional theatres' under the
control of London Unity (1991, 270). It is hard not to see this as
Unity positioning itself both to be visible to, and in imitation of,
the new structures.

The tendency of arts subsidy through the forties was towards
the accumulation and centralisation of cultural capital. This
involved jettisoning certain parts of its early operation and
ordering the new areas in vertical divisions. It is now necessary,
not least because of the Royal Court's claimed position of exteri-

ority to the West End, to examine the relationship between subsidised and commercial theatre.

West End

One of the first decisions that marked Keynes's chairmanship of CEMA was in response to an approach made in June 1942 by 'Binkie' Beaumont, managing director of H.M. Tennent Ltd. Beaumont was about to bring a touring production of *Macbeth*, starring John Gielgud, into the Piccadilly Theatre, London, and was sounding out the possibility of an association with CEMA. It may seem curious that a major West End producer should seek association with an organisation sponsoring small-scale community projects in industrial and rural areas; that is, until you consider Entertainment Tax.

Entertainment Tax was a levy placed on tickets, an emergency measure in 1916, designed to help the war effort, which had never gone away. A clause of the bill had exempted educational activities, which, for nearly twenty years, Customs and Excise tended to interpret very narrowly. In 1934, a landmark ruling by the Law Officers allowed the Old Vic exemption on the basis that it was a 'non-profit-distributing theatre' and that its dedication to producing the 'classics' amounted at least in part to an educational aim. This exemption was taken up by a small number of similar companies, like the Shakespeare Memorial Theatre. The 1916 rate was a little over 7 per cent, though by 1943, after Kingsley Wood, the wartime Chancellor of the Exchequer, had increased the rate in successive budgets, it was nearly 30 per cent (Herbert 1957, 27).

It was after the second of these increases in 1942 that Beaumont saw a loophole and applied to inhabit it. Although H.M. Tennent Ltd could not conceivably describe itself as non-profit-distributing, he realised that he could set up a subsidiary company, dedicated to work 'which conformed roughly to, say, that of the better class plays of the BBC' (Landstone 1953, 70), and apply for exemption. The problem was persuading Customs and Excise; Beaumont recognised that association with CEMA would probably shorten this process, since CEMA's stamp would guarantee its worthiness.[8]

Against the advice of Casson and Landstone, Keynes welcomed in Tennents. He felt that if CEMA were to have a long-term future, it 'must set a standard in London second to none. He believed that, for this purpose, the firm of Tennents was a ready instrument to his hand' (Landstone 1953, 73–74). Accordingly, Tennent Plays Ltd was established.

Apart from giving him a second management fee, the exemption did not profit Beaumont directly, since a condition was that the company be non-profit-distributing. The real benefit to Beaumont was that it allowed him bigger budgets to spend on cast, designers and writers. He was therefore able to attract bigger stars, playing on more lavish sets, in plays by more illustrious writers, and thus would be more likely to attract audiences. It gave him the financial margin to build a commanding share of the West End. The exemption ruling of 1934 had been on a production-by-production basis, but one of Keynes's last acts was to push through a change in the rules allowing *companies* exemption, which cemented Tennents' authority. After the war a number of commercial managements formed non-profit-distributing subsidiaries: Henry Sherek's 'Sherek Plays Ltd', John Clements's 'Associated Players' and the 'Company of Four' at the Lyric Hammersmith, which comprised Tennents, Glyndebourne, Cambridge Arts Theatre and Tyrone Guthrie. The 'Four' were to share the building, touring when they were not performing. But in all cases Tennents was ahead of the pack; Sherek and Clements, despite some success with *The Cocktail Party* (1949) and *The Beaux' Strategem* (1949) respectively, never threatened Beaumont's pre-eminence. Glyndebourne and Guthrie withdrew from the Company of Four within a year, and Cambridge a little after that, leaving Tennents fully in control at the Lyric.

At the same time, 'the Group' was building an empire in bricks-and-mortar. The financial arrangements of the theatres in the late forties are immensely complicated. The networks and chains of different parties can be bewildering; a play could be given a production by a non-profit-distributing company which is a subsidiary of another producing management, perhaps in association with a further management, occupying a theatre rented from the sub-lessee of the freeholder, who is in turn a subsidiary of a holding company, which is a subsidiary of a parent company. It is, however, striking how often these chains lead up to Prince Littler Consolidated Trust. By the early fifties, Prince Littler controlled over 50 per cent of the seats in London's West End, and dominated the number one provincial touring circuit. This was the 'Group'.

The 'Group' has become a byword for everything that was

wrong with the West End, and the extent of its influence – or 'dominance', or 'stranglehold' – is commonly imagined to have been total. The very name suggests the shroudedly sinister. For that reason, we should be precise about the nature of its monopoly. In the early fifties, the Federation of Theatre Unions conducted an investigation into this question, publishing a report, *Theatre Ownership in Britain*, in 1953. The first point it makes about the Group is that it actually put British theatre on 'a proper industrial footing, employing all the devices of horizontal and vertical combination that this involves' (7). The pre-war theatre was a mess of different interests; huge numbers of theatres were owned or controlled by companies whose primary commercial interest was entirely elsewhere, and who had, as a result, little interest in the upkeep of the theatres. These were the corporations who spent the thirties converting theatres into cinemas and dance-halls. The actions of the Group in buying up controlling interests in these companies could well be argued, in *this* sense, to have been in the interests of the theatre (cf. Elsom 1979, 13). The calculation that the Group ran almost seventy percent of the number one touring circuit has to be moderated by an acknowledgement that the sort of work the Group's associated managements were able to send into these venues *made* them 'number ones'.

The second charge often made against the Group was that it forced up rents and, through its associated managements, also forced up actors', designers' and writers' fees. While it is true that in certain well-publicised cases, Tennent Plays Ltd. was able to make unmatchable royalty offers for the British rights to plays like *Death of a Salesman* and *A Streetcar Named Desire*, there is no evidence that this had a generally inflationary effect. The Arts Council calculated that increases in total running costs meant that for every pound that was spent in 1939, £1 18s. 9d. had to be spent in 1954. But the increase in rents, production costs and production salaries actually rose considerably below this level (1954, 26). In fact, the Federation's report firmly refutes the charge that the Group raised their rents; indeed, since their theatres generally housed productions by associated managements it would not have been in their interests to do so. If anything, the non-Group theatre owners capitalised on the increased competition for their buildings by raising theirs (Federation of Theatre Unions 1953, 27).

For many writers, looking back on events, it is not Prince Littler but 'Binkie' Beaumont who was the face of the Group. This is certainly misplaced. Prince Littler controlled Howard and Wyndham Ltd. which held a sizeable stake in H.M. Tennent Ltd. This meant that he (or his associate A.S. Cruikshank) could sit on Tennents' board. But Beaumont was a manager, not a theatre owner, so to place him, as Hewison does, 'at the centre of the Group' (1988, 10), is misleading.

One problem is that many commentators on the period have collapsed these criticisms and these companies together, thus giving it even more monolithic an appearance than it actually deserves. During the forties, there was a different perspective. The main critics of Tennents itself were rival theatre managers. In 1949, there was a Select Parliamentary Subcommittee established to investigate claims of unfair advantage against the Tennents subsidiary; the Theatre Managers Association (TMA) prepared a statement, clearly aimed at Beaumont, suggesting that being a manager of a non-profit-distributing company and a commercial company allowed one to juggle productions between companies as a sophisticated means of tax-evasion (Federation of Theatre Unions 1953, 81). But the subcommittee found no evidence to support the charge; and even Charles Landstone, one of the severest critics of Tennents' association with CEMA, admits that 'my own investigations (I had many discussions with [...] Tennents' accountants) have satisfied me that the accounts would bear closest scrutiny' (1953, 80–81). Similarly the failed 1954 *Theatrical Companies Bill* which tried to break up Tennents was driven by a rival manager, Peter Cotes, who, it is suggested, was mainly motivated by a belief that a homosexual mafia with Beaumont as its Godfather ran British theatre (Duff 1995, 103).

There is, then, an important distinction to make. Landstone's objection is not to Tennents *per se*, but to the *idea* of a commercial company associating on a non-profit-distributing basis, since although no abuses had arisen in this actual instance, they *could* arise; it would never be easy to make the necessary distinction between non-educational and partly-educational, nor to decide whether to pay an unusually high royalty constituted distributing profits. The extreme concentration of capital in the hands of the Group was undoubtedly a danger for the theatre, but to infer directly from that to criticising the work of its associated producing managements is not self-evidently legitimate.

This distinction was expressly drawn at the time. In the late forties there were several calls for the Group's powers to be checked. But it is crucial to recognise that these were not aimed at

Tennents; in the pages of the left-wing *Theatre Newsletter*, Tennents was stoutly defended against the managers' charges and commended as one of the best companies in Britain.[9] The criticisms were exclusively and precisely directed towards the structures of ownership. The TUC Conference in 1944 called for the monopoly tendency in the entertainment industry to be broken up.[10] Over the next four years, several prominent figures urged some kind of statutory intervention. Sybil Thorndike, Freda Jackson called for theatre buildings to be nationalised, and Llewellyn Rees urged the managers to see that 'their policy is creating a situation to which nationalisation may prove to be the only solution'.[11] J.B. Priestley's proposal that the state regulate theatre buildings, was echoed by Basil Dean, Robert Morley and Peter Ustinov.[12]

This all came to a head in 1948 at the British Theatre Conference.

British Theatre Conference

In the terrible winter of 1946–1947, it was clear that the gains of the wartime period were under serious threat. In January 1947, J.B. Priestley in a letter to *Theatre Newsletter* argues that the problems facing the theatre could be addressed at an 'English Theatre Conference'.[13] The call was taken up by the editors of *New Theatre* and *Theatre Newsletter*.[14] In June a meeting was held between the editors of these two journals and a preparatory committee was established, which included representations from the TMA. In November the conference was announced for February of the next year. Soundings were taken from several groups, and representation organised from across the profession. With figures like Ralph Richardson, Edith Evans, Henry Sherek, Tyrone Guthrie, James Bridie and E. Martin Browne joining the usual names of Priestley, Willis, Ossia Trilling and Sybil Thorndike, the conference was supported universally.[15]

Well, almost universally. As the programme shaped up it became clear that demands for controls on theatre ownership would find their focus at the conference. The managers were rattled. They pulled out from the preparatory body and wrote a scathing denunciation of the organisers; their genuine fears are easily legible in their bizarre mixture of red-baiting and petty insult, moving between arguing that the agenda (which had not yet been formulated) was 'tinged with a left-wing aspect' to describing the conference as a response to the 'clamourings of the sandal-shod and corduroy-clad' (Collins 1947b, 5, 2).

Despite these attacks, the British Theatre Conference opened on 5 February 1948. The atmosphere, by all accounts, was inspirational. Alec Bernstein breathlessly reports, 'for fifty years theatre people have been raising their voices; but each in isolation, and with little result. This time everyone is pulling together' (1948, 11). Key recommendations included a body to control theatre rents, Entertainment Tax to be operated on a sliding scale, increasing as the run went on, and that Local Authorities be empowered to spend money on Civic Theatres. 'Everyone, even those most opposed to the whole idea, now admits the success of the British Theatre Conference', applauded *New Theatre*. 'The very existence of the conference represented the greatest step forward for the theatre in the past two decades'.[16]

At the conference, Stafford Cripps announced a clause in the *Local Government Bill* empowering Local Authorities to use 6d. in the pound to spend on civic entertainment. Contrary to some recollections (Landstone 1953, 182; Willis 1991, 44), Cripps did not act on the conference's recommendations; although he announced it at the conference, the decision had been made by the Minister of Health at the request of the Association of Municipal Corporations the day before the conference began (MacIver 1948, 6). The Association's approach was entirely separate from the Conference and had been prepared over the previous three years (Segal 1948, 3).

Nonetheless, it was welcomed as a victory for all who had campaigned for it. In a way it was, and yet it was also a very partial move. The *Local Government Act* suited the Arts Council's centralising strategy perfectly. By empowering local authorities to fund arts locally, it relieved the Council of the need to fund regional theatre projects, and allowed them to concentrate on the capital. In his speech, Cripps staunchly refused to entertain the idea of any further state controls on theatre buildings. His speech bears the traces of the renewed hostility to the Soviet Union, as he argues that the state should not be 'the *dictator* of the Arts but the wise patron' (1948, 9, my emphasis). This itself lines Cripps up with the TMA, which obsessively chased reds from under the Conference's bed. A review of Priestley's *Theatre Outlook* in their journal observes 'Mr Priestley's book costs 7s. 6d. (about nine roubles)'.[17]

Allowing local authorities to spend money on the arts might

THE DOCILE BODIES OF ARTS FUNDING

nonetheless be seen as a blow to the managers' dominance of the touring circuit. Initially the TMA seemed to think so; they distributed a circular to MPs raging against the new clause: 'Theatre Managers', it read, 'regard it as grossly unfair that as ratepayers they should have to contribute up to 6d. in the pound in order to enable their Local Authority to put them out of business'.[18] On 24 March, a deputation from the TMA met with the financial secretary to the Treasury, W. Glenvil Hall. Despite their bravado, they had clearly been scared by the Conference. Bronson Albery raised the matter of a rent control authority, and they asked for a reduction in Entertainment Tax. Percival Selby argued that this would help to reduce the competitive margin between them and the local authorities, whose projects would be automatically exempt.[19]

In the 1948 Budget, Entertainment Tax was reduced from 30 to 15 per cent.[20] There were some new exemptions, but none that would help the proposed civic theatres.[21] The only beneficiaries were the theatre owners. Not only did it reduce the margin between them and the non-profit-distributing companies, but agreements between producing managements and theatre owners usually took the form of a box-office split *after* tax (which an exempt producing management would get back) had been levied. The reduction meant that, relatively, more money went to the owner and less to the producing management.

The two actions meant that the Arts Council's increasing focus on London was confirmed and the theatre owners were better off than ever. It did not take long for this to sink in. By July 1948, *New Theatre* is raising concern that the Arts Council has not taken up the opportunities opened to it by the *Local Government Act* to co-fund the building of civic theatres.[22] Widespread press derision after large losses were incurred by the LCC's pageant *The London Story* and by Leyton Borough Council's *Aladdin,* both in late 1948, discouraged timid councils from taking up the new powers.[23] A subgroup set up to organise a successor conference fell into abeyance. Plans for a parliamentary working party, proposed by Hugh Dalton and supported by the conference to consider the problem of theatre finance, were put back a year and then quietly dropped.[24] At the end of the year, Robert Muller wrote 'I doubt if the year 1948 will bring tears of nostalgia to our eyes when we come to discuss its theatrical achievements twenty or thirty years hence. It has not been a very fruitful year' (1948, 3).

National theatre

In an editorial at the end of the war, *Theatre World* hailed the 'ambassadorial potency of the theatre'.[25] This captures the metropolitanism of the new Arts Council. After all, where do you site an embassy but in the capital? But the word 'ambassadorial' also signals an aim to preserve and promote Britain's national image.

Strains of 'English heritage' thinking were in CEMA from the start. Thomas Jones was given to bucolic fantasies, in which the Music Travellers were 'a dream of fair women singing their way through the villages of England until all the birds and all the shires joined the choir and filled the land with melody' (quoted, White 1975, 36); at the first meeting between the Board of Education and the Pilgrim Trust, he was enthused with images of 'Shakespear from the Old Vic., ballet from Sadler's Wells, shining canvasses from the Royal Academy, folk dancers from village greens – in fact, Merrie England' (Kisch 1943, 9).

In the ten years after the Second World War, national pride increasingly dominated discussion of arts policy. Basil Dean greets the news that the Royal Opera House is to be reopened with delight: it should be, he decides, a 'cultural centre for the British Empire [...] a noble conception, an Empire and Commonwealth memorial worthy of the achievements of the recent struggle, and of lasting benefit to the British race' (1945, 8). A variety of ventures, big and small, are fleetingly articulated in terms of their contribution to national pride. The Society for Theatre Research was founded in June 1948, *Theatre Today* trilling, 'all this is of immense importance, especially now when we have a theatre nearer to possessing national character than it has been for a long time but in danger of losing that character precisely because it is so unsure of its own traditions'.[26]

Commentators routinely appealed to the idea that we had lost touch with our heritage. More specifically, they claimed that it was still buried deep within the British character, but for various reasons we had lost the art of displaying our genius to the world. Priestley argued:

> playgoing with us is at a deeper and more instinctive level of behaviour than it is with most peoples [...] Not only are we not an undramatic people, but in some respects we are the most dramatic people left on earth. In

Shakespeare's time we sent plays and players all over Europe. We are still sending them.

(1947a, 16)

The boost to national pride offered by the war, offset by our increasing subservience to the United States, both economically and culturally, gave some to believe that it was time to rediscover Britain's dormant greatness.

The arguments for a National Theatre were pitched at this level. Stafford Cripps, announcing plans for legislation, predicts that it would 'set a standard for the production of drama in a national setting worthy of Shakespeare and the British tradition' (quoted, Minihan 1977, 237). Oliver Lyttleton declared on the *National Theatre Bill*'s second reading, 'A national theatre in Great Britain would help to keep undefiled the purity of the English language [...] by setting a standard springing from the glorious English of Shakespeare of which we are the proud but I must say somewhat negligent heirs'.[27]

Funds were not immediately made available for the National Theatre, as another celebration of Britannia was pending. As the *National Theatre Bill* passed its final reading, Herbert Morrison stood by the Thames while diggers waited to begin extending the river wall in preparation for the construction of the South Bank centre. 'What we are starting here today', he announced, 'must not be merely an embankment against mud and water, but a stronghold of the British way of life. This will be the site on which we shall show the world what we stand for' (1949, 14). The groundworks he was celebrating were the first visible preparations for the Festival of Britain. Planned to mark the centenary of the Great Exhibition, the Festival was conceived, as Michael Frayn put it, as 'a sort of national prestige advertisement' (1963, 322), or as the Arts Council had it, a means to 'display the genius of the nation' (1951, 5). Prestigious companies were invited to submit ideas for events. Four hundred thousand pounds was earmarked for the Festival, to be given to the most suitably ambassadorial proposals.

Theatre did not rise to the occasion. Olivier's Council-backed pairing of *Antony and Cleopatra* and *Caesar and Cleopatra* and Gielgud's *The Winter's Tale*, with Tennents money, were well-received.[28] But negotiations with other companies proved abortive and Alec Guinness's *Hamlet* was booed on the first night. Small grants were offered to regional repertories to commission new works for the festival, with patchy results. 'It was disappointing', admitted the Arts Council, 'that so few contemporary plays of merit emerged for the occasion' (1951, 7). This was the first blow to the Council's ambitions for cultural renewal. They continued dangling a series of baits in the water over the next few years: play competitions, earmarked money for repertory commissions, writers' bursaries. But the plays were not biting. This is not to say that there was no interesting theatre about, but the Council had certain views about what it did *not* want to see.

One strand of theatre that they conspicuously failed to support was the socialist theatre which had been strong in the forties. During the war the Army Education Corps were surprised by the soldiers' interest in learning and debating about the events they were involved in. To that end, and spurred by W.E. Williams of 'Art for the People', the Army Bureau of Current Affairs (ABCA) was set up. Besides producing pamphlets and lectures and discussions, in June 1944 ABCA established a small drama group. Remarkably, the writers asked to work for this company – Ted Willis, Jack Lindsay, Bridget Boland, André van Gyseghem, J.B. Priestley, Mulk Raj Anand – were largely from the political left, some from the far left, with an interest in using experimental forms often drawn from the socialist theatre of the thirties; under Stephen Murray and Michael Macowan, they produced plays like *What Are We Fighting For?*, *Where Do We Go from Here?*, *The Japanese Way*, and *It Started as Lend Lease: or, The Great Swap*. They were under investigation for political bias, during which the war ended, and they were quietly wound up.[29]

The wave of working-class militancy in the 1840s meant that there were a lot of centenaries to celebrate. The People's Entertainment Theatre offered Ann Lindsay's *The Rochdale Pioneers* (1944) about the mill-workers' revolt in 1844. Theatre '46 at the Scala offered *A Century for George* (1946) by Montagu Slater, to mark the centenary of the Amalgamated Engineering Union. L. du Garde Peach's *A Pageant of the People* (1946) celebrated one hundred years of the Co-operative movement. The *Our Time* reviewer gives us an irresistible glimpse of the latter, writing that the acting was good 'although most of the workers' chains clanked irritatingly in the wings through most of the performance, until we thankfully saw them removed to the strains of "England Arise" '.[30]

Other projects included *Exercise Bowler* (1941), an ABCAesque play about the dashed political hopes of a group of demobbed soldiers. On commission from the Ministry of Fuel and Power, Ted Willis and John Collier wrote a play called *The Precious Stone* (1946), making the case for coal. Collier reports in 1947 that 'other government departments are now nibbling at the idea of sponsoring such shows' (66).

They never did. The exigencies of the Cold War made that impossible. But Andrew Davies has argued that another reason for the sharp decline in left theatre at the end of the decade was exhaustion prompted by the refusal of the Arts Council to recognise their activities (1984, 78). Theatre Workshop, despite eminent recommendations to the Arts Council, from people like John Trevelyan, Kenneth Clark and Ivor Brown, an illustrious delegation to the Arts Council of Arthur Blenkinsop, Nye Bevan, Tom Driberg, Benn Levy, Ian Mikardo and Alf Robens, and a series of glowing endorsements in the theatre press,[31] never impressed the Council. Michael Macowan even took the trouble to write and tell them that their work was boring (Littlewood 1994, 226). Theatre Workshop split up again and again in the late forties and early fifties. Unity were virtually ignored. One by one, *Theatre Today*, *New Theatre*, *Our Time*, and Unity's professional companies folded.

If left-wing theatre was unsuitable, so too was the cloistered intellectualism of the club theatres. Ernest Pooley, the Arts Council Chair, ruminating on this point, remarked: 'I never quite know what "highbrow" exactly means, but in so far as it is a term of reproach, let us not be highbrow' (Arts Council 1949, 25). Given the Panoptical fear of darkened spaces and the demands of national advertisement, they gave short shrift to these small, experimental theatres. Priestley feels that 'the idea of these clubs is excellent [...but] the Theatre Club idea stands in need of both expansion and inspiration' (1947a, 42).

If suitable plays were slow in coming forward during the early fifties, the National Theatre project was also in trouble. In the forties, the Old Vic Company was being groomed to assume the mantle. The Old Vic was bomb-damaged early in the war, and the company set off on a regional tour, before settling in Burnley, with another company at the Liverpool Playhouse. But as sights began to be trained on London, Keynes invited the Old Vic to devise a 'large-minded scheme for a classical repertory in the West End', intimating that 'good round sums' would be available to support it (Landstone 1953, 148). Arrangements were made for Olivier and Richardson to be released from the RNVR (Royal Naval Volunteer

Reserve). The season that resulted at the New Theatre in 1944 easily fulfilled Keynes's hopes. *Peer Gynt*, *Richard III* and *Arms and the Man* were commercial and critical successes, and the Old Vic's position was cemented in January 1946 when the National Theatre Committee and the Old Vic formally associated. 'It was,' recalls Landstone, 'the prestige of Laurence Olivier and his Company that eventually decided the amalgamation' (1953, 157).

Then things started to go wrong. After another acclaimed post-war season, Olivier began dividing his time with other work. The governors of the Old Vic felt that a firmer hand was needed on the company, and Olivier was famously sacked by telegram while touring in Australia. In his place Llewellyn Rees was installed as administrator, with Hugh Hunt directing the Company. At the same time, a further arm of the company had been set up, The Old Vic Theatre Centre, under Michel Saint-Denis, Glen Byam Shaw and George Devine: the 'Three Boys'. They proposed a theatre school, a young people's theatre, and a company to be based at the Old Vic Theatre when it reopened. The idea was for the centre to work organically with the Company providing a testing ground for new actors, new audiences, and for less commercial work. But they could not work with Rees. They felt his position to be anomalous and they demanded control over administration and finance, threatening resignation if they didn't get it. Rees reacted by issuing a press release in May 1953, announcing their departure. The Governors, wishing to retain prestige rather than administrative experience, censured and finally sacked Rees. Guthrie returned to the Old Vic. In the mean-time, the seasons had been patchy, evidently affected by the backroom infighting.

This was worrying for the prospects of this National Theatre-in-waiting. The work of both companies was performing an admirably ambassadorial role, conducting prestigious foreign tours. But the internal instability precluded the Council making longer-term plans. This crisis in theatrical policy at the heights of government and the arts was lampooned by Unity in their show *What Next!* (1949), which featured a sketch entitled 'The Old Vic at Westminster; or, Labour's Lost Love', based on the premise that the establishment has judged Shakespeare's value as a prestigious cultural export too great to be left to theatre workers; accordingly, Cabinet Ministers, newspaper proprietors and members of MI5 act the plays themselves (Chambers 1989, 309–310).

What was needed was a prestigious, nationally-oriented theatre company that could crown what commentators after 1953 were beginning to call the 'New Elizabethan Age'. The ground had been prepared, but by the mid fifties, no company seemed able to occupy it. So when George Devine appeared with his plans for an English Stage Company, as Eric White says, 'it was a fortunate moment' (1975, 114).

The English Stage Company

The Company's roots lay in the early fifties, when Ronald Duncan devised plans for an 'English Stage Society' to tour new and uncommercial plays to different regional arts festivals, with a brief season in London. He sounded out the Arts Council. They were unenthusiastic, suggesting only that £500 might be made available (Duncan 1968, 376).

Over the next three years, however, as George Devine became involved, the idea for the company was entirely recast. In doing so, it intriguingly recapitulates the entire history of the Arts Council. Firstly they shifted the emphasis of the company firmly towards London. Devine briefly discussed with Anthony Quayle the possibility of linking up with the Shakespeare Memorial Theatre, acting as their London base, an arrangement which had been proposed for the Old Vic (Quayle 1990, 333; Arts Council 1952, 18). Neville Blond, when he was approached, agreed to sit on the Board, with the proviso that they find themselves a permanent theatre. 'Not much persuasion was necessary,' recalls Lewenstein (1994, 12). Secondly, when they held their first press conference in the bomb-damaged Kingsway Theatre, they were still emphasising their touring plans,[32] but by the time they decide to occupy the Royal Court theatre, these plans have been all but abandoned. This was a major change: as Wardle puts it, 'from a provincial festival service to a continuous metropolitan management' (1978, 164).

The aims of the English Stage Company (ESC) dovetailed beautifully with the policies of the Arts Council. The acclaimed 'right to fail' (Devine 1961, 132), was exactly the plan that the Council had for the National Theatre (see p. 49), and it is part of the same move away from touring and amateurs and towards metropolitan professionalism that characterised the first ten years of CEMA and the Arts Council.

Their relationship with the repertories recalls Arts Council policy of the mid forties. Wesker's *Chicken Soup with Barley* was produced at the Coventry Belgrade before transferring to the Royal Court. In fact, when Lindsay Anderson brought it to them, neither Richardson nor Devine took to the play; at the time, the Court was organising a short festival of plays from the repertories, and Devine persuaded Brian Bailey at the Belgrade to put the play on and then transfer it. This minimised costs, but also situated the repertory theatres as lower rungs of a ladder, offering them the chance to 'try out' a play which might then ascend to the metropolitan apex of the cultural pyramid.

The great play made of 'regional accents' should be set against the metropolitanisation of culture; that the Court is considered to have forced regional accents onto the stage, thus ignoring (most immediately) all the community work of the forties and early fifties, is a talisman of the way that London became a focus for displaying the nation. Stephen Joseph (1957) complained that those who are searching for new playwrights are simply ignoring the work of the regions and the little theatres. But by now 'new writing' is a construct of Arts Council policy, and therefore pivoted on the metropolis. The Royal Court's first season contained *The Crucible* and *The Mulberry Bush*, which several critics describe as British premières, despite the fact that they were both previously produced at the Bristol Old Vic.

Announcing the ESC in 1955, Devine echoed Ernest Pooley's disdain for club theatres; 'we are not going in for experiment for the sake of experiment. We are not an *avant-garde*, or highbrow, or a côterie set' (quoted, Browne 1975, 12). The ESC's policy was just serious enough to confer prestige; not highbrow, but perhaps upper-middlebrow. Devine also told Osborne that encouraging novelists to the theatre might be a useful way to stimulate new work, and Angus Wilson's *The Mulberry Bush* and Nigel Dennis's *Cards of Identity* were the fruit of this approach in the first season (Osborne 1991a, 15). This had been an Arts Council policy for three years (1953, 43).

Devine himself, though much is made of his wild hair, his look of vagueness, his pipe and so forth, was, in Lewenstein's words, an 'insider' who 'belonged to the central magic circle' (1994, 14). He had been involved in the first attempt to create a National Theatre, and had come out of it well. He was not a break with the previous structures, he was a link with them. The same is true of commentators' obsession with the apparent eccentricity of the ESC's management committee, comprising *inter alia* a queen's cousin, a schoolmaster, a communist entrepreneur, a verse dramatist and his friend, and the husband of the Marks and Spencers heiress (cf. Kitchin 1962, 99; Browne 1975, 1, 3; Findlater 1981, 14–15; Osborne 1991a, 16, 38, 47; Richardson 1993, 72–73). In fact, this was an excellent committee. Esdaile owned the Royal Court building; Lewenstein had years of managerial experience which would prove invaluable when organising West End transfers; Neville Blond was very rich. The board as a whole was made up of just the sort of people that the Arts Council liked. (It resembled, in many ways, the Old Vic's board of governors.)

The effect of seeing Devine and the board as eccentric is to perpetuate a mock-innocence that accentuates the 'shock' of the Court's success. Tynan displays just this historical trope when he writes, 'The Court is run by a stuffy committee and aided by a meagre subsidy from the Arts Council; even so it managed to stage [...]' (1964, 85).

That 'meagre subsidy' demands examination. Once Devine had become involved, the Court was offered £2500 start-up money and £7000 for its first year (Findlater 1981, 16). Yes, these were meagre by Continental standards; nonetheless during 1956–1957 the ESC was already the fifth largest recipient of money from the drama panel. By the second year only the Old Vic theatre and company got more (Arts Council 1956, 101; 1957, 83). Further, the ESC was not mentioned in the drama section of the *Annual Report* for 1956–1957 but rather in 'Notes of the Year', clearly having become a pivot of Arts Council funding strategy. In Autumn 1957, the Arts Council *itself* managed a tour of *Look Back in Anger* to Wales and the North-East (1958, 46).

Compare this with Theatre Workshop's unsuccessful attempts to secure subsidy throughout the forties. They eventually abandoned their touring plans and took up residence at the Theatre Royal, Stratford East. They applied again to the Arts Council, who made an offer of £500 a year but on the condition that they renovate the building. Eventually a grant for 1954 was settled at £150 (Goorney 1981, 214).[33] While their political stance was certainly an issue, John Bury suggests that 'it was the lack of accountability that worried them. There was a lot of fuss about the books and keeping it together, programming and playing. Joan would always be rude to them' (quoted, 138). In other words, it was their refusal to become docile objects of the Council's gaze that was the problem. After all, by the time they were settled in Stratford East, they had abandoned MacColl's more directly political plays, and were running the sort of repertoire of semi-forgotten classics which the Arts Council liked. They were acquiring considerable prestige abroad; they had toured Czechoslovakia and Sweden in the late forties and were a famous sensation at the Paris Festivals of 1955 and 1956. The Arts Council even lauds their success in its *Eleventh Annual Report* while skirting over its refusal to fund them (1956, 45). Eventually, in November 1957, after twelve years of work, Theatre Workshop was offered £1,000, with the condition that the Local Authority match it (Littlewood 1994, 496). It is against this background that we can assess what Richardson called the Court's 'pathetically small subsidies' (1993, 82).

The Royal Court was everything the Arts Council had been waiting for, in its project of national–cultural renewal. Indeed, the National Theatre was only established after this project had been consummated by the ESC; Olivier chose his directors and actors almost entirely from this new generation, and only failed to attract Devine because he didn't want to play second fiddle at the Old Vic when he could be first violinist at the Royal Court (Lewis 1990, 6–7).

In 1960, only four years after the foundation of the ESC, *Plays and Players* announced, 'Our drama has entered on its most vital period since the Elizabethan age'.[34] The reference to the Elizabethan period should be set in the context of earlier calls, by Findlater amongst others, for a 'new Elizabethan drama' (1953, 468; 1954b, 372): a theatre which could rise to the emblematic example of the Coronation of a second Queen Elizabeth. The frequently employed term 'renaissance' (e.g. Tynan 1957, 122; Hinchliffe 1974, 22; Brown 1982, vii) carries the same resonance. Lindsay Anderson and John Arden often placed their work within a Shakespearean tradition (*Sergeant Musgrave at the Court* 1990; Arden 1960, 13).

Priestley had claimed that the British retained within their national character a flamboyance and confidence that 'could astonish the world' (1947a, 53). This evokes an opposition between inside and outside, private and public that we have met before. The New Wave shared a belief that our publicly apparent affluence was only masking the slow decline of something inside us all. It is not obvious whether Osborne and his contemporaries, who conspicuously lacked the economic perspectives and arguments of the New Left, were more sympathetic to the left- or right-wing versions of this story (though I shall return to this question in Chapter 5). Certainly, the Court played a considerable part in cementing the changes of arts policy undergone over the previous fifteen years, which included a reorganisation of cultural activity so as to inaugurate a prestigious national culture which could be the envy of the world.

What, then, of the Court's declared opposition to the West End? Crucially it is rather compromised by the fact that the funding structure underpinning their work was a product of a history in which the West End played a vital, productive part. Arguably, without the West End, Keynes may not have been able to push through his agenda. And without that, the Royal Court may not have happened. CEMA would certainly never have subsidised an English Stage Company.

It is also striking that, unlike those made ten years before, criticisms of the West End now focus exclusively on the *plays*. This editorial from *Encore* is typical: 'Our times are big. But our plays are small [...] Sleeping princes, reluctant debutantes, guys and dolls spending days by the sea, confidential clerks padding about living rooms'.[35] Another asserts that whatever one says about *The Entertainer* 'it is worth a thousand nude débutantes with or without violin'.[36] The concentration of theatre ownership, the operation of cartels between owners and producers, none of this enters into the discussion. Compared with the atmosphere of 1948, Raymond Williams, calling for nationalisation of the theatres in *The Long Revolution*, is spitting in the wind (1992, 341).

It is instructive to consider why the plays and production processes themselves should draw so much more fire than the structures of ownership. A key to this might be that where the angry young men strove to reunify purpose and expression, inside and out, private and public, the 'emotional repression' of writers like Coward and Rattigan, the 'excessive' decoration of the West End, and the 'self-indulgence' of the star system, only seemed to drive them further apart. Given this, it may be the case that their real criticism of the West End was not that it unthinkingly endorsed and promoted a complacent vision of cultural superiority, but that it didn't do it enough.

The West End was exposing gaps between inside and out, undoing the possibilities of sincere unity between intention and expression, opening theatrical plays to the play of theatricality. Why this might have been, and what the Court did about it, is the subject of my next chapter.

Figure 3.1 Ralph Richardson in J.B. Priestley's *Johnson over Jordan*
(February 1939, New Theatre)

3

A WRITER'S THEATRE
The professionalisation of the playwright

> We want a Theatre that is [...] a place where serious professional men and women, properly trained and well equipped, go to work, as surgeons and physicians go to work in a hospital.
>
> (J.B. Priestley, *Theatre Outlook*, 1947a, 53)

The concerns raised by the New Wave about the perceived failings of British theatre drew on a sense that it was incapable of offering the cultural vitality, the national strength, that could display Britain's greatness to the world. While this certainly focused on the plays, underlying this was a broader concern with the status accorded the playwright in the matrix of theatrical production. The premiere of J.B. Priestley's *Johnson over Jordan* (1939) illustrates both a call to change the status of the playwright, and the irreconcilability of this shift with theatre practice of the time.

Johnson over Jordan is a poetically abstracted narrative of an Everyman figure, passing from death to *Bardo*, a vision of the afterlife drawn from the Tibetan Book of the Dead. In the process Johnson examines his life in a series of expressionistic flashbacks, before, as shown in the photograph opposite, passing into the Beyond.

Priestley was deliberately trying to write a play which would challenge and extend the boundaries of theatre practice. By forcing the theatre's technical and design teams to work beyond their usual limits, the playwright would be leading the way in extending the practical limits of theatrical imagination. The director Basil Dean, excited by the opportunities this afforded him to 'resume my experiments in new production methods' (Cheshire 1984, 15), called in Edward Carrick, Gordon Craig's son. His lighting was highly innovative; this was one of the first productions to use 1,000 watt lanterns designed by Louis Hartmann, David Belasco's lighting engineer, and they had to be specially built by Strand Electric. At the time, lighting would usually only be considered by the director in the final week; here, Carrick designed an integrated pattern of reflected light throughout, giving a soft, numinous quality to the illumination, shaping atmosphere and mood, a development beyond the functionalism which dominated lighting in the thirties.

Craig's influence was felt in the set's huge curtains of canvas and hessian. Two independently-lit cycloramas fluidly enabled the lights to change the dimensions of the playing area. Setting was pared down, relying on a few well-chosen pieces to convey location. Elizabeth Haffenden's masks drew on Expressionist techniques to people the infernal nightclub which appears to Johnson. Antony Tudor's choreography conjured a Tolleresque vision of workplace regimentation. Benjamin Britten was invited to write a continuous score, which quoted from a variety of styles, from the lyricism of Johnson's passage into Bardo, to the angular jazz of the nightclub. Ivor Brown hailed Priestley's 'blue-prints for a theatrical revolution'.[1]

The production was not a success. Lavish theatrical resources of this kind required audiences to respond in equal measure. Reviews were mixed, and the production closed within a month. A revival of the same production a month later was no more successful.

In large part, *Johnson over Jordan* was flawed by a central contradiction within its conception. That Priestley was bidding for the writer's supremacy is clear. He saw his writing as the centre of the production process; for example, Britten's score was 'dramatically apt and nothing more', his talents were 'placed unreservedly at the author's disposal'.[2] But if he thought that trying to test the inventiveness of theatre practice would enshrine the writer's text at its head, he finally managed to lose that text in a welter of competing attractions.

This tension is borne out by the reviews; *The Times* was distracted by the masks, the *Tatler* by the choreography, and the *Observer* by both. The production prompted Ivor Brown to imagine 'plays in which "the lighting plot" may be as important as the verbal plot'. Ralph Richardson's universal praise in the lead role led Priestley to wonder morosely, 'if what this fine actor had to do and to say in the play had not at least some small share in his triumph' (1948a, x).

In this production, two incompatible visions of theatrical work are seen at work. One places the writer as the beating heart of theatrical creativity, with all other elements arraigned around him or her. The second reveals a more dispersed network of theatre workers, offering independent attractions to the audience. When these models were overlaid on one another, as they were here, this dispersal seemed to offer rival and competing claims, and the coherence of the theatrical experience was undermined. Those campaigners who favoured the first model got their victory in the mid fifties at the Royal Court. This reformation of theatre practice is rarely commented on, except to offer generalised approval, but how and why it happened is decisive in revealing the intimate connection between the creative structures of the Royal Court and the broader cultural anxieties that were being articulated and expressed on its stages.

The author and the actor

In the ten years before *Look Back in Anger*, the status of the actor was very high. J.C. Trewin, looking back at the years since 1945, declared that it became 'increasingly obvious that we were entering a period of fine theatrical acting' (1951, 8). The actor, in Hugh Hunt's words, was acknowledged to be on the 'front end' of theatrical production, offering the 'ephemeral but vital contact which gives life to a play' (1954, 73). And, since it was thought right that everyone's energies be focused around this moment of contact, the actor's pre-eminence was unquestioned; as Landstone puts it, the public's only concern 'is with the actors and actresses, and, quite rightly, no one else holds any interest for them' (1948, 67). When Phyllis Hartnoll published the first edition of the *Oxford Companion to the Theatre* in 1951, she explained that, since her aim in the selection of entries was to reflect what 'was most likely to interest the English-speaking reader [...] actors have been rated above dramatists' (v).

The retrospective diagnosis of many commentators is that the supposed distinction of British acting actually inhibited the production of good plays. Clive Barker describes two types of acting that had once dominated the theatre, 'the one school completely discounting personal characteristics, the other blatantly hiding behind a display of them'. The result either way, he contends, 'is to concentrate attention on the actor, and to divert attention from the play' (1966, 368). When a starry production of

Enid Bagnold's *The Last Joke* (1960) failed, *Plays and Players* rejoiced that 'playgoers are beginning to appreciate that the play's the thing, and not the stars who happen to be appearing in it'. It asserts that the revival of British theatre is due to the fact that 'the power of the star has begun to fade. For the stars, though they have proved over and over again in the past that they draw the crowds, have not always been very good for our drama'.[3]

It is commonplace to observe that the fifties saw a great re-emergence of British playwriting. But, as Foucault has observed, 'what we have to do with banal facts is to discover – or try to discover – which specific and perhaps original problem is connected with them' (1982, 210). It is easy to assume that the history of writing is an undeviating regularity, that 1956 saw only a new chapter in the chronicles of inspiration, in which writers managed to throw off their shackles and emerge into the light. Such an account constitutes playwrights in the depths of the old theatre and becomes the story of their liberation. But, following Foucault, we should question whether writing really possessed this kind of underlying continuity, and explore instead 'how the author was individualized in a culture such as ours; the status we have given the author [...]; the systems of valorization in which he [*sic*] was included' (1977b, 115). It is important, then, that we pay careful attention to the different conceptions of writing and acting before and after 1956.

In the forties, playwriting was generally discussed as a technical craft. Falkland L. Cary's manual *Practical Playwriting* (1945) compares writing to architecture:

> whilst the architect must have the licence that allows the fullest play of his [*sic*] art, he must bind himself by certain rules and to certain boundaries in order that the palace he is building does not finally emerge as a pigsty – or the pigsty as a palace.
>
> (71)

When in *The Art of the Play* (1948), Hermon Ould spends time discussing the problem of resolving plot strands in the last act, it is clear that he sees these as technical problems (60).

Playwriting manuals might be expected to picture the drama-tist's task like this, but several playwrights offer similar perspectives. J.B. Priestley suggested that 'a good dramatist has to work on two different levels of his [*sic*] mind [...] the warm-imaginative-creative-deep level, and the cold-crafty-technical-upper level. A good play needs both' (1941, 445). Peter Ustinov, in an article calling for innovation, observes that this 'does not mean a decay in technique, it just means the substitution of a new technique for an outworn one' (1948, 5). Rattigan contended that 'certain elementary rules of construction and stagecraft have to be learned (and possibly later discarded!) by all playwrights' (Dent 1951, 28).

Acquiring these rules comes from practice. In 1951, a group of British playwrights were asked whether authors needed first-hand experience of the theatre. While Rattigan is categoric – 'Most emphatically, yes' – Christopher Fry is insistent – 'yes, yes, yes, yes' (Dent 1951, 30). Charles Landstone argues that authors should 'work as ASMs or small-part actors in order to gain knowledge of their craft' (1948, 16). This is the advice that Garry Essendine gives the experimental young writer, Roland Maule, in Coward's *Present Laughter* (1943): 'Go and get yourself a job as a butler in a repertory company if they'll have you. Learn from the ground up how plays are constructed and what is actable and what isn't. Then sit down and write at least twenty plays one after the other' (Coward 1990, 173).

To modern ears, sitting down and writing twenty plays in succession might seem bizarre. However, by internalising these rules, writers could write very fast. Priestley recalls writing *Dangerous Corner* (1932) 'very quickly, as a technical experiment and as proof that I could write for the stage' (1962, 199). He also acknowledged having written *Time and the Conways* (1937), *An Inspector Calls* (1946), and *The Linden Tree* (1947) each in 'about ten days' (Muller 1958, 59). Giving us a sense of how this technique operated, he describes writing *An Inspector Calls* 'at great speed, blinding on past all manner of obstacles and pitfalls and only realising afterwards how dangerous they might have proved' (quoted, Brome 1988, 283). Cecil Beaton once asked Noël Coward about his writing process:

> but he elaborates little on the birth pangs of creation for the reason that there are none, or if so, they are not interesting to him. 'If I type easily then I know the stuff is good!' The way he goes over the appalling obstacles of play construction is done with the ease of a surf-rider skimming the Honolulu waves.
>
> (1965, 119)

Coward wrote *Blithe Spirit* in six days, *Private Lives* (1930) in four.

Look Back in Anger only took Osborne seventeen days, and *The Entertainer* eleven (Osborne 1991a, 1; Ritchie 1988, 128). But Osborne's speed is not Priestley's. While Priestley writes with technical assurance, Osborne writes in the white heat of passion. It was, he says, a 'solo dash [...] fuelled by a reckless *untutored* frenzy' (1991a, 1, my emphasis). His fervent playwriting is seen as an insatiable desire to express oneself truthfully, 'a crude, almost animal, inability to dissemble' (9). This speed has everything to do with inspiration and nothing to do with technique.

Technique was a leading figure in the new generation's expansive demonology. Osborne denounces 'playmaking' as 'a home craft like fretwork or pottery'; he notes of his predecessors that 'construction was the centre of all their faith and was invoked like the Resurrection or Redemption' (1981a, 196). In *Declaration*, he scorned those who 'bumbled out the usual stock words like "construction"' (1957a, 68). Alan Ross, writing in *London Magazine*, insisted that 'preoccupation with technique, in all the arts, usually coincides with a weakness of impulse' (1960, 7). Lindsay Anderson denounces a play produced in this way as 'an expert machine' (1957, 45).

Anderson's metaphor is an accusation about human presence. Technique canalises human feeling, compromising and weakening it by forcing it into predefined forms, displacing the authentic vitality of the author's voice. Once again we confront this image of a highly-polished outside flourishing at the expense of inner feeling. The cultural anxieties articulated by both the Arts Council and the New Wave find their target in the predominance of technical construction in the theatre. Tynan noted the perpetual danger of theatre being 'parasitic on life' rather than embodying 'the human situation', and asked 'whether we want our drama to batten onto the lipstick of life or on the blood of it' (1958, 11).

While Tynan's call is for a one-to-one contact between author and audience, technique, like lipstick, adorns the surface, hides the interior. It operates laterally, opens a gap between feeling and expression; it allows that there are a number of technical ways to say the same thing, that one can say something without meaning it, even that one can say one thing and mean another. This opens speech up to repetition and substitution, what Derrida calls 'iterability', which is inimical to the desired integration of thought and expression. Wesker makes this point when he argues that 'Art is the re-creation of experience, not the copying of it' (quoted, Taylor 1963, 146). And technique is not the only theatrical force that threatens to adorn and hide the surface; directors, designers and actors may also make their dangerously artful interventions.

But there is no escaping the play of technique, even in the most heartfelt utterance. I argued in Chapter 1 that the formal proper-ties of language, the rules under which it operates, make the rigorous exclusion of 'iterability' inconceivable, since it is a feature of textuality itself. It is striking then, how this problem is displaced onto those other figures. All theatre workers are redescribed as potential threats to vitality and their functions have to be subordinated to the writer's 'voice'. Indeed, each of these theatrical roles became a talisman of raging forces within textu-ality.

Devine was insistent on the primacy of writers' intentions at the Court. Osborne recalls that 'you always knew he was on the writer's side' (1981b, 22). *Theatre World* previewed the new venture:

> *The play's the thing* is the guiding slogan of the English Stage Company [...] the Court is an author's rather than a producer's theatre; a stage upon which the author is treated with respect and everything is done to transmit his [*sic*] intentions to the audience.[4]

A year after the English Stage Company's occupancy of the Court, Devine judged that the perfect theatrical condition for the writer is 'a place where the dramatist is acknowledged for what he [*sic*] is – the fundamental creative force in the theatre' (1957, 153). Jocelyn Herbert also remembers how 'the author was served by all who worked at the Court' (1981, 85–86).

In the late forties, playwrights still conventionally paid for their seats on the opening night (Landstone 1948, 5). At the Royal Court, from Autumn 1957, writers were issued with a pass that gave them free admission to any production or rehearsal, and also to weekly policy and planning meetings. Thus, the entire opera-tion was brought under the author's gaze. Symptomatically, productions were referred to by the playwrights' names (Doty and Harbin 1990, 50).

By 1961, the status of the writer was such that *Plays and Players* could editorialise furiously on the absence of playwrights in the New Year's Honours list:

This seems particularly unfair since it is the playwright who is ultimately responsible for what is best in the theatre. Actors and directors, however brilliant and dedicated they may be, can only reach the highest distinction through the dramatic material they are given by the writer. And it is the dramatist who always leads the way. [...] Gradually our actors are falling into step, but it was not they who took the lead.[5]

This is a long way from Hunt's vision of the theatre as a collaborative activity (1954, 1).

The period, then, sees a marked change in the conception of the writer away from technique and towards personal vision. It has been easy to assume that the history of acting in the fifties is animated simply by the sudden emergence of good plays, and that, bowing to the inevitable, actors realised that the game was up. But in fact the role of the actor underwent a parallel transformation.

Actors were retrospectively blamed for the weakness of mid-century theatre. There were two points of criticism. The first, once again, condemned the dominance of technique. Clive Barker describes the previous generation as relying 'less on acting than on the power to appear quizzical, bland, perplexed, and triumphant in turn, and to time lines well' (1966, 367). The infamy of good timing is nothing to Marowitz's harrowing indictment of the British actor: 'he [sic] knows his way around a stage, and can simulate almost any emotion demanded of him' (1958, 21). When Barker insists that plays in the early fifties 'called upon the actor to have a considerable technique' (367), once again we find that underlying these curious objections is the sense that acting must be freed from iterability.

Charles Marowitz made a name for himself in the late fifties with his criticisms of British acting. He contrasted the 'artifice' and 'superficiality' of British technique with the 'vigour and vitality' of the Method (1957, 10). British acting was a matter of short-cuts, he declared, reduced to 'a mechanical process of Buzz and Flash. Buzz: the cliché-symbol is transmitted; Flash: the cliché-symbol is received' (1958, 20). The problem is once again mechanisation and technique; these short cuts do not require *feeling*.

The second focus for criticism was the star system. Visible in *Plays and Players*'s remarks, quoted above, this took the form of a charge that stars had become a sole focus of attraction for audiences who would disregard the plays in which these gigantic presences had inadvertently found themselves. But this is to misunderstand the mid-century relationship between actor and audience. Acting involved (when does it not?) a dialectic between actor and character, such that 'there is not one interpretation of Nora in *A Doll's House*, but hundreds' (Hunt 1954, 30). The relation between the performer and the performance was, to a considerable extent, arbitrary; Athene Seyler explained acting as 'not a question of physical limitation as much as of spiritual range'.[6] Thorndike concurs: 'An actor has to be ready to be any sort of person'.[7]

The 'star' took this to a particularly heightened level. Harold Downs describes a common way of passing the time before curtain up: 'recalling the plays and the theatres in which we last saw some of the players [...or reading] an autobiography of one of the members of the cast' (1951, 65). This suggests an intensification of an audience's ordinary awareness of the performer's own status. The star wielded their own set of signs, their 'persona', which could be read *alongside* the performance they gave. Thus the arbitrary relation between actor and character becomes a site for the enjoyment of artifice, of pleasurably playing off actor against character. It accounts for the high profile given to classical revivals in which the audience could inscribe the performance into intertextual skeins of prior experience *both* of the play and the actor.

To the Court, this ripped apart those vital unities of meaning and expression, interposing artifice, arbitrariness, and iterability. Hence it was this pleasurable artifice that they sought to abolish. The star system was the first to go. Actors were encouraged to withdraw from the audience into the text in an inspiring act of indivisible vitality. Albert Finney recalls meeting Devine for lunch while working at the Court on *The Lily White Boys* (1960). Devine told him,

> being the leading man is not just a question of having the best part [...] It is not just having the most lines or the most laughs, the number one dressing room, or the name in lights over the title [... It means] showing how much you care for the thing. To encourage your fellow actors to stretch and to dig into the text by demonstrably doing that yourself.
>
> (1981, 88–89)

Figures 3.2 and 3.3 Laurence Olivier's transition from 'star' persona to immersion in character as Archie in *The Entertainer* (film, 1960)

Lindsay Anderson demanded of actors 'humility before the words, truthfulness to character, complete purity of feeling' (1957, 43). This purity was a bulwark against the actor developing an independent 'star' persona.

Actors were to be perceptually indistinguishable from their characters. Towards the end of the fifties, Derek Granger wrote an article featuring up-and-coming performers and notes the closeness of Kenneth Haigh to Jimmy Porter, describing him as 'the speaking likeness of this gritty-minded, nerve-twanging malcontent'. The complete identity between them is further reinforced when Granger starts describing Haigh in terms reminiscent of Jimmy's own critical clichés: Haigh has 'a sour, moody integrity' and 'a streak of the Romantic in him which he keeps heavily muffled'. Generally he observes of his finds,

> look how strongly they can be identified with the new movement in the theatre; even, in a more general sense, with the attitudes and temper of their own generation [...] even their looks and speech seem to reflect the young intellectual climate of the time.
>
> (1958, 6)

This identity of performer and performance was secured in other ways. The first cast of *Look Back in Anger* included Haigh as Jimmy and Alan Bates as Cliff. If the audience had seen the first two English Stage Company productions, they might have seen them, but not otherwise. Mary Ure, as Alison, on the other hand, was already very successful; she had scored a major West End success in Anouilh's *Time Remembered* (1954). Consequently, Jimmy and Cliff appeared to come out of nowhere, while Alison had just come out of another theatre. This play of personas and non-personas helped to fix the authenticity of the male characters, establishing them in metonymic contrast with the West End.

The new actor was someone who lent his or her body to the text, became guarantor of its authenticity, and through it transformed him or herself into its symptoms; consequently they came to be more authentic people. Laurence Olivier had perhaps the most highly developed star persona of them all: in the fifties, you could even buy cigarettes named after him; but even Olivier recalls how *The Entertainer* affected him: 'I began to feel already the promise of a new, vitally changed, entirely unfamiliar *Me* [...] I now belonged to an entirely different generation' (1981, 40–41).

A symptomatic effect was a new attitude to make-up. Horace Sequiera in a make-up manual from 1953 argues that a distinction should be drawn between 'straight' and 'character' make-up: 'roughly, anything that differs from one's own self is character' (37). Charles Thomas, a British Drama League staff tutor, regards this distinction as questionable: 'Every make-up should be regarded as a character make-up since we are all characters of some kind' (1951, 12). The stage is then a place of artifice where one's make-up is designed either to signify one's star persona (39), or the character, and probably both. In sharp contrast, photographs of Royal Court productions suggest that most make-up was straight (the precise opposite of Thomas's point), thus blurring the identity of the actor and reducing it to a function of their character.

Actors, and stars in particular, threatened the unity of thought and feeling which the New Wave wished to preserve. The actor's inevitable use of resources outside of the text itself (technique, experience, persona) reveals – like Derrida's 'supplement' – the precarious instability and incompleteness of a text. To reduce this danger, the Court positioned the actor in a new relation to the character, effectively subsuming them within it. What is at stake, then, in the 'revolution' of 1956, is not simply the singular emergence of the repressed playwright, but a reconstruction of the writer's role, and a reorganisation of the working relationships in which it functioned. In this sense, it constituted a change in the writer's professional status.

Professionalisation

What professionalisation involves has been much debated. Max Weber (1930) and Talcott Parsons (1968) describe it as an ultimately benign and inevitable consequence of rationalisation (Cooper and Burrell 1988, 93). More recently, some sociologists inspired by Foucault's work have shifted emphasis; where the professional's *expertise* had been seen to define professional status, writers like Freidson have stressed the professional's '*control* of the division of labour' (Freidson 1970, 48).

Against the 'service' ethic stressed by previous commentators, Freidson argues that a profession is 'an occupation which has assumed a dominant position in a division of labour, so that it gains control over the determination of the substance of its own work' (xvii). Furthermore, 'the profession claims to be the most reliable authority on the nature of the reality it deals with' (xvii). The profession gains a monopoly over the work, and *also* takes upon itself the duty of regulating its own practice.

The lure of professionalism was extremely strong in the forties and fifties. Greenwood and Parsons both refer explicitly to theatre as an area ripe for professional reorganisation (1957, 46–47; 1968, 546), and, as my epigraph illustrates, the acknowledged professions were frequently models for ideal theatre practice. Many theatrical occupations underwent changes typical of professionalisation. There was an extensive retitling of rôles. The producer became the director, the electrician the lighting designer, the stage designer simply the designer, the stage director the stage manager, and the manager the producer. As has often been argued, these apparently superficial changes can indicate much broader transformations (Greenwood 1957, 52). Professional bodies like the Director's Guild and Society of British Lighting Designers, which also emerged in this period, indicate the same thing. But while many theatre workers hankered after professional status, they did not all get it.

Autonomy was crucial to the changes in theatre practice. In the forties, Charles Landstone suggested that one of the main problems that beset the theatre was that the director of a theatre company and the controller of a building were separate people: 'one day that halcyon period will arrive when the producing manager and the "bricks and mortar" are one and the same person, and then all will be well' (1948, 63; see also Priestley 1947a, 36–38). This chimed well with the Arts Council's emphasis on buildings rather than tours. With this 'state sanction', the Royal Court was able to choose what to produce. The dawning of subsidy brings with it the artistic director, who combines the production and regulation of the work, thus creating a new autonomy for the artistic process. Freidson argues that the granting of autonomy by the state is a necessary precondition to the process of professionalisation. (And how nicely appropriate it is to see Devine, in the film of *Look Back in Anger*, playing a doctor.)

Sociologists often stress the importance of training to professional identification. Its significance is less to do with the complexity of the tasks in hand than the impression generated that the profession possesses formalised skills and a body of knowledge that need to be acquired by serious, disinterested study. As one sociologist observes, 'knowledge is a symbolic value' (Torstendahl and Burrage 1990, 3). George Devine, who was described by Osborne as 'a natural teacher' (1991a, 260), tried to formalise a more 'serious' kind of actor training in the thirties with his London Theatre Studio, co-run with Michel Saint-Denis between 1935 and 1939. From 1945 to 1952, they also established and ran the Old Vic Theatre School.

At the Royal Court, the educational atmosphere was pervasive. As Devine described it, 'this place is a sort of *school*, after all' (1961, 129). He set up regular classes for the company in the early days. Osborne describes these as 'less arduous than PT and more tedious than morning assembly. At least it made you feel that term had started' (1991a, 18). Twenty-five years later, Joan Plowright recalled that while at the Court, 'I was getting a very broad education and also getting paid for it' (1981, 32). Nicholas Wright, later co-artistic director of the Court, claimed, 'When I have to fill out a form, and it says "Where educated?" I always think I ought to put down, "Royal Court"' (1981, 185).

Formal and informal social groups also have the function of building a professional culture (Greenwood 1957, 52). A good example of this is the Writer's Group. Set up in January 1958, it lasted two years and marked the emphasis on training that characterises the profession, but was also of value in its informal rôle: 'to be a member of the group', recalls Jellicoe, 'was terribly important because one could establish and develop friendships' (Doty and Harbin 1990, 86), Wesker valued 'the ritual of going and seeing one's friends' (quoted, Jellicoe 1981, 56). Arden puts his development as a playwright down to his informal presence in and around the Court (1960, 14). Such informal groups were very important and Jellicoe notes how many writers used the casting director Miriam Brickman's office to meet and chat (Doty and Harbin 1990, 89). Osborne himself was brought into the acting company; he also read new scripts, and ran auditions.

Harold Wilensky describes one of the main factors of professionalisation as the move to being full time. In the theatre before 1956, writers like Peter Ustinov, Noël Coward and Emlyn Williams were equally well-known performers; others, like Priestley, Wynyard Browne and Charles Morgan, were novelists. Devine's initial plan had been to approach novelists and actors for plays (Osborne 1991a, 15, 7). Osborne himself had been an actor touring in rep. and at the Court he performed in *Cards of Identity*, *Don Juan* and *The Death of Satan* and *The Good Woman of Setzuan* (1956). (He also understudied for *Look Back in Anger*.)

But soon writing became his dominant profession, and certainly amongst subsequent playwrights, only Jellicoe and Howarth took on other rôles, and both have acknowledged that it was only by writing that they got a chance to direct (Doty and Harbin 1990, 148). The reverse did not occur until the late sixties when Nicholas Wright's first play was produced; none of the first wave of directors at the Court ever wrote a play. Even more indicative is that while *Look Back in Anger* took twelve days to write, *Inadmissible Evidence* (1964) took a little under two years (Osborne 1991a, 242–244).

But for an occupational field to include professional members, there must be those who are *not* so blessed. As Freidson argues, in respect of medicine, the responsibility for curing the sick involves a large number of other people; nurses, pharmacists, porters, volunteers, ambulance drivers, etc. However, the doctor's aspiration to professional autonomy may be challenged by these occupations. Hence the BMA's continuing resistance to extending the responsibilities of nurse or pharmacist. Freidson argues that professional status confers the ability to control these supplementary rôles, which both prevents them from threatening the doctor's autonomy, and reinforces his or her power (1970, 47–49). The professional achieves what Foucault calls 'government', not the simple or top-heavy curtailment of another's freedom, but the power 'to structure the possible field of action of others' (1982, 221).

Over the previous fifty years there had already been a considerable reordering of tasks. As Findlater noted,

> Specialisation of function has destroyed the old theatrical unity, in which Mr. Henry Sherek, for example, would own the Lyric Theatre; direct *The Confidential Clerk*, instead of engaging Mr. Martin Browne; and, perhaps, take a leading role, in place of Mr. Paul Rogers – or Mr. Denholm Elliott
>
> (1954a, 162)

Further and decisive changes were made during the 1950s which fully professionalised the playwright and sharply delimited the creative freedom of all but a select few theatre workers.

Elsom's claim that Osborne 'revitalized the star system' (1979, 79) is misleading. Although actors like Alan Bates or Peter O'Toole went on to establish personas of their own, it was at the cost of pruning the status and resources of the actor to below those of the writer. Even the badge of the actor's own triumph, the seriousness of the Method, was ditched if it ever came into conflict with the playwright's holy writ. Osborne is scornful even of his first Jimmy Porter, Kenneth Haigh, whose version of Methodism would lead him to cut lines if he 'wasn't feeling it'; ' "What do you want me to do? Tell the audience a lie?" Yes, by all means, Ken. They won't know the difference' (1991a, 57). This ambivalent transformation, a shift involving simultaneous gain and loss, is paradigmatic of the changes which took place in most theatre occupations.

The director and the stage

Over the first fifty years of the twentieth century, after the decline of the actor-manager, the tasks of actor and director became increasingly separated and distinguished. By the early fifties, the director's status could be very high; Tyrone Guthrie and Peter Brook were often as well-known as their leading actors. Findlater admits, however, that some actors saw directors as 'jacks-in-office, superfluities in nature, arty interlopers whose days are numbered; they pine for the return to power of the actor-manager, or for some blissful but unspecified state of Thespian self-government in spontaneous combustion' (1954a, 161).

The director's authority was defended on the sound theoretical principle that written texts are capable of sustaining a wide range of possible interpretations. Brook opined 'There is no perfect production of any play [...] nor is there any final one; like a musician's interpretation, its existence is inseparable from its performance' (quoted, Findlater 1954a, 165–166). To those writers who complain of distortion, Hugh Hunt asks 'If the author objects to the imaginative interpretation of his [*sic*] play, then why is he writing for a medium which requires it?' (1954, 52). Priestley apparently had so much faith in the director's contribution that he deliberately over-wrote so that a play could be cut when the particular production's shape began to emerge (36).

A claim to professional status is involved here, as many commentators urge that the director is the person best suited to oversee the activities of all theatre workers, including the playwright. Landstone suggests in 1948 that directors ought to receive a proportion of the author's royalties from subsequent productions (1948, 46). By the mid fifties, directors received a fee of five guineas from a publisher who printed an acting edition using his or her production (Hunt 1954, 60). The same move to 'full-time' status that the playwright underwent took place as a wave of directors, like Peter Hall and Peter Brook, emerged who were not themselves actors. Hunt believed that directors should also design the shows (56). Brook designed and even wrote music for some of his productions.

Several directors were amongst those calling for new forms of theatre architecture, new stage configurations. Intriguingly, a Royal Academy exhibition after the war suggested that these would 'in turn evolve new forms of drama' (British Drama League 1945, 3). Richard Southern's Rockefeller lectures at Bristol University claimed that the three-sided stage would allow for more experimental writing (1953, 14). Guthrie fostered such innovation with Tanya Moiseiwitsch at Stratford, where they collaborated on producing a thrust stage for his production of the Shakespeare history cycle in 1951, a design which Moiseiwitsch reproduced in her plans for the Shakespeare Festival Theatre, built in 1957, and the Guthrie Theatre, Minneapolis, in 1963. The director seemed to be emerging as the figure best placed to determine the development of the theatre, of the stage, and, so it seemed, of plays.

This initiative seems to have evaporated at the Court. The director was no longer translating a written text into a performance; the Court's director had the responsibility of finding a production that was, in some sense, already there in the text. The first Royal Court directors were in accord: Lindsay Anderson insisted, 'what is important is not the "sort of theatre" – but the PLAY' (1957, 43), and Bill Gaskill defined 'the Court's real aims – to present new writing in a form of staging centred in the play and without any extraneous decoration from the director or the designer' (1981, 61). The director's work was now to subdue any other sign-system than that of the author, whose intentions, in a familiarly repressive metaphor, could thereby be 'revealed'.

In May 1957, the English Stage Company instituted its 'Sunday Nights without Décor', designed famously to try out new writing in the raw, so to speak. In an article in *Encore*, one critic described the plan as an example of George Devine's notion of 'essentialism', that plays should be performed with the most economic use of setting possible (Adler 1957, 24–25). Terry Browne glosses the strength of the Sunday Nights as being that 'the play cannot be "dolled up" by production and hence both its strong points and its weak points are plainly visible' (1975, 37).

The rhetoric vaguely suggests Copeau's notion of the *tréteau nu*. Browne's words do seem to be echoing Copeau's testimony in 1917, 'I want the stage to be naked and neutral in order that every fault may stand out; in order that the dramatic work may have a chance in a neutral atmosphere' (1990, 82). But by 'dramatic work' Copeau seems to be including the performer, and three years later he recalled how 'this instrument brings a sense of exultation to the actors' performance' (83). And like Richard Southern, he insists that this new stage is 'bound up with the problem of the new dramatic form which it will *engender*' (87, my emphasis). Copeau's *tréteau* is another aesthetic, not a purer one; it is aimed at creating new dramatic forms rather than revealing prior ones. But by the time this idea has passed by way of Copeau's nephew Michel Saint-Denis and his Compagnie des Quinze to George Devine, it is an unparalleled means of disclosing the truth of a play.

Considering how often directors tried to explore how different stages enable different kinds of play before 1956, the Royal Court's attitude to its own stage is surprising. Findlater suggests that the Court stage is 'a test-bench of stage theory' (1981, 7) and the scientific metaphor is revealing. Just as a scientific instrument is designed so as not to contaminate or affect the things with which it comes into contact, so the Royal Court stage is being treated as a neutral means of revealing the plays in some kind of 'pure' state. Max Stafford-Clark has described the stage at the Court as 'a fine instrument – a microscope that examines and presents the detail of the work placed upon it and exposes the flaws' (198). Devine had the proscenium ripped out and added an apron stage. While adding height to the visible stage area, it is, in its basic audience–stage relation, still a proscenium theatre. Nonetheless, Osborne declared 'I don't care what the constraints of the old proscenium arch are, that people go on about so much, because I think you can do *anything* on that kind of stage' (1981b, 26).

The discourse of the Royal Court stage silences the complex process which has involved transforming one signifying system (a written text) into another (the performed text) to claim that it has directly performed the play-in-itself. The role of the director becomes directly analogous to that of the scientist, whose rôle is simply to eliminate background noise (set and lighting design, the actor's charisma, and indeed his or her own directorial decisions) to let the play speak for itself. Lindsay Anderson spoke of his own desire for invisibility when he gave his view that 'the best "notice" that a director can get is praise for his [*sic*] playwright and praise for his players' (1981, 148). Note that when in 1979 John Dexter tried to argue for a royalty on further productions of plays he had directed first, the idea was treated with incredulity (Hall 1983, 445).

The director had a certain status, but it was as a border guard, protecting the playwright from anyone who would challenge their sovereignty. And this is done in the name of preserving and presenting the playwright's work 'in itself', so that nothing can threaten its vital unities, its sense of life.

The lighting designer

Typically, changes in lighting design and operation are thought to be exhaustively accounted for by technological advance. The standard accounts will narrate this history as a series of 'discoveries'; the move from gas to limelight in the 1820s, the Savoy Theatre's installation of full electric lighting in 1881, the development of reflecting lanterns and dimmable and gas-filled bulbs in the 1910s, the consequent development of gels, and the invention of remote control boards in the 1930s.

But technology is only part of a system that involves human agency, demands and desires, and theatre technology is no different. British theatre workers involved with lighting design and operation viewed the situation in the 1940s with disquiet. Lighting was rarely 'designed' beforehand, and tended to get left to the lighting rehearsal. There the director or the designer would create lighting effects through trial and error, aided by the theatre's electrician, who would mechanically put these effects into practice.

In the late forties and early fifties theatre lighting workers put in a bid for recognition as professionals with as strong an artistic contribution to make as anyone else. The leading figures in this were Percy Corry and Frederick Bentham, of the Strand Electric and Engineering Corporation. Corry commented that the electrician is responsible for 'lighting, heating and ventilating the whole theatre. His [*sic*] main concern with stage lighting is usually with its technique rather than its artistry'. He observes that the person responsible for the lighting has no named function and suggests that, along the lines of the stage and costume designer, he or she should be termed a 'lighting designer' (1954, ix).

Encouragement for this shift came from abroad. Komisarjevsky

Figure 3.4 The Light Console, modelled on a cinema organ, with a full
view of the stage

was famous for the concern he took over the lighting and we have
seen how Basil Dean and his electrician Bill Lorraine used some of
Belasco and Hartmann's innovations in *Johnson over Jordan*. In
the forties, H.M. Tennent produced many American plays, and Joe
Davis, their resident technician, adapted many of the original

lighting designs for London. Thus in the late forties the work of Jo Mielziner, Norman Bel Geddes and Robert Edmond Jones added to the range of effects already developed by pioneers like F.S. Aldred and Harold Ridge at the Festival Theatre in Cambridge. Productions of *Our Town* (1946), *The Glass Menagerie*, *Death of a Salesman* and *I Remember Mama* (1948) used lighting to define space and mood; and these techniques then filtered into the Tennent productions of *Crime and Punishment* (1946) and *Love in Albania* (1949) amongst others (Davis 1949, 6).

In the thirties the dominant form of lighting control was the Grand Master Control. This was a huge installation which would usually fill a wall in the wings, on which banks of levers locked electromagnetic clutches onto a master wheel, which could thus operate groups of dimmers. This needed to be operated by several people at once and made it difficult to execute subtle lighting effects because of the length of time it took to perform a single cue. Bentham argued that two preconditions needed to be met before lighting design and operation could be accorded artistic status. The first was that the board be operable by one person and the second was that a system be devised so that the operator has full view of the stage (1950, 110).

To this end, Bentham, who was working in the research department at Strand, invented the Light Console. This was a remote board designed to be operated by one person. As can be seen from the picture opposite, it was modelled on a cinema organ and featured a piano-like keyboard coupled to several stops and a foot pedal. It was designed to be operated from the auditorium so that the effect of any lighting change could immediately be seen.

There is one further respect in which the Light Console constituted its operator as an artist. It had no facility for operating pre-set cues which Bentham thought were part of the ungainly apparatus of the Grand Master system. This meant that design and operation were virtually indistinguishable processes, and indeed he recommended that they be carried out by the same person (251). For Bentham's Console, operating the lights is not the execution of a series of pre-set cues, but rather the manipulation of a continual lighting track. The designer-operator is thus capable of improvising and altering the design for every performance: 'In the same way that each night the actors bring life to their rôles for the audience, so do the scene shifters bring to life their scenes and the lighting staff their lighting' (129). Bentham also suggests that, just as actors learn their lines, the lighting plot should be memorised (252). In this way the designer becomes less of a technician and more of an artist; Bentham frequently compares the designer to a fine artist 'painting the stage with light' (141).[8]

Crucially, the conception of this operating system seems to entail the lighting designer's autonomy from the director and the writer. It even opens up the possibility that lighting itself may one day 'play the principal role' in the theatre (1). Bentham's confidence may be judged by his response to one eminent questioner after a lecture he gave at the end of the thirties: 'At the end Shaw got up and in that wonderfully soft Irish voice of his spoke about stage lighting, concluding, not unnaturally, with an admonition that lighting such as mine would be a distraction to his plays. My own diffident but firm riposte was that his plays would be a distraction to my lighting' (1992, 92). Light Consoles were installed in several theatres during the forties and early fifties. By 1952, there were such boards in the London Palladium, Drury Lane, Stoll Theatre, Coliseum and Covent Garden. In the early fifties Strand stopped manufacturing the Grand Master Control.

The Light Console existed at the crux of a complex negotiation of power between writers, designers, directors and lighting technicians. The struggle for control polarised views. Tyrone Guthrie was thoroughly opposed to these developments, wishing instead that theatres were roofless, and maintaining that unavoidably important though lighting was, the job was 'technical – to make the lights work as required by the Producer and Designer. His [sic] status is analogous to the carpenter, dressmaker and painter [...] it is technical rather than creative'. He claimed to have little technical knowledge and candidly admitted that he was 'inclined to think electric light a recession from gas' (1952, 11). Hilton Edwards, of Dublin's Gate Theatre, also viewed technical developments with suspicion, notably in the proliferation of gels. He denounced the more subtle gradations as ' "delightful affectations." So prejudiced am I that when in my moments of doubt the electrician has murmured to me – "why not try a surprise pink?" I am so horrified that I order a black-out immediately and start again' (1946, 26).

The same sentiments, though without Edwards' fine sense of camp, were voiced by George Devine. His initial, somewhat vague, objection is to a lack of rhythm in its operation (1948a, 19). Perhaps the problem was: whose rhythm? In an interview for the Strand house magazine he commended any developments which would add 'precision and subtlety in operation as well as accuracy in timing', but opined 'I do not visualise a long-haired genius "playing the lights" as his [sic] feelings take him' (1948b, 23). Nonetheless, at the end of the interview he arranges to watch a demonstration of the Light Console (26). This clearly did not impress him as in his review of Bentham's *Stage Lighting* (1950), which pushed the merits of the Light Console, he firmly resisted the lighting designer's push for enlarged influence: 'When he is within his title, a large enough subject in all conscience, Mr Bentham is always interesting, knowledgeable and stimulating. I do not, however, feel that he is entitled to assume the same authority on other allied subjects' (1950, 31).

As Devine clearly perceived, in Bentham's insistence that 'there was, in the emotions evoked by changes of colour, intensity and direction of light, something too important to be forever shackled to mere illumination of actors and scenery' (1992, 92), here was a play for full creative recognition, and one which threatened to transpire without the full control of the director. As we have seen, the function of the director at the Court was primarily to moderate between all levels of artistic endeavour to ensure that they channelled their energies purely to convey the author's intentions.

As a result, there was no Light Console at the Court. Indeed, what some critics have seen as the influence of Devine's 1955 visit to the Berliner Ensemble in his use of harsh white lighting in fact goes back to his championing in 1953 of the 'Pageant' lantern which gave out just such a light (6). It is part of that desire to assert the dominance of director over designer that also sees Guthrie condemn 'fancy' designs, and maintain that 'I think you should put on all the white light you have, and leave it on' (1952, 10). The position of the lighting board at the Court in a corner at the side of the upper circle meant that Bentham's dream of the designer-operator could not practically be achieved, and Devine dominated the lighting at the Court until his retirement.

No doubt it was the broad holding action against Bentham's vision that stopped the Light Console in its tracks. In 1957, Richard Pilbrow designed the Lightboard. This new board had much of the flexibility of the Light Console but crucially included presets. Although they were capable of being overridden in an emergency, the preset states represent the triumph of the director who could once again dictate the operation of the lights in the lighting plot; the actions of the operator were easily distributed into correct and mistaken actions, a division under the control of the director, and cemented by the development of the computer memory board (Pilbrow 1979, 155). The 1961 Strand Electric catalogue treats the Light Console as a piece of lighting history (16).

The lighting designer achieved certain things, a national association, a job title, but at the cost of any further creative development and autonomy. In 1970, Bentham notes that while technology has developed enormously, 'in the process of turning the career of the technician into something worthwhile we have done virtually nothing'. So nine years after *Plays and Players* blazed at the failure of the Queen to give honours to playwrights, for the lighting technician 'training is little and chancy, the hours of work long, and the pay bad – all this to work mainly in ill-lit and ill-ventilated backstage slums with poor future prospects' (59).

The designer

Such is the disdain now shown for theatre design in the period before *Look Back in Anger*, that it is automatic to imagine it as a design era of tyrannical and monstrous scoundrelry. The Royal Court, on the other hand, is widely held to have been the place where theatre design, in the capable hands of Jocelyn Herbert, Richard Negri, Alan Tagg and others, grew up.

The metaphors which tend to describe this previous era are of the stage being 'cluttered' or 'swamped' by 'unnecessary clobber' (Anderson 1981, 148; Herbert 1981, 84; Gaskill 1988, 20). Yet again, what is discernible here is a retrospective reading that assumes the priority of the playwright's text, and then sees any designer who independently attracts the audience's attention as floridly self-indulgent.

However, most audiences in the forties saw sets and costumes as attractions, not distractions. The widespread practice of applauding the sets does not suggest a receptive body yearning for naked scrutiny of the playwright's art (Sarron 1945, 2). The drama critic R.D. Charques, writing shortly before the Second World War, denounced the detractors of design as 'the old puritan writ large' arguing,

> it is surely senseless to protest, as the high-minded often
> do, that we ought to swap fashion on the stage for more

soul. Both have a place there. It is the indifference or insensitiveness of the high-minded critic to the elementary magic of the stage – its evocation of elegance and beauty.

(1938, 12)

In 1954, George Devine gave a British Drama League lecture to schoolchildren, which was reported in *The Times*.[9] His insistence on theatrical illusion was roundly condemned by a letter from C.B. Purdom who insisted that 'the concern of the drama is with truth, its exploration and apprehension'.[10] The designer Laurence Irving, who had chaired the lecture, weighed in to defend Devine:

What is the truth that Mr Purdom protests? Will he dispute that truth is beauty? [...] Where else than in the theatre can so many senses be stimulated at the same time by a collaboration of those whose business is the pursuit and creation of beauty?

He lines up the desire for 'austerity in performance' with 'low theatre-goers' and suggests that the 'high theatre-goers [...] welcome the addition of colour and music to the ritual of make-believe'.[11]

In the forties a number of productions gave prominence to the design. In an International Theatre Institute survey of British theatre designers between the mid thirties and mid fifties, Aubrey Ensor praises Cecil Beaton's set design for a tour of *School for Scandal* which was largely a monochrome backcloth 'against which his lovely 18th century dresses showed to perfection' (1956, 25). Other designers are identified in similar ways: Oliver Messel's 'splendour' and 'opulence' (26), often in his use of gauzes to create a glittering fairy-tale feel, as in *Ring Round the Moon* (1950, see Figure 3.5), Roger Furse's bold use of colour (26), John Piper's 'unmistakable' style, and Leslie Hurry's 'triumph of splendour and beauty' in a revival of *Tamburlaine the Great* (1951) at the Old Vic (27). Heavy rich swagging, ropes and ornate wooden tent poles created the on-stage military encampment, set against a backdrop which emphasised the already distorted perspective of the camp, with a raging purple sky and black-edged, gold-crowned tents receding into the distance (27, see Figure 3.6). The Old Vic and the Shakespeare Memorial Theatre took great pride in giving designers this opportunity to produce such lavish sets; Laurence Irving,

Reginald Woolley and Reece Pemberton were amongst several other designers to whom the Old Vic gave such an opening, and Stratford showcased the work of Loudon Sainthill, James Bailey, Kenneth Rowell and Malcolm Pride, as well as Tanya Moiseiwitsch. As Irving stated above, 'serious' theatre was by no means incompatible with conspicuous design.

What is perhaps most striking is that Irving is stressing the *audience*'s desire for flamboyant design. Devine himself, in his original lecture, claimed that the audience's wishes governed visual conventions. The prominence of the designer's text was largely to do with the fact that designers had reputations outside the theatre. John Piper and Edward Burra were respected artists, Cecil Beaton a photographer and columnist, William Chappel and Motley also ran dressmaking firms. In the late fifties, a gallery opened, selling set and costume designs by Piper, Hurry, Beaton, Furse and others.[12] In a certain sense, these designers possessed the same kind of star personas as actors. Many had trademark scenic elements with which they independently claimed the attention of an audience, and which provided a visual theatrical history of prior and independent playgoing experiences. Cecil Beaton's design for *Lady Windermere's Fan* (1945) was an 'opulent ball-room filled with masses of roses' and 'magnificent dresses' on which the rose motif was picked up (Ensor 1956, 25); the costumes and set, then, signalled each other, creating a circuit of reference achieved without the intercession of actor or director, and only the lightest hint from Wilde. Robert Forman wrote at the end of the forties that 'your scenery, like the players, is acting a definite part and just as the actor is inspired so also must your efforts be' (1950, vi).

Unsurprisingly, the charismatic attractions of the star designer found no home at the austere Court.[13] Gaskill recalls their insistence that there would be 'no Cecil Beaton flower arrangements, no Leslie Hurry backdrops, no Oliver Messel gauzes' (1988, 20). Devine's vision of the Royal Court stage was one where design would take a firm second place. Jocelyn Herbert noted his desire:

> to get away from swamping the stage with decorative and naturalistic scenery; to let in light and air; to take the stage away from the director and designer and restore it to the actor and the text. This meant leaving space around the actors, and that meant the minimum of scenery and props, i.e. only those that served the actors and the play:

Figures 3.5 and 3.6 (top) Oliver Messel's design for *Ring Round the Moon*; (bottom) Leslie Hurry's design for *Tamburlaine the Great*

nothing that was for decorative purposes only, unless the text, or the style of the play, demanded it.

(1981, 84)

The early Court directors were in accord. Jocelyn Herbert has remarked that Lindsay Anderson was very suspicious of design (*Sergeant Musgrave at the Court* 1990), and Gaskill has stated unequivocally that 'we were constantly fixed on the idea of the play and that nothing should interfere with the play, nothing should make a statement beyond the play, and the design was always at the service of the play' (Doty and Harbin 1990, 185).

It has become a commonplace to describe Royal Court designs as being decisively influenced by the work of Brecht. Devine explained the lesson of the Berliner Ensemble to Bill Gaskill, 'If there has to be a door, you see, it has to be a real door but nothing else' (Gaskill 1981, 59). This delight in real objects would have been inexplicable in the early fifties. Hugh Hunt, like a good semiotician, observed that 'on the stage a spade is no longer of value as a spade, it is only valuable if it is a theatrical spade' (1954, 3). Similarly one manual for costume designers insists that 'real clothes are seldom theatrically effective, any more than real faces are without clever make-up' (Green 1941, 22). Yet at the Court, real objects were a staple feature of design. Joan Plowright recalls a 'real sink on stage, not to mention a real stove, on which real liver and onions were cooked' (1981, 34). This is despite the fact that Hugh Hunt's assertion is in one important sense correct; there is no way of telling the difference between a real stove on stage and an elaborate piece of stage managerial trickery.

While there was surely admiration for Brecht's work, they did not share Brecht's own objective of showing the origin of objects in the social world of human activity; Devine instead seemed to be more interested in effacing the presence of human activity in design, bypassing human craft through 'reality'. Again this positions the stage as neutral, erasing the constructedness of production, in the name of the author. Not for nothing was Jocelyn Herbert described as the invisible designer.[14]

The initial plan for the Court, also inspired by the Berliner Ensemble, was for a permanent surround. It was designed by Margaret Harris of the 'Motley' design firm, and comprised three side walls of white canvas, with gaps for two upstage entrances on either side and two further long s-shaped pieces downstage left and right. This canvas was then covered with fine black fish-netting to break up its solidity (Doty and Harbin 1990, 173–175). It was used for the opening two productions, *The Mulberry Bush* and *The Crucible*, but when it came to *Look Back in Anger*, the designer, Alan Tagg, insisted that this surround clashed with the intentions of the text. The permanent surround was bypassed (175). Gradually more and more productions ignored it in deference to authorial intention, and by the end of the decade it had been abandoned (Browne 1975, 30).

The new generation acted on the wider determination to restore sincere, authentic unity to the voices of the national culture. The discursive proliferation characteristic of the previous generation's theatrical practice was incompatible with this ambition, since its playful exploitation of the tensions within theatricality opened up tensions within utterance itself, accentuating the interdependence of artifice and realism. It could be countered that a Cecil Beaton rose motif or a gauzy Oliver Messel backdrop seem small prices to pay for the sophistication of *The Entertainer* or *Serjeant Musgrave's Dance* (1959). However, as I shall describe in my final two chapters, there were broader kinds of subversion implicit in this apparently frivolous theatricality.

For the moment, we should recognise that the brave causes of 1956 depended on a selective adjustment of the processes of theatrical production. Yet it needs also to be acknowledged that the disciplining of meanings on stage could only be completed by a disciplining of meanings off stage, and that the goal of cultural revitalisation involved the playwright's governance extending into the auditorium itself.

Figure 4.1 The opening night of *Blithe Spirit* (1941): Noël Coward, Fay Compton and Kay Hammond

4

OH FOR EMPTY SEATS
The Royal Court and its audiences

> The culture is not neutral, but flogs its publics into obei-
> sance to governing modes, political, aesthetic systems of
> seeing, hearing, demanding.
> (Howard Barker, *Arguments for a Theatre*, 1993, 134)

If we should want any evidence of the Royal Court's success in reuniting author and text in a tightly authentic unity, we need look no further than Arnold Wesker's *Roots*. Virtually all critics have commended the play's emotional authenticity: the *Guardian* review found it full of 'urgent sincerity' (Lloyd Evans and Lloyd Evans 1985, 85). Worsley adds that it is 'realistically and freshly observed' (Leeming 1985, 17), and Findlater saw it as 'stamped with authentic freshness of observation' (Elsom 1981, 94).

Such comments are not merely observations. To call a speech 'genuine', as, say, the *Guardian* did, involves a degree of interpre- tation. Interestingly, these predicates are all of the kind normally associated with people rather than things, and as such this critical response demonstrates the close relation between Wesker and his play. Just as interesting is the relative lack of lingering comment on set and costume that characterised reviews from the forties. Even when an actor is praised it is implicitly for their authentic presentation of the text; it would, after all, be hard to imagine someone being praised for sincerity in an insincere play. Such changes bear witness to the success of the new generation in uniting a world of feeling with those of speech and action.

It would be a mistake to assume the author to be a historically invariable category. In theatrical performance there are several authors, and I have shown that the relations between them can be captured historically. But the curtailment of West End signi- fying practices involves only one half of the communicative process. Derrida's critique of Austin, discussed in Chapter 1, insists on the impossibility of finally closing speaking and hearing, intention and understanding, within a perfect unity. But he does not suggest that we must therefore abandon intentionality, meaning, communication. He insisted, after all, that under the gaze of deconstruction, 'the category of intention will not disappear; it will have its place, but from that place it will no longer be able to govern the entire scene and system of utterance' (1988, 18). But what is that 'place'? Without determining this, without an eye to the 'indispensable guardrail' (1976, 158) of conventional readings, one may fail to assign it a place at all. While there is no doubt a kind of rapture to be gained from letting go of the guardrail and launching oneself into the purer air of infinite polysemy and freeplay, imagining an interpretation exhilaratingly free of history and culture, this is not reading. A recognition of the tensions and contradictions within theatrical experience must unfold alongside a detailed account of the specific relations of theatrical perception.

Literary agency

One of the many targets of Osborne's autobiographical spleen was the literary agent. 'To be dependent on an agent', he characteristically opines, 'is like entrusting your most precious future to your mother-in-law or your bookmaker' (1991a, 12). He notes Devine's resigned acceptance of their necessity, while maintaining that they 'despise both innovation and tradition, protecting the laws of deceit, avarice and self-aggrandizement of those they "represent"' (13). Those telling inverted commas mark one of the New Wave's great fears: being represented. Representation sits uneasily with the desire to reunify intention, feeling and expression, because it seems to prise open this unity. To use Derrida's term, it *grafts* utterances and events into new contexts, speaks without meaning it. To the playwright dedicated to exorcising such cultural maladies, representation is a parasitic threat. Osborne's determination was to 'ban the presence of the bat-like predator agent from first nights' (13).

In Osborne and Creighton's *An Epitaph for George Dillon* (1958), a surly young playwright, George Dillon, is visited by a producer, Barney Evans. As a producer, Evans is a conduit through which Dillon's play may be (re)presented. But, like the agent, he has the power to transform what he touches.

Barney: [...] this play of yours. I think it's got possibilities, but it needs rewriting. Act One and Two won't be so bad, provided you cut out all the high-brow stuff, give it pace – you know: dirty it up a bit, you see.

George: I see.

Barney: Third Act's construction is weak. I could help you there – and I'd do it for quite a small consideration because I think you've got something. You know that's a very good idea – getting the girl in the family way.

George: You think so?

Barney: Never fails. Get someone in the family way in the Third Act – you're halfway there.

(Osborne 1993, 167–168)

Later in the third act Josie, whom Dillon has slept with, is revealed to be pregnant. This poses an intriguing question that puts the whole theatrical frame in question; has Evans got to Osborne, as he tries to get to Dillon?

The circularity is one that resonates with the central dilemmas of the new generation. They wish to believe these plays are complete in themselves, but in which case why perform them? Performance endangers the stability of these plays' meanings, opens up, as we have seen, a cleft in the structure of utterance itself; any utterance 'can be *cited*, put between quotation marks; in doing so it can break with every given context, engendering an infinity of new contexts' (Derrida 1988, 12). The fact that plays can be given a vast number of different productions is not an external or secondary fact about theatrical production, it is a condition of plays themselves, and the structures of language in which they are written. And if these multiple new versions are in some sense drawing on forces within any play, the stability of the New Wave's texts is in doubt, as performance itself threatens to flout the very vitality it is meant to affirm.

Karl Mannheim, in *Ideology and Utopia*, argues that debate over the meaning of a text, action or object cannot be resolved by looking at 'the "object in itself"' (if it were, it would be impossible to understand why the object should appear in so many refractions)' (1960, 241). The Court's striking way through the impasse was to reverse this process: to clamp down on the surrounding 'refractions' in order to constitute 'the object in itself'. As a result there were furious penalties placed on those who might multiply the meanings of *Look Back in Anger*. Banning agents from the theatre is paradigmatic of what was to come.

The audience

In 1941, Noël Coward's *Blithe Spirit* opened in Manchester at the beginning of its pre-London tour. At the end, Coward joined the cast on stage and gave a brief speech to the audience.[1] I want to note three aspects of the speech; firstly, Coward is anxious to thank the audience for their appreciation; he repeatedly acknowledges their applause, and pays tribute to Manchester and its wartime spirit. Secondly, the character on stage is not so much Noël Coward as 'Noël Coward', the well-known performer, dramatist and song-writer. He can assume that they know about his trip to Australia and New Zealand; he can talk personally about his love for the theatre and he recalls his first play. Lastly, in the speech he says nothing about *Blithe Spirit*; he makes no attempts to explain, justify or expand on what the audience has seen. Such a speech would have been unthinkable fifteen years later.

Theatregoing in the forties and early fifties was a profoundly social activity. The earlier start of evening performances, a continuation of wartime curfew restrictions, meant that it was going to the theatre, rather than a meal or a drink, that marked the move from work to leisure. Audiences would often eat chocolate or drink tea or coffee in their seats (Steinbeck 1952). Wendy Trewin notes that intervals would be used to seek out old friends (1954, 219). Downs describes the moments before curtain-up spent reading the newspaper or recalling past performances (1951, 65). Further, the patterns of wartime and post-war leisure encouraged other activities around the performances, like the pit queue. John Sommerfield watched a number of these queues for Mass Observation and could observe as many as 150 audience members, chatting for over an hour, often about other plays they had seen.[2]

A result of this is that audiences were highly conscious of themselves as an audience. Wendy Trewin states that on first nights photographers would compete with autograph hunters to catch any celebrities in attendance (1954, 218). The performance was then not the sole focus of the theatrical event, but part of a web of pleasurable activities: eating, smoking, drinking, meeting friends, reminiscing and gossip. One writer saw intervals as crucial parts of the experience:

attendance at the play is the celebration of a rite and rites require rituals. Ritual is repetitive behaviour, which serves to recall and recreate an emotional response whenever it is needed. The striking up of the band, the glow of the foot-lights on the curtain, the parading and regaling in the intervals, the urgent rings of the bar bells, the talk and laughter silenced as the lights go down – all these slight things are a part of the rite of the play.

(Pullein-Thompson 1947, 6)

These words in the left-leaning *Theatre Newsletter* remind us that this self-consciousness in the audience is a recognition of collective identity and collective power.

Another characteristic of mid-century audiences was a shift in their class formation. The Bancrofts' policy at the Prince of Wales in the late nineteenth century of targeting middle-class audience goers had encouraged, on class lines, a division between 'art' and 'entertainment'; from this evolved two traditions of audience behaviour: while popular entertainments, variety and music hall, tended to invite a more demonstrative following, the West End saw 'the disappearance of emotional responses from audiences' (Baer 1992, 167). The pre-war years had seen this opposition deepen.

But this changed during the war. Bringing the curtain time forward from 8.30 to 6.00 meant that people could go directly from work and use public transport to get home afterwards. The requirements of rationing mean that the exclusive convention of wearing evening dress fell into disuse. And, as the war squeezed people's earnings, theatres lowered their prices.[3] The dangers and limitations of operating in the centre of London during the Blitz encouraged some managers to send tours around the country of plays which would previously have sat in West End houses for the entirety of their runs or had, at most, the 'glorified dress rehearsal' of a pre-London tour (Landstone 1953, 14). Major productions toured to towns which had previously had to content itself with No. 2 repertory; the freshness and glamour of these productions made theatregoing newly attractive. CEMA complemented this work with its tours to factories, canteens, workers hostels and canteens, where they found audiences, most of whom had never seen a play before.[4] The forces were encouraged to go to the theatre; in early 1945, the Old Vic reserved 10 per cent of its seats for members of the armed forces.[5] Despite a decline after the war, this new audience was substantially retained (Landstone 1952, 4). Findlater and Darlington note a younger audience, with a broader class base, than before the war (1952, 195; 1954, 124).

One result of this was that plays began to receive noisier receptions than they had done previously. Audiences would show their appreciation of a fine speech, a performer's entrance and exit, and even, on occasion, a particularly impressive set.[6] Plays were structured to evoke these kinds of response: the second act curtain of Rattigan's *The Winslow Boy* (1946), in which Sir Robert Morton agrees unexpectedly to take on Ronnie's case against the Admiralty, was greeted with an enormous relieved ovation. Typical was the reaction to Robert Donat's return from Hollywood to play in *Murder at the Cathedral* at the Old Vic in 1953: 'when Donat stepped forward to speak [...] somebody got in, loudly and clearly, a "Welcome back!" To which he replied, greatly moved, "It's wonderful to be back – and in this theatre"' (Wendy Trewin 1954, 223).

These collective responses were not always in support. Wendy Trewin notes that 'on an unfortunate night one always wonders in the second interval whether the gallery has decided to boo. The third act is the crucial time; if there are those inarticulate sounds of derision, then trouble at curtain-fall is sure' (219–220). There are reports of individual actors being heckled (Miller 1957, 167), and sometimes the content of the plays would be attacked; at the première of *Her Excellency* (1949) (a musical starring Cicely Courtneidge as a British Ambassador to a South American state, trying to arrange a meat contract) the play was marred by crudely nationalist sentiment and the gallery jeered it to an early closure (Wilson 1949a, 244). J.C. Trewin recalls that *Look Back in Anger* received 'ironical laughter' during its closing scenes (1957, 6).

Predictably, this new audience was not always welcomed, and middle-class resentment took the form of a debate about the rights and wrongs of booing. J.B. Morton (Beachcomber) wrote in the late forties that 'it is a healthy sign that booing and yells of disapproval are returning to the theatre. An audience should not sit like a herd of milksops enduring boredom or active discomfort in genteel silence'.[7] A.E. Wilson insisted, 'an audience has as much right to express its disapproval as it has to express its admiration of any play, and I can sympathise with any playgoer who has been fobbed off with something which is not worth the price of admission' (1949b, 159). But one Mass Observation reporter, watching a play at the Bedford Theatre, Camden (a Music Hall which in its dying days was used for plays), shows unease at the contested theatrical territory: 'the audience was very appreciative – generally in the right places – but as one would guess in Camden Town, [there were] certain loud laughs by a few people, at the worst swearing, or the silliest jokes'.[8] The same reporter seems faintly aware of this class struggle when remarking of the response to *Oklahoma!* 'it reminded me more of a pantomime audience'.[9]

These remarks should be seen in the context of a (then) general belief that an audience is the ultimate arbiter of a performance's quality. J.B. Priestley affirmed that:

> you cannot write plays without the willing co-operation of the audience [...] if he [*sic*] is creating situations that leave the audience yawning and coughing, he will see the yawns and hear the coughs. This behaviour of the audience is the real dramatic criticism.
>
> (1948b, 46)

Coward burst forth in the early sixties with this paean to the audience's taste: 'The Public! Exacting, careless, discerning, indiscriminating, capricious, loyal and unpredictable' and ends with this advice: 'never bore the living hell out of it' (1962, 180).

For a more elegant exposition of this view, we should turn to Rattigan's Aunt Edna. The quite unjustified mockery that this invention brought upon Rattigan's head can be explained as the clash between two quite different attitudes to the audience. Prefacing the second volume of his *Collected Plays*, Rattigan suggests that while in certain spheres of creativity, one may be freer to ignore one's potential audience, theatre is a public art and the reactions of the audience are unavoidably part of the experience. He therefore sets out to characterise a section of the theatre's audience as 'Aunt Edna': 'a nice, respectable, middle-class, middle-aged, maiden lady, with time on her hands and the money to help her pass it' (1953, vol. II, xi–xii). She has little time for modernist painting ('those dreadful reds, my dear, and why three noses?'), and she likes a good story. In short, she is a 'hopeless lowbrow' (xii).

Edna became a stick to beat Rattigan with. It was assumed that Rattigan must either be patronising this figure or slavishly writing down to her level. Yet neither is the case. In the first place, he makes clear that he has learnt a great deal from her; in his early theatregoing experiences, he was exploring his own emotions through her theatrical responses: 'I was experiencing emotions which, though no doubt insincere of origin in that they were induced and coloured by the adult emotions around me, were none the less most deeply felt' (xiv). But neither is Rattigan recommending that writers must satisfy Edna by conforming to her every expectation: 'although Aunt Edna must never be made mock of, or bored, or befuddled, she must equally not be wooed, or pandered to, or cosseted' (xvi). Instead, the playwright is engaged in a kind of *pas de deux* with Edna, with whom he or she must maintain a certain distance, working with and pushing against the limits of her tolerance and understanding. He remarks that critics, notably Tynan, who had wanted a play like *The Deep Blue Sea* (1952) to end in Hester's suicide were themselves being somewhat Edna-like in preferring a neatly tragic conclusion to the grim starkness of Hester's decision to live.

Rattigan's conviction that the audience is essential to the life of the play means yielding to them the right of judgement. A.E. Wilson agreed: 'I would not deny the right of any member of the audience to express an opinion upon what he or she has to see' (1949b, 159). But others were not so sure. *Punch* reported a 'seasoned actress' complaining that 'the manners of London first-night audiences had never, in her experience, been worse'.[10] Philip Hope-Wallace admitted himself aghast to hear

> (as increasingly I do hear) people talking to one another during the course of a play in perfectly normal, clear conversational voices. I cannot imagine myself ever speaking above a substage whisper, once the curtain was up on that warmest of all hearths, a living stage.
>
> (18)

Steps were taken to silence the audience. Specifically targeting the young, a number of British Drama League lectures were given by leading theatre practitioners in 1953 and 1954. At these lectures, much time was spent on theatre behaviour. Particular emphasis was placed on noisy eating; Sybil Thorndike storms, 'Sometimes I feel like spitting at the audience because of the noise made by unwrapping chocolates'.[11] At another discussion, Richard Burton and Claire Bloom, then co-starring at the Old Vic, develop Thorndike's criticisms to 700 London schoolchildren; 'I love to eat chocolates when I'm in the audience,' admits Burton. 'But I take it as a favour if the audience doesn't when I'm on stage'; 'A lot depends,' adds Bloom sagely, 'on whether the choco-lates are in silver paper'.[12] *Plays and Players* noted this campaign but defended the audience, maintaining 'that there can be no tampering with the right of the gallery to express its views on first nights'.[13]

It was into this debate that the Royal Court entered. In the publicity inaugurating the English Stage Company, George Devine declared that he 'would like to build up a public who *always* go to the Court, similar to the patrons who *always* go to the Old Vic'.[14] And, as if taking their cue from Tynan's calculation that there were 6,733,000 people who ought to see *Look Back in Anger*, they focused their energies on finding a new audience, not regular West End theatregoers. An 'audience organiser' was employed to arrange group visits (Browne 1975, 25).

Apart from a simple desire to tap a new market, this policy functioned to reinforce the authenticity of the plays against theatre convention. At a public symposium at the Royal Court in September 1956, Wolf Mankowitz attacked the average West End audiences as 'a kind of "lumpen" *bourgeoisie* (*Laughter and applause*) which of course hasn't had to think for a very long time whether it was hungry or not (*Laughter and applause*)'.[15] Osborne, in his contribution to *Declaration*, marked his constituency by commenting that 'the boys in the orchestra at the Royal Court Theatre were capable of judging, and they did: "*We've been through it and we know what it is like*"' (1957a, 79). He deploys a comparable strategy when he observes that 'the people I should like to contact – if I knew how – aren't likely to be reading this book anyway' (64), thus appealing over the heads of the actual readers. *Encore* fell in line, titling its editorial column 'View from the Gods', and incongruously signing it 'Groundling'.

There were early successes. The televised extract from *Look Back in Anger* was watched by five million viewers, several of whom came to see the play at the Court, boosting the box office and the play's public profile. In early 1957, Devine was confident enough to claim that the Court has 'begun to create an audience which will patronise our theatre for the quality of our work, regardless of its "attraction value"' (161).

This was premature. The starry revival of *The Country Wife* in December 1956 drew 95 per cent attendance, but did not rely on or create this new audience. Towards the end of 1957, houses began to decline. A note in the Council's minutes observes that gross takings were sometimes as low as £19 for an evening performance (and £6 for a mid-week matinee), adding 'this does not indicate much of a following' (Findlater 1981, 51). The audience organiser was dismissed. In November of that year, Lindsay Anderson complained that the Sunday Nights without Décor

> can only really fulfil their function with audiences who come, not with the passive expectation of 'entertainment,' nor just with mouths wide open for another slab of minority culture, but themselves prepared to give something, to work, with minds open and alert, themselves creative (*Judge Not* should be inscribed on the programme). But this kind of audience – I am driven to conclude – does not exist in London. If it did exist, you would surely expect to find it at, or around, the Royal Court. No single management (nor all the others put together, for that matter) has given us such intelligent stimulus in the last eighteen months.
>
> (1957, 46)

Anderson does not see the lack of public enthusiasm as saying something about the plays themselves, because the audience's function is not to judge. Instead, he is proposing a new conception of the relation between stage and auditorium.

The debate may be illuminated by considering Derrida's discussion of 'supplementarity'. In *Of Grammatology*, he notes that 'supplement' has two meanings; a supplement can be an object which simply adds to something which is complete in itself, 'a surplus, a plenitude enriching another plenitude' (1976, 144); but the supplement may also be something which adds to something to make it complete, indicating that there is something lacking in the structure that it adds to. It is this ambiguous object, the supplement, neither properly internal nor external to a structure, that deconstruction classically fastens upon. The danger posed by the supplement may be seen in that original concern about representation and agency; the Royal Courtiers wanted their unique and self-present moments of pure expressivity to be seen – in other words, they wanted an audience – but if an audience is *required*, how can the 'original' object be complete? A theatre that requires an audience's approval locates that audience on the interior of its texts, allows it to mark an absence within the text, requiring completion and confirmation (which is Rattigan's conception of Aunt Edna); but if that text is already complete, the audience is exiled to a position of pure exteriority, leaving the integrity of the text intact.

A move between notions of the supplement is involved in the move to professional status discussed in Chapter 3. Greenwood notes that occupations generally treat those who use their services as *customers*; professions regard them as *clients*. The change is not merely terminological. He lists two attributes of the customer: he or she (a) has the capacity 'to judge the potential of the service or of the commodity to satisfy them [...] epitomized in the slogan: "The customer is always right!" ', and (b) is believed fully able to 'evaluate the calibre of the professional service he [*sic*] receives' (1957, 48).

Clients do not possess these attributes. The prized autonomy of the profession dictates that its knowledge is a closed system which may only be assessed by other professionals. The client does not have sufficient competence to make his or her own decisions. A broad divide opens up between the professional and his or her own client, who lacks the skills to choose, praise or criticise what they receive.

This is what Anderson's words signal. The ESC initially sought approval from its audience, albeit an audience which did not usually go to the theatre. But that this audience did not finally appear does not imply criticism of the Court, but of the public themselves. The quality of the work is unquestioned, indeed is not dependent on the audience recognising it at all. It rather recalls Brecht's ironic remark that if 'The People' should prove themselves unworthy of their democratic responsibilities, the government should dissolve them and elect another.

This soon developed into a new hostility towards audiences; this hostility, by modelling itself on a battle, constitutes performance and audience as two opposed, hence separate, combatants. George Dillon's description of acting sets the tone:

> whenever I step out on to those boards – immediately, from the very first moment I show my face – I know I've got to fight almost every one of those people in the audi-torium. Right from the stalls to the gallery, to the Vestal Virgins in the boxes! My God, it's a gladiatorial combat! Me against Them! Me and mighty Them!
>
> (Osborne 1993, 147)

In his autobiography Osborne compares his playwriting to his tactics in school boxing matches, in which 'a bloody technical knock-out could result with negligible injury to oneself' (1981a, 142). Devine had also come to see the theatre and its audience in these oppositional terms. Osborne recalls finding him before the première of *The Entertainer*, peering gleefully through the curtain:

> 'There you are, dear boy, take a look out there. [...] There they are. All waiting for *you*. All of us, come to that. What do you think, eh? Same old pack of cunts, fashionable arseholes. Just more of them than usual, that's all'
>
> (47)

Arden, the notorious box office failure of the early Court, believed that drama was 'a public art' and thus should 'appeal to more than a minority if it is to remain healthy' but finds that this must be tempered by a recognition of 'public taste as corrupt' (1960, 14). Perhaps it is this raging perplexity that underlies one of the most famous theatrical images of the late fifties: Serjeant Musgrave's Gatling Gun trained on the audience.

The Royal Court's way out of this dilemma was to separate the play's quality from audience approval. Devine believed that the bottom line was that a play was 'basically authentic in itself and worth doing in the first place'. That 'first place' draws a line in the sand between artistic judgements and audience judgements. The kinds of vocal and physical criticism that an audience might make are therefore secondary, and caring about them a sign of weakness. Osborne rightly links 'craft' to a desire for no one to walk out, inversely suggesting that his own pugnacious disregard of the audience is a sign of uncrafted vitality (1981a, 211). In *Déjàvu*, Osborne's oddly Pirandellian Porter proudly claims to be 'accustomed to the banging of uptipped seats' (1993, 338).

Even more strikingly, walking out was redescribed as an *effect* of performance, indeed as a sign of its success. As Lindsay Anderson put it, 'if a play was successful, you heard the seats banging up as people walked out'.[16] Osborne recalls that during the premiere of Charles Wood's *Meals on Wheels* (1965), which Osborne directed, Devine said, ' "They're *hating* it, aren't they?" And he didn't say this at all despondently; he was delighted because they were hating it for the right reasons, responding *as we had anticipated*' (1981b, 24, my emphasis). Joan Plowright remembers that as the audience went 'shouting and grumbling into Sloane Square, George would watch through his window and smoke his pipe and think "That's what I'm here for" ' (Wardle 1978, 204).

The Arts Council was fundamentally in agreement. Still smarting from its Council-sponsored *Hamlet* being booed at the Festival of Britain, it speculated whether ticket prices should be raised, on the grounds that we esteem more highly what we strive to achieve. The exponential increase in the Council's grant to the ESC, by insulating it from audience disapproval, further cemented the abandonment of CEMA's original aim of widening access. In this sense, the famous 'right to fail' is a doctrine aimed directly *against* audiences. This reached perhaps its apotheosis in Peter Brook's deeply autocratic *Encore* article, 'Oh For Empty Seats', where he calls for a theatre funded so heavily that no one need attend its productions.

The factors that encouraged the audience's self-consciousness in the early fifties were suppressed at the Court. Devine's persuasion that 'the Royal Court ideal is to be likened to an art gallery or a literary magazine' (1957, 154) or his more famous counsel that 'you should choose your theatre like you choose a religion' (Wardle 1978, 279) have been taken as tokens of the seriousness of his endeavours. But perhaps they also slyly intimate his preferred audience behaviour, aspiring to the silence of the art gallery, the hush of a church, or the private study of the literary journal.

Devine acknowledged shortly before his death, 'I wanted to change the attitude of the public towards the theatre. All I did was to change the attitude of the theatre towards the public' (Wardle 1978, 279). The desire for vital theatre presumed a tight unity of feeling and expression in the productions, which could not be disturbed or judged by outsiders. So the activities of the audience are effaced and marginalised. A decade after Devine's death, audience behaviour had been entirely transformed: 'voices aloft have ceased to complain', remarks one commentator; booing 'is the thinnest half-whisper of what it was'.[17]

Proscenium

If the audience's independent right to judgement was expropriated by the stage, it is also important to show how authorised judgements were put in their place. And here we return to those problematic figures that interpose themselves between author and audience. Figures like the critic, publicist, publisher, even the box-office staff and programme seller act as intermediaries between audience and stage, framing and perhaps shaping the theatrical event. These too were drawn into the author's sphere of control.

In his analysis of Kant's *Critique of Judgement*, Derrida focuses on a short passage in which Kant is attempting to distinguish pure judgements of taste from empirical judgements of what is beautiful:

> Even what we call *ornaments* (*parerga*), i.e., what does not belong to the whole presentation of the object as an intrinsic constituent, but [is] only an extrinsic addition, does indeed increase our taste's liking, and yet it too does so only by its form, as in the case of picture frames, or drapery on statues, or colonnades around magnificent buildings.
>
> (Kant 1987, 72)

In this, Kant is trying to distinguish an inside and an outside to art; these frames, he says, commend the object to our attention, prepare it for aesthetic contemplation, but are not properly part of the object itself. Derrida notes that these parasitical frames, these *parerga*, perform a crucial function in Western philosophical aesthetics, since a 'permanent requirement – to distinguish between the internal or proper sense and the circumstance of the object being talked about – organizes all philosophical discourses on art'. To divide art from non-art, to divide the purely beautiful from the empirically beautiful, requires 'a discourse on the limit between the inside and outside of the art object, here a *discourse on the frame*' (1987, 45). Paradoxically, then, Kantian aesthetics, in the very attempt to make a strict distinction between inside and out, is forced to concede the existence of a third phenomenon; the frame, which is both inside (it is an essential part of presenting the object to us) and outside the object ('only an extrinsic addition').

There are affinities with the Court's project here. Just as Kant wants us to focus our attention exclusively on the object itself, the Court was determined to organise and restrict the meanings within theatrical representation. Kant's 'golden frame' has its theatrical counterpart in the spatial limit that divides the performance area from the auditorium: the proscenium. As John Frow observes, changes in the architectural theatre frame (are) accompanied (by) changes in the 'whole status of the scenic illusion' (1986, 223).

114

When the English Stage Company first moved into the Court they found a late Victorian theatre, complete with house tabs, an orchestra pit, and a golden proscenium with boxes immediately beside it left and right. Devine's response was to cover over the orchestra pit, providing a small forestage, and convert the side boxes into downstage entrances. He also took one look at the proscenium and declared 'Well, that will have to come down. We don't want the border' (Doty and Harbin 1990, 40). The cloud of plaster dust raised by the demolition of the frame hung, ghost-like, in the theatre for weeks afterwards.

This ghostly frame is a fitting image of the Court's requirements. The discourse that wants to present and preserve the purity of the performance text needs a simultaneously absent and present frame. It must be there, maintaining its rigid distinction between text and non-text, but must not draw attention to its role in constituting the integrity of that text; 'the *parergon* is a form which has as its traditional determination not that it stands out but that it disappears, buries itself, effaces itself, melts away at the moment it deploys its greatest energy' (Derrida 1987, 61). We have seen this in the rearticulation of certain theatre occupations, where, in effect, their job specification is fundamentally altered in such a way as to efface both their activity and, hence, the activity of rearticulation *itself*.

The proscenial frame comprises the sphere of theatrical activity that circulates around the performance and in which the performance itself circulates: reviews, posters, programmes, publishing, discussion, criticism. John Urry has noted the way in which these kinds of texts help us to imaginatively pre-figure an event, which that event then has to live up to; 'and even when the object fails to live up to its representation it is the latter which will stay in people's minds, as what they have really "seen"' (1990, 86). This circulation creates a semantic economy in which a performance can be articulated, negotiated and shared between members of an audience – and indeed people who never went to the performance at all, since the performance event is only one place within a much wider circulation. Osborne once commented that the number of people who told him they attended the first night of *Look Back in Anger* would have filled the Albert Hall (Ritchie 1988, 126).

This is why the proscenium is so unsettling for the New Wave. Once again, they are faced with a force within theatrical experience that threatens to multiply the meanings of the performance, affect their interpretation, graft the text into new, unanticipated contexts. A talisman of the change is the front-of-house worker. Before 1956, especially given the importance accorded to the spectator, and the social aspects of theatregoing, they had a decisive contribution to make. Tolmie calls the box-office manager 'one of the most important and responsible officials in a theatre' (1946, 34). With a different class emphasis, Gerry Raffles laid great stress on the accessibility and friendliness of the Theatre Royal Stratford East, where they had a low-pricing policy, sold tickets through social clubs and factories, and endeavoured to ensure that 'every person is welcome' (1956, 229–230).

The Court inherited a small, cramped building, but its priority was not audience comfort. The foyer remained dark, narrow and hot. Jokes were played on the audience, like playing the national anthem too fast or too slow. In the early sixties, its one concession to audience comfort was a revamp of the bar. But by installing large windows looking into the auditorium, the Court ensured that even when having an interval drink, the stage was still the single focus of your evening (Tschudin 1972, 21).

A more obviously dangerous figure is the publicist; not only does he or she have the parasitic task of 'representing' your play to others, but he or she affronts the convention of the professional that you do not advertise. As Greenwood points out, 'if a profession were to advertise, it would, in effect, impute to the potential client the discriminating ability to select from competing forms of service' (1957, 48). Hence, Osborne is particularly venomous in his description of George Fearon, the part-time press officer for the ESC. He was 'overpaid', 'ineffective', says Osborne, who remembers meeting him to discuss publicising *Look Back in Anger*:

> He equivocated shiftily, even for one in his trade, and then told me with some relish how much he disliked the play and how he had no idea how he could possibly publicize it successfully. The prospect began to puff him up with rare pleasure. He looked at me cheerfully as if he were Albert Pierrepoint guessing my weight. 'I suppose you're really – an angry young man...'
>
> (1991a, 20)

To describe the man who invented the term 'angry young man' as an ineffective publicist is perverse enough, but several of those who were brought under this label censured this 'journalistic stunt' (Wain 1957, 91), the 'journalistic swindle' and 'cheap journalistic fiction' (Osborne 1957c, 4) of grouping together various writers 'without so much as an attempt at understanding' (Maschler 1957, 7).

Ironically, Wain and Maschler's remarks are both taken from *Declaration*, a volume which brought together a group of writers on the same grounds as did the label 'angry young man'. Osborne himself, while deriding the term, was often happy to popularise, and even claim authorship of the phrase.[18] These paradoxes are undoubtedly the paradoxes of the frame; but, like the treatment of the audience and these writers' fellow theatre workers, they resolve this paradox by insisting that publicity is riding on a momentum that the text already possesses. Fearon's equivocation is flattened by the sheer, unequivocal power of the play.

Worse even than the dangers threatened by the publicist is the power of the critic. To appreciate the peril they represented for the New Wave, their function in the years before 1956 needs clarification. There was a close affinity between the audience and the critic; Philip Hope-Wallace describes the critic as 'on the side of the audience' (Roud 1958, 28). They offered advice and commentary for the audience. Parallel to this, an audience's hostile first-night response would often be noted in a review as a 'mixed reception'.

Their role was unabashedly not merely to inform but to mediate. Worsley saw his role as to 'start discussion rolling' (Roud 1958, 27). It was often stated that critics were not right or wrong, but simply delivering one person's opinion (e.g. Brown 1960, 29). 'The professional critic', wrote Harold Downs, '[...] writes in accordance with his conception of truth – but the truth has many sides' (1951, 29). Immediately, this seems to offer a dangerous proliferation of response, what Osborne dismissed as 'too much commentary and clamour' (1991a, 32).

The danger is that the critic may be what Worsley called 'an interpreter between the theatre and the public' (quoted, Gilliatt 1959, 24). As Lindsay Anderson lamented, 'if you cut yourself off from them, how do you reach an audience at all? But if you subscribe to them [...] then you are caught in a trap. Because how are you represented by them?' (1958a, 7). The critics' danger, like the supplement, like the *parergon*, is that they exist both outside and inside the work; adding commentary to it, but in the process revealing ambiguity and incompleteness within it. And like those other supplements, the bat-like agent, and the hangman publicist, they threaten to break up the vital, living quality of these texts:

'the critic's state is related to the artist's as inseparably as a para-site's to his [*sic*] host's' (Gilliatt 1959, 22).

As usual, the strategy is hostility and scorn. If Osborne is not threatening them with expulsion (1968, 69), he is deriding their powers of commentary: they 'misinterpret one's intentions, partly from insensibility, but also from simple, unacknowledged igno-rance' (1957a, 78). His aggression towards the critics culminated in *The World of Paul Slickey*, cholerically dedicated to journalists and 'their boredom, their incomprehension, their distaste' (1993, 188). While the play itself deals mainly with a gossip columnist, it contains a number of asides at the expense of critics, including the anti-hero's confession that 'I take the theatre too seriously to be a dramatic critic [...] and I know too much about it' (196), and a despised servant named Trewin.

The allegation that critics know too little about the theatre is in sharp contrast with the earlier view that they were representing the audience's interests. Penelope Gilliatt confesses that the call to commitment is 'commitment *to our side*. We want allies, flag-wavers and objection-waivers, to support our belief in a pungent, vivid popular drama' and adds that 'we would trust them [critics] all the more if they evidently had technical knowledge of the theatre' (1959, 21–22). Gilliatt was herself a critic for the *Observer*, alongside Tynan, though that 'our side' indicates that she had already followed her own advice. She elaborated her demands in claiming that 'the born dramatic critic should share enough of the theatre's extroversion for it to be possible to imagine him [*sic*] on a stage without embarrassment' (25). (This preposterous requirement has the sole function of further endorsing the flamboyant Tynan).

Tynan was, without a doubt, the model of a modern major critic. With a blend of humility to stage and disregard of the audience, he stated, in an address to a Foyle's literary luncheon, 'the critic must not attempt to teach playwright and actor their jobs [...] The last thing a critic ought to be concerned with is the people who read him first. He should write for posterity' (1988, 101–102). His review of *Look Back in Anger* strikes an unusual note when he discloses that 'I doubt if I could love anyone who did not wish to see *Look Back in Anger*' (1964, 42). While this is unlikely to bother you unless you yearn to be loved by Kenneth Tynan, it is clear that he is set on confronting his readership, not speaking for them. It was even clearer two years later when he described the critic's function as making up for the inadequacies of the audience (Roud 1958, 29).

Of course, the critics did not immediately fall into line. Greenwood notes that the professional community will band together to protect any of its members whose authority is attacked from outside (1957, 51). And following terrible reviews of *Serjeant Musgrave's Dance* Lindsay Anderson, the play's director, went on the offensive, producing a leaflet entitled 'What kind of a theatre do you want?', attacking the critics.[19] It set what George Devine tellingly called 'authoritative opinions against press criticisms' (1960, 26); a number of theatre workers wrote brief statements in praise of the work, amongst them Peggy Ashcroft, Doris Lessing, Christopher Logue, N.F. Simpson, Arnold Wesker, John Osbourne [sic] and Wolf Mankowitz (all of them involved with the Court). A year later but in the same vein, he had Alan Sillitoe write in defence of Arden's *The Happy Haven* (1960) and at the annual lunch for the press, after a panning of Delaney's *The Lion in Love* (1960), Devine made his displeasure clearly felt (Osborne 1991a, 172).

This campaign did have its affects. The new generation of critics – Gilliatt, Derek Granger, Alan Brien, Irving Wardle – followed Tynan's model, and had all been supportive of the Royal Court. Their allegiance to the stage rather than the auditorium, however, did not always make for independent judgement. In the mid sixties an Australian critic visiting London complained: 'the sheer cowardice, lack of independence and band-wagon-jumping of even "responsible" London critics has been the most disillusioning of my theatrical experiences of the last four years' (Seymour 1965, 62).

Ephemera and memorabilia

In 1958, Robert Bolt described the new vitality and commitment required of the playwright: 'the playwright must, so to speak, be present on the stage no less than his [sic] cast and more than they must risk making a fool of himself on just those issues where he feels most solemn' (Bolt 1958, 144). Bolt's 'so to speak' brings us back to Noël Coward at *Blithe Spirit*, and reminds us that the author was once literally on the stage. The practice of the first night curtain speech endured through the forties and early fifties. Wendy Trewin recalls Eliot giving a speech after *The Cocktail Party* in 1950, but not after *The Confidential Clerk* in 1953, although Carl Zuckmayer at the London première of *The Devil's General* in the same month did (1954, 220, 222). In general terms, the curtain speech bowed out throughout the fifties.

This might seem surprising; one might be tempted to imagine that the author's curtain speech was precisely the kind of veneration of authorship encouraged at the Court. But this would be mistaken. The problem of the curtain speech is that the author seems to be opening him or herself for judgement. Firstly, this violates his or her professional status; as Freidson puts it, 'being visible when the work itself requires it or when one himself [*sic*] so requests is acceptable, but anything more is uncomfortable, if not demeaning' (1970, 180). The author can find him/herself in a tricky situation, as William Douglas Home discovered after *Ambassador Extraordinary* (1948), when he tried to face down a unitedly hostile gallery. Secondly, the author who wishes to limit and control the meanings of his or her text risks opening up the same kind of extra-textual 'noise' that accompanies the actor in the form of a star persona. They may unwillingly become part of the object being judged, and thus be dragged into the theatre's relentless performativity. Of course, before 1956, this was simply not a consideration, and many playwrights, like Clemence Dane, relished the opportunity to sparkle in a well-turned curtain speech.

The opposite extreme, complete authorial silence, runs the risk of allowing a play to be taken any old way. The dilemma is by now familiar; the playwright who wishes to protect the vitality of their writing can neither be the fully visible focus of that vitality, nor can they silently let the play speak for itself, either option opening the play to the mercy of the graft, to reinterpretation. They need, in fact, to operate both inside and outside their play. This is, of course, the space of the proscenium.

The author began to inhabit precisely this liminal space. Authors began to make their interventions from social spaces like newspapers, theatre programmes, television interviews. Their proscenial quality is that they appear and disappear: the newspaper is read and thrown away, the programme is read in between watching the stage, the interview disappears as it is broadcast. They pass from ephemera to memorabilia (though are neither forgotten nor fully remembered, since their principal function relies on us forgetting remembering them).

The theatre programme is one of the most common members of this class of objects. In the early fifties, they were very flimsy documents offering little information beyond cast, order of scenes, producers and suppliers of props. While some criticised the practice of charging 6d for such a meagre document,[20] the description of scenes and, in particular, the listing of songs in the musical allowed the audience to anticipate and imagine the events that might take place, a kind of independent speculation that the Royal Courtiers would have shuddered at.

In fact, rather than abandon programmes or proclaim their functional exteriority by giving them away, the Royal Court expanded the programme through the late fifties and early sixties. It began to hold comments by the writer, contextual information to aid the audience's understanding, appreciations by director and designer, etc. As such it develops from texts like Lindsay Anderson's leaflet in defence of *Serjeant Musgrave's Dance* or the brochure produced to celebrate the English Stage Company's third season (*Royal Court Theatre*, 1960), and, like those, is a document designed to restrict, rather than open up, the audience's understanding of the play.

Another theatrical document that underwent major changes in the fifties, directly prompted by the work of the Royal Court, was the printed playtext. In the forties, few publishers systematically published plays. Those that did – Evans Plays, English Theatre Guild, Samuel French – published them as virtual model-books of the original production. The director's blocking would be printed, indistinguishable from the author's stage directions; a photograph of the set would be placed against the first page of text, and the set dressings, props, and lighting, sound and flying cues would be listed at the back. In the published text of Colin Morris's *Reluctant Heroes* (1950), the play which inaugurated Brian Rix's twenty-year residency of the Whitehall Theatre, it is even indicated where the major laughs are. The pragmatic reason why published plays took this form was the fast turnaround of much repertory theatre. If an entire production needed to be mounted from scratch in a week, such texts were invaluable. However, for a generation whose theatrical philosophy was founded on the self-sufficiency of the playwright's work, this riotous intermingling of signifying systems was intolerable.

Tom Maschler, the editor of *Declaration*, approached E. Martin Browne, by now an editor at Penguin, with a proposal to publish a volume of three plays, by Doris Lessing, Arnold Wesker and Bernard Kops. This volume was the first in a series entitled *New English Dramatists* which ran to some fourteen volumes and encouraged the establishment of a 'Penguin Plays' imprint, systematically publishing authors introduced in the *New English Dramatists* series. The Penguin edition of the *Wesker Trilogy* would go on to sell approaching half a million copies. In 1939,

Methuen had around eighty-five plays in their list, but only five of these (two each by Arnold Bennett and Ivor Novello, and one by Wodehouse) could remotely be considered contemporary (Methuen 1939). In the mid-fifties, however, they announced an ambitious project of publishing contemporary drama. Their first two catalogues announce plays by Behan, Delaney, Anouilh, Brecht and Pinter (Methuen 1959, 1960). And while only one play from the 1939 catalogue is still in print, today we can still buy the vast majority of plays published in the first two years of the Methuen new drama list.

Their systematic publication has no doubt contributed to their wider longevity, which in turn has helped the publishers keep them in print. But it is also important to examine the style of publication chosen at the time. The Samuel French 'model book' approach is rejected. Gone are the props lists, lighting cues, and hints at how audiences once responded. The only trace of the original production is a list of the original cast and director, and perhaps a photograph on the cover. The playwright's is the only set of theatrical signs made available to us, and it now has a much wider circulation than that of the director. Whereas previously, one might easily have been able to compare revivals with the decisions taken by earlier directors and designers, now their work disappears as the run ends.

Newspaper interviews and journalistic commentary is the third proscenial space occupied by the playwright. The vital unity of feeling, experience and expression, is sanctioned by continual assertions of the proximity of these playwrights to their subject matter. These fragments have become clichés for anyone discussing the period: Shelagh Delaney may always be a nineteen-year-old typist from Salford, Wesker and Pinter eternally from East End Jewish families; in one virtuoso essay, Charles Landstone adroitly situates Bernard Kops in similar surroundings to Wesker, Donald Howarth as 'barman and clerk' (1959, 212), and Delaney as daughter of a Manchester bus driver and working in an engineering factory (215). Landstone then deftly ties this experience directly to the plays, insisting that they are the product of playwrights 'more intuitive than skilled', products of a 'new democracy [...] concerned simply with the living of life amongst the masses' (216). These are different from star personas because rather than read the life dialectically against the work, you look at the life and are sent, heartened, back to the work.

These borderline interventions helped flesh out the sometimes sketchy characterisations of the plays. The off-stage Mrs Tanner, in *Look Back in Anger*, is a case in point. We learn that she is a charwoman who married an actor (Osborne 1993, 62) and has consequently been poor all her life (44). She has an off-stage stroke near the middle of Act Two (60) which she dies from twelve pages later. She also owns Jimmy's sweet-stall (31), though the precise nature of their financial relationship is unclear (she may have offered Jimmy a block grant or a guarantee-against-loss, but either way he presumably has a right to fail). But this all seems more persuasive when we read Osborne's mawkish statement that 'I have learnt more about theatre from old women in public bars and upstairs concert-rooms all over England than I shall ever learn from reading the left and right reviews on a Friday' (1957b, 10). One contemporary article revealed that *Look Back in Anger* reflected Osborne's home life, in a room shared with Pamela Lane and Anthony Creighton (Hopkins 1959). In other words, the vitality of these plays is assured by the repetition of statements about their personal origin.

It is Wesker who is, in many respects, the most intense site for these authentication practices. Landstone notes that Wesker has done 'every job from pastrycook to plumber's mate' (1959, 210) (we are to assume that this is not meant alphabetically). These facts which circulate around the proscenium reach into his plays (especially the trilogy), invisibly conferring upon them their vitality. As we saw at the beginning of the chapter, this is reflected clearly in the critical reception which unanimously found the play sincere and genuine. *Roots* is indeed a particularly interesting example of how this play of proscenium and performance, inside and outside, text and context, works to constitute a play which is both about and embodies this vitality.

In *Roots* Beatie Bryant returns to her family in Norfolk for a visit. She has been living with Ronnie, whom she met while working as a waitress, whose ideas on art, society and love she tries to press upon her sceptical family. In the final scene, the family are preparing for Ronnie's arrival when a letter appears in his place; in it, Ronnie says that his ideas are barren and that they are finished. Initially devastated, and scorned by her family, Beatie begins to see that she must find roots of her own. Her desperate pleas for support build in anger and confidence culminating in a lengthy call for working people to lift themselves from cultural impoverishment. At that moment, she finds herself.

The structure of *Roots* is based on a series of oppositions. High culture versus mass culture, authenticity versus artifice, and, vitally, speaking for yourself versus quoting. In each case the play values the first term at the expense of the second. Beatie criticises the pop song her mother is singing because it is 'like twenty other songs, it don't mean anything and it's sloshy and sickly' (Wesker 1964, 114). Her mother's defence of the lyrics is, like so much else in the play, ironically damning: 'them's as good words as any' (115). Beatie recalls days at a holiday camp discussing with the other girls what to put in their letters home;

> an' we all agreed, all on us, that we started: 'Just a few lines to let you know', and then we get on to the weather and we get stuck so we write about each other and after a page an' half of big scrawl end up: 'Hoping this finds you as well as it leaves me.' There! We couldn't say any more. Thousands of things happening at this holiday camp and we couldn't find words for them. All of us the same.
>
> (127–128)

In each case, it is repetition and substitution that is marked out for criticism.

Beatie's family repeat words rather than mean them; their dialogue is full of secondhand sentiments from right-wing newspapers and endlessly recycled folk wisdom. Furthermore, they repeat themselves; Mrs Bryant's view that the pain in her back is indigestion and Jenny's response is given three times (86, 87–88, 125) and Mrs Bryant's expounding of the bus timetable is offered twice (109, 117). Sometimes they repeat gossip, which suggests an even longer chain of repetition. Beatie confronts her mother on this point; 'you *still* talk to me of Jimmy Skelton and the ole woman in the tub. Do you know I've heard that story a dozen times. A dozen times. Can't you hear yourself Mother?' (128).

Ironically, though, Beatie is herself quoting, and her source is Ronnie. Pearl spots this when Beatie chides her for gossiping. Pearl retorts, 'Well that's a heap sight bettern' quotin' all the time'. Beatie's response betrays her confusion: 'I don't quote all the time, I just tell you what Ronnie say' (139). And when Ronnie's letter is read out, it becomes clear that everything Beatie has criticised her family for, she was guilty of herself. As Mrs Bryant puts it,

> When you tell me I was stubborn, what you mean is that *he* told you *you* was stubborn – eh? When you tell me I

don't understand you mean *you* don't understand isn't it?
When you tell me I don't make no effort you mean *you*
don't make no effort.

(145)

Beatie admits that this is true; quoting Ronnie is no different from
quoting gossip.

The process that the play dramatises is Beatie's movement from
dependence on Ronnie to her autonomy. Her intertextual ties are
severed when the letter arrives (a particularly shocking moment;
writing substituting for the real man, absence displacing his presence). She begins to talk about 'roots! The things you come from,
the things that feed you. The things that make you proud of yourself – roots!' (145). She dwells on the irony that despite coming
from a farm workers' family, she has no roots in anything. This
'vertical' image contrasts with the horizontal chains of intertextual
substitution (gossip, formulaic pop songs, quoting). And at the
end of the play, she discovers the roots within herself, and vertically ('on my own two feet') her words are finally her own: 'I'm
talking, Jenny, Frankie, Mother – I'm not quoting no more' (148).

But how do we know that this is authentic? The problem is that
no object or event on stage can guarantee its own authenticity.
Look at the instances of 'work' that appear through the play.
Wesker is often praised for his use of real action on stage. When
someone bakes bread in a Wesker play, they *really* bake bread.
This conceit suggests a full identity between reality and representation, a moment of pure presence. But this ignores the fact that
the signs function on stage independently of the presence of their
referents; Wesker's oven has a structural position, no guaranteed
positive identity. In practical terms, the audience might not know
(and *need* not know) if the oven is real or simulated.

The same problem attends Beatie's moment of self-identity,
where she begins talking for herself. A key to this lies in a textu-
ally very marginal moment; a note within a stage direction. In Act
Two, Beatie has produced a couple of her own paintings: 'They
are primitive designs in bold masses, rather well-balanced shapes
and bright poster colours – red, black and yellow – see Dusty
Bicker's work' (112). Before you go rushing to a reference book, I
should say that Dusty Bicker had become Dusty Wesker a year
before *Roots*'s premiere. She came from a Norfolk farm workers'
family, and met Arnold Wesker when working as a waitress. And
the anagrammatic Ronald shares with Arnold most of his ideas,[21]

an East End background, being Jewish and working as a pastrycook. This is what confers Beatie's authenticity on her; Wesker is writing a situation that he knows about, characters he has met. This apparently external knowledge, circulating around the play, operates at its heart, rooting its experience.

John Mander has praised the way Wesker (through Ronnie's letter) backs out of the play, allowing Beatie her own space: 'no playwright could do more to relativize his [sic] own ideas, and to alienate the autobiographical element by the use of critical irony' (1961, 198). But this isn't quite right. It is crucial to the play that we know this *is* autobiographical; we need the guaranteeing Wesker, even as we reject him. He backs out, but remains; rejected and retained, inside and out, Wesker haunts the play from the proscenium.

This also reminds us of the ultimate impossibility of the project. The same moment, in fact, that grants Beatie her independence and originality reveals her to be quoting again. Before his letter arrives, Ronnie is the absent origin of her speech, forcing her into these intertextual chains of quoting and substitution. Her ultimate attempt to put down roots and establish her own identity only makes sense with reference to the guaranteeing, proscenial Wesker. But since Arnold has been pretending to be Ronald all along, it seems that for her speech to be judged authentic, she must also be revealed still to be quoting. The very moment that asserts the authenticity of the event does so only by deferring to the absent Wesker. The claim to presence and self-identity is established through absence and repetition.

The long search on the part of the arts administrators for a theatre that would demonstrate British national strength was rewarded by the New Wave. The desire to see thought and feeling reunited, the inner bound tightly and unequivocally to the outer, was fulfilled by their plays. But this was not, as is so often stated, merely a matter of writing good plays. Working against the very problematics raised by theatrical practice in the forties, this idea could only be achieved by a fundamental realignment of theatrical signifying practice. It might be objected that while the new genera-tion benefited from the state's desire for national renewal, they did not adhere to such beliefs themselves. Precisely how the New Wave's work fitted into the wider picture of British national iden-tity, and the way in which that picture frame reaches into that work, is the subject of my next chapter.

5

SOMETHING ENGLISH
The repatriation of European drama

Jimmy:	[...] Why *do* I do this every Sunday? (*Pause.*) I keep thinking it's Friday.
Cliff:	Well, it's Sunday.
Jimmy:	*La Paix du dimanche.*
Cliff:	What's that?
Jimmy:	Some cunning French play I expect. All bombast and logic and no balls.

(John Osborne, *Déjàvu*, 1991b, 3)

Osborne's sequel to *Look Back in Anger* opens with a witty visual pun. As the curtain rises, despite the intervening forty years, nothing appears to have changed. Jimmy and Cliff still sprawl beneath their newspapers, Alison – albeit a different Alison – is still doing the ironing. However, Jimmy Porter is now a fully acknowledged fiction; he has lived a life on stage. This allows Osborne to direct Jimmy's rhetorical fire at changes in the theatrical culture since his last appearance, articulating the kinds of cultural disdain which had formerly been left to his author. In 1956 it was Osborne, not Jimmy, who was busy demonising French theatre.

In the thirty years before 1956, European theatre became more and more prominent on British stages. Club theatres like the Gate in the twenties and thirties had championed Symbolist and Expressionist playwrights like Kaiser, Toller, Wedekind and Maeterlinck (Marshall 1947, 45). As West End managers increasingly used club theatres to scout for possible new material, the techniques of European Modernism began to be felt on larger stages. Priestley's *Johnson over Jordan* was a clear instance of this, and in 1943 his *They Came to a City* showed Craig's influence in Michael Relph's bold design, comprising sombre monochrome

127

flats and steps, and lit with bold, stark planes of light. On the eve of *Look Back in Anger*, Peter Brook claimed that

> the ideas that Craig stated, shouted, loaded into blunder-busses and shot into the air, ideas that went to Russia, then to Germany, and eventually reached England and America with Craig's name no longer attached, these revolutions are now everyday axioms in the designer's language.
>
> (1955, 33)

When Peter Daubeny and others began bringing European companies to Britain as part of the 'World Theatre' seasons, the influence became even more direct.

This impact was felt even more forcibly in the repertoire. In the early fifties, probably the most successful playwright in Britain was Jean Anouilh. In 1954, Harold Hobson could note that London had already seen *Ardèle, Ring Round the Moon, Thieves' Carnival, Antigone, Fading Mansion, Colombe*, and *Point of Departure*; the Bristol Old Vic had produced *Traveller without Luggage* and the BBC Third Programme had broadcast *The Waltz of the Toreadors* (1954, 233). By the end of the decade, you could add to that *Time Remembered, The Lark, Restless Heart* and *Dinner with the Family*. *Point of Departure* was revived at the Glasgow Citizens Theatre and *The Waltz of the Toreadors* at the Arts, the latter transferring to the West End in 1956.

Anouilh was in good company. Jean Giraudoux had around eight major productions of his plays in London, including *The Madwoman of Chaillot, Tiger at the Gates* and *Duel of Angels*. The playwrights who would later become known as Absurdists gave their British debuts in the fifties; they included Genet's *Les Bonnes* and *The Balcony*, Ionesco's *The Lesson, The Bald Prima Donna* and *The New Tenant*, and pre-eminently, Beckett's *Waiting for Godot*, which ran successfully in the West End. Sartre, Cocteau and Obey were championed by smaller theatres like the Arts, before gaining main stage productions at theatres like the Lyric, Hammersmith, where Wolfit also produced Montherlant's *Malatesta* and *Master of Santiago*.

The presence of French dramatists was not confined to such major figures; André Roussin had successes with *The Little Hut, Figure of Fun, Nina* and *Hook, Line and Sinker*. In 1952 alone, audiences could see Jean Bernard Luc's *The Happy Marriage*,

Roger-Ferdinand's *Husbands Don't Count* and Barillet and Grédy's *A Kiss for Adèle*. By the end of the decade, writers including Marcel Aymé, Albert Husson, Julien Green, Felicien Marceau, Claude Magnier, Max Regnier, Marcel Achard, Alexandre Breffort and Marguerite Monnot had seen work on London stages.

A token of the love affair between British and French theatre is the way that revues and musicals could appear *chic* by being given some (occasionally spurious, often suggestive) French connection. Emulating the success of Maurice Chevalier's cabaret performances or Robert Dhéry's celebrated *La Plume de Ma Tante*, performances appeared entitled, *Hors D'Oeuvres*, *Paris by Night*, *Pardon my French*, *From the French*, *Paris '90*, *Wedding in Paris*, and *Plaisirs de Paris*. Bolstered by annual runs early in the decade by the Folies-Bergères and Latin Quarter series, a mixture of wit, sex and spectacle meant that an association with things Parisian became *le dernier mot* in sophistication.

France was not the only source of this theatrical Europhilia. In 1955, Ugo Betti received great acclaim for three plays, *The Queen and the Rebels*, *Summertime* and *The Burnt Flower Bed*, leading Ivor Brown to claim that he had 'replaced Anouilh as the critics' darling' (1955, 11). British audiences could see work by Benedetti, Fabbri, Zuckmayer, Huizinga, Hochwalder; most influentially, Brecht had his major London breakthrough in 1956.

That Britain's stages appeared to be dominated from abroad did not go unnoticed. Ivor Brown admits that when it comes to writing, 'in contemporary work the praise has gone to the imported article' (1955, 11). Another critic puts it more strongly: 'the only plays worth seeing are by authors long dead or by Mr Eliot' (Hamilton 1956, 124). A young girl innocently makes the same point in Joan Temple's *No Room at the Inn* (1945); asked to define a classic she promptly responds, 'something by a dead Englishman or a live foreigner' (1946, 199).

Some believed that this situation should not be allowed to continue, that it was a national humiliation. Tynan lamented in 1956 that 'the general impotence of our theatre [...] is the laughing-stock of the Continent' (1964, 39). On the occasion of the Brook-directed *King Lear* touring to Moscow, *Plays and Players* urged,

> Let us strike while the iron is hot, stepping up this theatrical export drive on an organised basis. It should

not be left to any individual managements to carry out such an important task. A plan should be prepared by a national body such as the British Council to take the best of British plays and players to the Continent.'[1]

There is a clear agenda being set by terms like 'export drive', 'national', and 'important task', which takes us back to the campaign for national renewal, embodied in the actions of the Arts Council. One of its original functions was to provide material for the British Council to show off abroad. The substance of Ivor Brown's complaint is that the British Council's drama fund was insufficient to counterbalance the theatrical imports flooding across the Channel.

The Arts Council's project of reversing our cultural decline imagined it to take the form of a fragmentation in the British identity, one exacerbated and encouraged by the dominant modes of theatrical practice. I have described the Court's methods of protecting this identity against repetition, substitution, supplementarity and the graft. But in what way did this respond to the actual situation of Britain in the world? Where does the New Wave fit politically in this debate? And how ought we understand the generally unremarked repatriation of French drama from British stages?

Cockpit

The Allied victory in 1945 seemed to confirm Britain's status as a major world power; it had emerged with its Empire intact – in some areas even enlarged – and its moral authority seemingly enhanced. However, within twenty years the British Empire would be reduced to a handful of territories scattered across the world. To trace the effect of these events on British theatre, it is essential to observe their impact on Britain's self-image; and, remarkably enough, we find that the collapse of Empire proceeded virtually unnoticed.

Well into the Second World War, the perception which Britain actively promoted of its actions in the colonial territories was that it ruled by a system of benevolent trusteeship (Robinson 1979; Gallagher 1982, 142). Britain was holding these territories in trust until such a time as the natives had developed sufficiently to take over the running of these domains themselves. This attempted to give an altruistic air to colonial rule, though no criteria were given for what would constitute sufficient development. It was assumed that they would never 'catch up' and that any *forcible* attempt to seize power was construed as self-evident proof of barbarian unfitness for rule.

The task of preserving the Empire could be described in terms of trying to maintain authority and prestige. Before the war, these two terms seemed to many people mutually reinforcing, sutured by the notion of racial hierarchy. Britain's prestige was dependent on the way it guided these 'primitive' peoples towards parliamentary democracy. Its authority was thus rendered acceptable by the long-term humanitarian aims that Britain appeared to have for its dependents.

This neat legitimising structure started coming rapidly undone during the Second World War. The affinities between the doctrine of racial superiority and Nazism were picked up by colonial nationalists very early on (Howe 1993, 108). The radicalism of wartime saw a growth in anticolonial feeling at home, indicated by the success of the Common Wealth party which stood partly on a policy of dissolving the Empire (124–126). In 1942, the Atlantic Charter included an agreement 'to see sovereign rights and self-government restored to those who have been forcibly deprived of them'; this was probably meant to refer to nations occupied by the Axis powers, but the fact that clarification had to be sought indicates how evident the corollary was (141). The problem was intensified as the Cold War blocs were set in place, and ideological opposition to Soviet empire-building put Britain in a similarly uncomfortable position. With racial superiority no longer a credible justification, prestige and authority were soon seen as contrary aims, with damaging results.

The thinness of the British claim to moral supremacy, and the way it became drawn into European ideological battles is captured brilliantly by Bridget Boland's *Cockpit* (1948). It is set in a theatre in Germany just after the war; a large number of refugees – displaced persons – from various European countries have been rounded up and are being held in the theatre by the British army, prior to their passage back home. The play stages and works through the implications and contradictions of Britain's attempt to claim ascendency over the ideological conflicts that erupt in the theatre.

The British officers' right to oversee the squabbles and rivalries between different groups (collaborators and resistance fighters, Serbs and Croats, Poles and Russians, etc.) depends on being 'above' the cultural and political differences between the refugees. It is through British omniscience that conflicting interests are judged and resolved at a higher, disinterested level. Duval, a French farmer accused of complicity with the invading German forces, urges that 'you must listen to me', and earns Ridley's lofty reply, 'I am listening to everybody' (62). When a few of the refugees suggest that they might be equally unbiased there is laughter; Marie (a French communist) proposes Peter, the Soviet farm worker, as an impartial figure, and occasions derision; 'God Almighty!' roars Ridley. 'Blimey!' agrees Barnes (63).

The actions of the officers are informed throughout by the sense of imperial mission that animated Britain abroad. They believe that British parliamentary democracy transcends all difference, that it is the point to which all other systems tend, and at which they *must* arrive if they are to be given control of their own lives. As with the Kenyans, Ugandans and Malayans, this would, if necessary, be forcibly imposed. 'It doesn't matter a hoot in hell what your politics are', says Ridley, 'or your profession, or your religions. Will you get that into your heads? Democracy is what you have been fighting for, and Democracy is what you're going to get' (63). As this passage suggests, the right of the British to keep everyone else under control is backed up in the last instance by force. On their first appearance 'Both are armed, Barnes with a Sten' (31).

The means used by the officers to establish their authority inter-twine with the theatrical setting of the play in a way that deepens and complicates the debate about Britain's world role. The play begins with a tumble of different languages, which is silenced by Barnes's 'parade ground voice' yelling, 'Shut up!' (30). He goes on to establish rules of behaviour in the theatre, but also the rules of theatrical representation. Standing on stage, addressing the displaced persons (but also us), he explains that 'I'm English, a British officer. I am sorry to have to talk to you like this in German, but it's the only language we've got in common [...] I am talking in German to help you' (32). Secondly, and in place of the disorderly confusion of languages, they describe the stage as their 'Orderly Room' and order the refugees off it (39). Thirdly, from this position, the rest of the theatre can be organised Panoptically from the stage – 'we can keep an eye on things from here' (33) – and different refugee groups can be observed and controlled. Barnes reels off a list:

> Poles, Dutch and Belgians in the Circle, Norwegians and Russians in the gallery. Bulgars and some Italians in the Circle Bar. Roumanians and some more Italians in the Stalls Bar and the foyer; and the dressing rooms are full of a bloody mixed bag.
>
> (31)

With the stage as the still centre, the building is disciplined, inside and out, with two neat sets of Eastbound and Westbound convoys preparing to take the refugees home.

The play stages the breakdown of British legitimacy, as Britain's right to govern and its power to govern become turned against one another. The French communist, Marie, denounces the British officers:

> You want an efficient organisation and peace and quiet and you have stood about for the last three-quarters of an hour stirring up trouble in every part of this theatre [...] You English have spent hundreds of years playing Empire Builders all over the world. What do you know about us at home in Europe? [...] Who are you to know what's good for us? *We're* the people to judge that.
>
> (65–66)

The crisis threatens to get out of control until a Polish doctor thinks he has discovered a case of Bubonic plague. Under this new crisis, hostilities are suspended, and enemies work together to prevent the infection spreading. The scientific diagnosis replaces British moral impartiality as the principle sustaining the hierarchies between officer and refugee. Nonetheless, tiny ironies tilt the play against the British; when they are considering how to share out the food, the communists offer to take charge of the division. Ridley thinks he is deftly countering him: 'Listen. Everything we've got must be pooled and shared equally' (83).

A further crisis looms as the dying man is properly diagnosed and found only to have a severe case of tetanus. The general relief is soon followed by suspicion; did the professor invent the plague to draw attention away from the charge of collaboration against him? The neutral authority of the professor is reinscribed within the play of ideologies, and the play does not tell us what his real motives were. This has serious consequences for the British whose authority, having been invested in the professor's impartiality, collapses.

The ambiguous status of the scientific diagnosis extends to the theatre; immediately the doctor's mistake is revealed the British desperately acquiesce in a plan to bring the refugees together in staging a short extract from an opera, but was this performance also a collaborationist strategy? After all, it was prompted and facilitated by Bauer, the German stage manager, whose enthusiasm for the stage cannot quite mask a conspicuous silence about his own political allegiances. Further, it was he who earlier created their 'Orderly Room' on stage by giving them pieces of stage furniture and props (35); the opera, their attempt to control the theatre, and, more broadly, the status of the theatrical illusion, are placed under question.

The three tenets of their control evaporate: their ability to gaze on everything disappears: Marie is murdered off-stage, and refugees talk amongst themselves and out of their earshot. Secondly, as if responding to this, the calm intelligibility of the theatre's geography collapses as Ridley announces 'those damned Westerners – they're rushing the Eastbound trucks' (116). Finally, the discourse of the play turns against them as Ridley urges their restless semi-captives to work together: 'It can be done, you've seen it done! You worked together, you're still the same people.... There'll be no shooting'. Immediately the stage direction announces '*Shooting*' (118).

The irony of this moment marks the final breakdown of the British claim to omniscience; they have become displaced persons. The end of the play is left open, but the decisive reversal of the officers' gaze marks a fundamental change, as the armed refugees 'look at each other. Slowly they all look back at Ridley and Barnes. Slow Curtain' (118).

The threatened violence of the end of the play is very prescient about what happened in the fifties with the emergence of radical nationalist groups in many of the territories. After 1952, when Mau Mau began their campaign of violence in Kenya, government figures tried unsuccessfully to employ the old images of racial degeneracy to vilify them and Jomo Kenyatta (Darwin 1988, 187; 1991, 20). Reports emerged of British colonial atrocities in Cyprus, then at Hola Camp and under emergency rule in Nyasaland, which the Devlin Report in 1959 accused of being spuriously established and run like a police state (Darwin 1991, 20). This use of authority, which had been designed to preserve Britain's prestige, was now seen to be fatally damaging to it.

Paradoxically, then, the relinquishing of Empire by successive British governments could be seen as yielding authority to *preserve* prestige. It was calculated that less damage would be done to Britain's image by acquiescing in the colonies' desire for independence than by trying to retain them by force. The end of Empire was presented as the logical completion of Britain's historical mission. When the Labour cabinet was discussing how it wanted to present the withdrawal from India, they agreed that they wanted to avoid any sense of a 'scuttle'; instead it was to be seen as 'a voluntary transfer of power to a democratic government' (quoted, Darwin 1988, 94). This was a continuation of the 'benevolent trustee' thesis; as Macmillan wrote in his memoirs,

> The British people [...] had not lost the will or even the power to rule. But they did not conceive of themselves as having the right to govern in perpetuity. It was rather their duty to spread to other nations those advantages which through the course of centuries they had won for themselves.
>
> (Darwin 1982, 188)

In fact, the arrangements for decolonisation were often hastily drawn up, in an impetuous attempt to install friendly rulers who would allow some of the formal structures of imperial privilege to continue informally, with catastrophic results. But for a while the real loss of imperial preference, access to real estate, natural resources, workpower, markets and military bases, was successfully presented at home as a convincing demonstration of Britain's enduring moral supremacy.

Evidence of the success of this strategy may be found in the fact that, compared with France and Portugal, British decolonisation was fairly undisruptive at home. As John Darwin argues, 'the disappearance of the empire, of global power and the "world rôle", the stuff of political rhetoric since time-out-of-mind, left scarcely any visible political traces and cast no serious shadow on the viability of British institutions' (1986, 29). This was supported by the general public apathy and ignorance about colonial issues (Howe 1993, 326), the impenetrably obscure kinds of decolonising relationships (Darwin 1986, 42), and also the lack of predatory rival powers who would make decolonisation more sharply wounding to national pride. 'Few empires', writes Darwin, 'have been granted such generous terms on which to negotiate their own demise' (41).

A loss of will to rule

The only major flashpoint came with the Suez crises of 1956. But even here we must be cautious before ascribing long-term significance; after all, despite a small number of resignations and the deselection of a couple of dissident MPs, Suez was not an election issue in 1959 and those Tories who resigned the whip in protest at the apparent capitulation returned to the fold soon after (Kyle 1991, 489–491; Darwin 1986, 38). Public opinion throughout the crisis was divided.[2] However, Suez did become a focus for resistance to colonial policy for some. Opposition was inchoate, but three kinds of opposition may be discerned.

The most widespread criticism of Britain's actions hinged on their duplicity. Eden defended Britain's offensive on the grounds that Israel had attacked Egypt and that Britain and France's only role in Egypt was to 'separate the combatants'. This was a lie: an agreement signed at Sèvres on 24 October 1956 had arranged for Israel to invade so as to provide a pretext for Britain and France's action. The ultimate aim of the action, as far as the inner cabinet were concerned, was to bring down the Egyptian government (Kyle 1991, 148). Hiding the collusion was in no one's interests but Britain's, and the real aims were easily readable when Britain unusually failed to condemn the Israeli military action and separated the combatants by bombing Egyptian airfields.

With the smell of collusion in the air, critics were pitiless in their condemnation. At an anti-Suez rally in Trafalgar Square it was declared that either Eden was sincere, and therefore stupid, or he was clever, but duplicitous, neither option boding terribly well for Britain's image as moral guardian of the Middle East's better interests. Nor did ITN pictures of the aftermath of the Port Said landings, showing the charred bodies of Egyptian civilians (Shaw 1995, 337). A permanent secretary in the Foreign Office, writing with 'heavy heart' admitted feeling that 'whatever our motives, we have terribly damaged our reputation' (quoted, Hennessy and Laity 1987, 5).

Suez was also opposed by groups to the left of the Labour Party, like the Movement for Colonial Freedom. Their general argument criticised Britain's residually imperialist assumptions about the Middle East. This fed into New Left thinking, for whom 'what continued to resonate was the deeply held view that colonialism was an evil for British society, as well as for the colonised, because it was morally corrupting, inimical to the better self of British, or English, national identity' (Howe 1993, 301).

On the right, however, the Suez escapade was condemned, as part of a pro-imperialist analysis, for the damage it did to Britain's world standing. In 1954, as Britain agreed a timetable of withdrawal from the Canal zone, a group of Empire nostalgists and hawkish young Tories, still shaken by the loss of India, urged the vital strategic importance of a Canal presence. They dubbed the agreement 'Operation Scuttle' and denounced it as 'evidence of the loss of the will to rule' (Kyle 1991, 43; Darwin 1986, 37). This sentiment was widespread on the right wing of the party, and required continual rebuttal by ministers. Their response to the collapse of the Anglo-French mission was 'deeply-felt humiliation' (Darwin 1988, 229). The rest of the party seemed keen and able to shrug off the Suez defeat; there was no enquiry into the fiasco, and after the resignation of Eden, the party quickly regrouped around Macmillan (ironically one of the most hawkish members of the Egypt Committee). So why did the Empire diehards feel Suez so keenly?

The far right of the party perceived Suez at an intersection of a number of forces. The Commonwealth was projected by some as a continuation of Empire by other means. But there were a number of rival blocs threatening its supremacy, principally the European

Community. For many, not just the far right, joining the European Community was unthinkable, since this would involve signing up to the Customs Union, which, in turn, would mean surrendering Britain's preferential tariff arrangements with the Commonwealth (Kahler 1984, 134–135). The right recognised that participating fully in the EC would be an irreversible acceptance of the new alignment. Many members of the British government held out against European integration in the hope that Britain may be able to act as a fulcrum between the Commonwealth, the EC, and the United States. Macmillan even entertained the thought that the Commonwealth and the EC might join together in 'some still wider common market' (Porter and Stockwell 1989, 424).

In fact, Suez hastened the abandonment of this objective, as Britain alienated everyone whose forces it had hoped to marshal to its side. America forced a cease-fire by refusing to support sterling; in the Commonwealth, Britain faced near-universal censure (cf. Lyon 1989). Britain had spent some years resisting pressure from a United Nations hostile to its colonial influence. After Suez, Britain was far less able to prevent the UN calling it to account (Goldsworthy 1994, xliv–xlv). Lastly, Britain's relations with France, which had throughout the crisis been mistrustful, collapsed, as France turned towards Germany as its chief ally in Europe (Vaïsse 1989, 337).

For the right, then, the tragedy of Suez was that at the very point where Britain could have asserted its focal position between the West's major power blocs, it actually found itself entirely isolated, thus accelerating its slide from Empire status. And because the right obstinately saw Britain as a nation with a historical destiny to rule the waves, reasons for the ultimate failure were not located outside but *within*, in a 'failure of "will" on the part of a society the moral foundations of which had been weakened by rampant materialism, lack of discipline, and a declining acceptance of Judaeo-Christian values' (Murphy 1995, 9). The right's explanation for the collapse of British imperial interests was finally domestic, rooted in a degeneration of certain values and strengths, in 'betrayal [...] loss of nerve or cowardice' (Howe 1993, 11).

The argument is elaborated by Corelli Barnett in *The Collapse of British Power* (1972). He argues that the foundations of the British Empire lay in the strong character of the eighteenth-century ruling classes, 'squirearchy, merchants, aristocracy [...] men hard of mind and hard of will'. Under their grasp, 'England grew from a second-rank nation on the periphery of the Continent into a great power whose wealth, stability and liberty were the envy of Europe' (20). Throughout the nineteenth century the buccaneering self-interest of these men was weakened by the moral righteousness of Methodism and Evangelism, the anti-materialism of Romanticism, the 'middle-class sentimentality' of people like Dickens (23), and the high-minded idealism embodied in the public schools and classical education. Moral purpose began to be considered a part of English policy-making, resulting in a 'feeble and nerveless' (19) refusal to accept 'the ugly truths of human behaviour' (61) and soon international relations were shaped by 'the Utopian fantasies of the "tender-minded" ' (53).

The contrast with the New Left is striking. While the latter saw the Empire having a corrupting effect on British culture, the right saw a corruption within British culture causing the decline of Empire. This establishes either end of a spectrum of positions, and we can now examine where the New Wave fits into all this. After one particularly blimpish condemnation of the Angry Young Men in the *Spectator*, one letter-writer notes with exasperation that these writers 'cannot be expected to look back to Imperial Britain'.[3] This is a curious defence, since that is precisely what many of them did.

The Entertainer is one of a number of plays from the period that address colonial politics. It was immediately recognised as being concerned not merely with a particular family, nor even the music hall, but a play in which the characters comprise a 'national microcosm' (Tynan 1964, 49), 'a drama which could image the nation to itself' (Ronald Bryden, quoted, Page 1988, 49). Set against the backdrop of the (unnamed) Suez crisis, the play raises questions about imperial attitudes and national character. But what does it say about them? Archie's jingoistic stage act is undermined by its evident badness. Jean and Frank occasionally voice criticisms of platitudinous nationalism; Jean responds to Billy's patriotic rant with sarcasm, 'Nothing to worry about. *We're* all right. God save the Queen!' (1998, 26). Later, Frank scorns emotional restraint: 'That's right chaps – remember we're British!' (52). Near the end of the play, the criticism of contemporary Britain is given its most explicit symbol in the Nude Britannia (80). Through a kind of reinvention of the Emperor's New Clothes, this image captures the shifting relations between authority and prestige. Prestige is all that Britain has left, but when even that evaporates, as it did during Suez, we are revealed naked underneath the tattered finery.

The target in all these cases, however, is not so much the patriotism, as the *emptiness* of the patriotism. It is this emptiness that recurs throughout the play, in Archie's eyes, Phoebe's vacuous film, the meaningless patter. More important, the play hardly seems to side with the left's anti-Suez campaigners: the speech Osborne gives Jean about the Trafalgar Square rally is ostentatiously vapid: 'somehow', she says, 'with a whole lot of other people, strange as it may seem – I managed to get myself steamed up about the way things were going' (23). And Jean and Archie both compare this action unfavourably with 'real' feeling (64, 65). For Osborne, the 40,000 strong anti-Suez rally is part of the problem, not part of the solution.

Crucially, the play gives us a vision of *decline*, and the criticisms are of *contemporary* patriotism. Nowhere does Osborne suggest that patriotism has always been an evil. Just as the halls have become a hollow shell of their former glory, so has England. His note which prefaces the play begins, 'The music hall is dying, and, with it, a significant part of England. Some of the heart of England has gone' (3). Elsewhere he elaborates; in the halls 'you can see part of England dying before your eyes [...] Sometimes I have watched it in tears' (1957b, 10). Billy, who played the halls when they were in better health, is now reduced to living on past triumphs; but nowhere are those triumphs themselves criticised. And the metonymic slide between the halls and Britain itself suggests that Osborne may not be crowing over but tearfully mourning the denudement of Britannia.

This is fully visible in the film of *The Entertainer*. The sequence contrasting Archie's dried-out routine, 'Thank God I'm Normal', with Billy's spontaneous pub performance, shows us a fragment of Billy's music hall act, a song called 'Don't Let Them Scrap the British Navy'. In rhythm and style, the song is a clear pastiche of G.H. McDermott's famous song from 1877, 'We don't want to fight / But, by Jingo, if we do / We've got the ships, we've got the men, we've got the money too...' (cf. Summerfield 1986). Both songs hark back to a peak of British colonial confidence. The projected moment of authenticity and vitality that Osborne imagines for the music hall is also a high point of imperialist swagger.

Much the same may be said of *Look Back in Anger* which sees Porter fondly imagining life under the *Raj*: 'high summer, the long days in the sun, slim volumes of verse, crisp linen, the smell of starch'. Although he recognises the incompleteness of this picture, he admits that 'even I regret it somehow, phoney or not' (13). It has often been commented that the only character Porter treats as a kindred spirit is Alison's ex-colonial father. Perhaps these facets of his character lead Helena to suggest that Jimmy was 'born out of his time' and to describe him as an 'Eminent Victorian' (88–89). Critics have pointed to the contradiction that 'Jimmy feels himself powerfully drawn – even as he mocks them – to images of British imperial rule in India' (Davies and Saunders 1983, 27). But this is not really a contradiction: Jimmy is drawn to the Empire, but mocks the *contemporary* version of it. The title of Osborne's play suggests someone looking back, but their anger being directed at the failure of the present to live up to the past.

In this context, it is striking how Osborne's work seems to correspond to the right's view of decolonisation rather than the left's. The sense of cultural crisis that animated the New Wave took the form of a belief that our culture had severed thought from feeling, intention from expression. This has at least affinities with Barnett's rage against the enervation of Great Britain, since Osborne represents the causes of imperial decline as deep within British culture. Tynan revealingly suggested in 1958 that the new generation is characterised by feelings of 'uselessness and impotence' which are 'intensified by the knowledge that Britain no longer had a voice strong enough to forbid chaos if, by some horrific chance, it should impend' (1964, 55–56). The slide between moral and military strength is telling.

The same can be seen in Willis Hall's *The Long and the Short and the Tall*. The play is set in the Malayan jungle during the Second World War, but contemporary echoes abound; at one point, for example, we see a soldier reading a serialised war story about a soldier on a special mission to blow up an airfield in North Africa (1961, 23). Much of the force of the play lies in the iconoclasm of the group of racist, foul-mouthed soldiers with no idea of what they are doing: 'so far on this outing out,' says one of them, 'it's been the biggest muck-up in the history of the British Army, and that's saying a lot' (52). On one level the play cries out for the combatants to recognise each other as human beings. Macleish and Mitchem discuss whether they could really kill; Macleish insists that he could as long as he didn't look into his target's eyes (63). When the men discover their Japanese prisoner's family photographs, another moment of near-understanding passes them by (76–77). On another level the play seems to suggest that the personal weaknesses of these men are responsible for their eventual chaotic demise. The final image of the play is a dying soldier, stealing a cigarette from his dead prisoner, then his scarf, and raising it as an improvised white flag. The soldier's capitulation is such that he even takes the means of his surrender from those he once ruled.

But the two levels of the play do not sit together easily. Firstly, it is not clear that greater humanity on the part of these soldiers would have prevented their deaths or the final surrender. Secondly, it is actually the introduction of moral debates that contribute to their confusion: the more liberal Bamforth throws himself in front of the gun, and a struggle ensues in which their prisoner is shot (89). The play might indeed be seen as endorsing Barnett's position: that the surrender of the colonialists to their colonial subjects was at least in part due to a fatal dose of moral squeamishness.

This is not to suggest that Osborne and Hall, or even the Suez Group, secretly longed for a retaking of Pakistan and Burma. As one historian has argued, few people ever actually opposed colonial withdrawals, recognising the 'powerful internal dynamic' that was driving it (Murphy 1995, 11). This did not stop them watching this irresistible process with impotent fury. This structure – rage at the direction of a society, yet a recognition that the past cannot be recaptured – characterises the whole of *Look Back in Anger*: Porter fumes at the inadequacy and nervelessness of the people around him (look at the way he describes his brother-in-law, Nigel), hankers after the certainty of the Edwardians, but knows it has gone for good. Osborne is more interested in searching out the causes of decline, which he finds *within* British culture.

Once we recognise this, other features of the New Wave fall into place. More particularly we can see structural reasons for the hostility towards Europe and how their criticisms of European drama are tied up with the New Wave's obsessive hunting out of enervation, equivocation and performativity.

Something strong, something simple, something English

The hostility towards European drama, then, is precisely tied to the threat that integration with Europe posed for the survival of Empire status. Repelling this advance, by asserting the independence of British culture, was a symptom of this fear of national decline. Osborne's lifelong hostility to the Common Market was often cast in a right-wing Eurosceptic mould (e.g. 1994, 197, 202, 214–218, 222), but given the belief that the causes of decline were ultimately internal, we should also see French theatre as a talisman of forces within British theatrical culture. Expelling the French meant doing battle with an enemy within.

In *Look Back in Anger*, Jimmy Porter reads the *Radio Times* to see if there is a concert on. He is relieved to discover that 'There's a Vaughan Williams. Well, that's something, anyway. Something strong, something simple, something English' (18). This moment of direct comparison provides three clear terms which I shall use to consider how this figuration operated.

The Englishness of the new culture was, of course, fundamental. As *Plays and Players* argued editorially in early 1956, 'Season after season almost every serious play London has seen has come from Paris or, less frequently, New York, while our own writers have been represented by mechanically constructed thrillers or pot-boiling comedies'.[4] The perceived weakness is here constructed differentially, on the basis of an embattled opposition to another culture. But this play of cultural difference is inescapable. As Malcolm Crick puts it, 'A culture experiences itself *as* a culture by contrast with other ways of life' (1985, 76). Paradoxically, even the mission to (re)establish a self-identical, autonomous British culture had to be established in relation to another. In British theatre, this other culture was French, and asserting Britain's cultural *strength* meant a transformation of cultural relations to situate French culture as weak.

Right across this period, French theatre is identified as drama of the intellect. In Parisian theatre, argues one critic, a 'tradition of the poetic and intellectual theatre has persisted from Hugo, and Musset to Giraudoux and Anouilh' (Warnke 1959, 30). The profoundly Francophile (and Christian) Harold Hobson observes that 'the characteristic note of the French stage of today is religious [... it] asks the religious questions and gives no religious answer' (1954, 242–243). Even those who excoriate French drama still insist upon its intellectual character, the other side of the coin of intellectual rigour being aloof abstractness. 'The French,' declares Adrian Brine, 'do not regard social responsibility as a virtue' (1961, 36).

Against this, Porter's demand for English *simplicity* suggests a repudiation of French intellectualising. The New Wave's belief that Britain had suffered by separating its thought and feeling found a new target in the fashion for all things French, which they represented as a kind of parasite, sucking the blood of English vitality. In *Look Back in Anger*, Jimmy Porter rages, 'I've just read three whole columns on the English Novel. Half of it's in French' (1993, 6). In his autobiography, Osborne explains,

> The literary and academic classes seemed to have been tyrannized by the French. The 'posh papers' every Sunday blubbered with self-abasement in the face of the bombast of the French language and its absurd posture as the torch-bearer of Logic, which apparently was something to which no one in these islands had access.

Disparagingly he parodies the view that 'what we all needed was a short, sharp shock of clear-round-the-bend French logic' (1991a, 11). The recurrence of the word 'logic' indicates what is at stake here: European casuistry against British common sense or what Roland Barthes called 'the old reactionary myth of heart against head' (1975, 22), not that this *maître à penser* would have cut much ice with Osborne.

To repel the French, they reasserted *feeling*. In 1960, Jeremy Kingston noted that:

> a stress on the need for an emotional response – and the lack of emphasis on the need for an associated intellectual one – is a characteristic of many writers today [...] There is a fairly contemporary slogan (circa 1958?): Think less and feel more!
>
> (21)

In *Declaration*, Osborne famously wrote:

> I want to make people feel, to give them lessons in feeling. They can think afterwards. In some countries this could be a dangerous approach, but there seems little danger of people feeling too much – at least not in England as I am writing.
>
> (1957a, 65)

Jellicoe claimed that 'these plays are directed at your emotions, to your ears, to your eyes [...] directly to emotions, to sense, to common feelings' (Burton 1959, 30).

This manifests itself in the whole approach to representation, in which reality is portrayed as graspably pre-intellectual. Wesker's note to his trilogy states, 'My people are not caricatures, they are real (though fiction)' (1964, 7). How the 'real' and the 'fictional' could be reconciled was not something the new generation cared to examine too closely. Rather, the hostility to the French was a way of ruling this whole question out of court. Vaughan Williams, in this sense, is 'simple' by contrast with the 'liturgical' Beckett, the 'discordant wilfulness' of Ionesco, and the 'peremptory sourness' of Brecht (Osborne 1991a, 105).

In this, Osborne clashed with Devine whose own association with Michel Saint-Denis gave him access to a chain of continental influence and innovation that included Copeau, Dullin, Jouvet, Artaud, Vilar, Barrault and Strehler; and the first two seasons of the English Stage Company at the Royal Court Theatre included Brecht's *The Good Woman of Setzuan* (1956), Ionesco's *The Chairs* (1957), Beckett's *Fin de Partie* (in French) and *Acte Sans Paroles* (1957), Giraudoux's *The Apollo de Bellac* (1957) and Sartre's *Nekrassov* (1957). Osborne withholds no derision for Devine's preferences, and the tide began to turn his way. In their early days, there was felt to be some overlap between the work of Beckett and Ionesco and the movement inspired by *Look Back in Anger*. J.W. Lambert jokingly suggested in 1956 that *Look Back in Anger* 'might have been subtitled *Waiting for Godot in Wolverhampton*' (14). Ivor Brown saw in both *Godot* and *Anger* 'a genuine appetite for the seamy and the shabby sides of life. Glamour is "out" and grubbiness is "in"!' (1956, 7). This was a brief moment of undifferentiation where the ideas of experiment and innovation seemed to cross boundaries of cultural identity, a moment of parity in the economy of the other – before the sudden devaluation of the franc.

The philosophical scepticism that threads through the Absurdists' dramaturgy was itself judged to show a degenerate attenuation of feeling, and the questions which it raised scornfully dismissed. In *Declaration* Kenneth Tynan threatens, 'The sort of temperament that prefers to steer clear of reality had better steer clear of the drama', advising that ultimately this type of thinking leads to 'the belief, not uncommon in certain Parisian circles, that communication between human beings is impossible' (1957, 111). Tynan's strictures seem elsewhere less harsh; a play should show people 'in a desperate condition, which it must always explain and should, if possible, resolve' (109).

The openness of that 'if possible' was hardened into flat rejection one year later when Tynan locked theoretical horns with Ionesco, whom he had once championed (1964, 196–198, 201). In a review of *The Chairs* and *The Lesson* at the Royal Court, Tynan repeated his charge about the nihilistic attitude to communication, and censured Ionesco's philosophy and dramaturgy as 'a self-imposed vacuum, wherein the author ominously bids us to observe the absence of air' (Ionesco 1964, 92). Dismissing 'the ostriches of our theatrical intelligentsia', he declared 'this was an Ionesco cult, and in it I smell danger' (90). Ionesco's reply took Tynan to task for his impoverished conceptions of art, reality, language, progress, and society, arguing that 'if anything needs demystifying it is our ideologies, which offer ready-made solutions (which history quickly overtakes and refutes) and a language that congeals *as soon as it is formulated*' (95). This debate, which brought contributions from Philip Toynbee, John Berger and Orson Welles, amongst others, marked the growing incompatibility of the two theatrical strands.

Instead of seeing these plays as questioning whether authenticity in feeling, perception and representation is possible, the New Wave brushed these concerns aside only to use them again as arguments against their authors. Marowitz described *Rhinoceros* as 'cerebral', 'contrived' and 'spiritless' (1960, 161); what is lacking from his writing is the unity of thought and feeling: 'Ionesco has contemplated anguish in tranquillity and then gone about simulating it' (163). The key word is 'simulating'. Once again, it is the iterability of a theatrical practice which is to be feared; there is no indissociable link between Ionesco and his plays. Throughout Marowitz's review he returns to this theme: the play's style is only 'dramatic trellis-work' not 'the creative heat of the true artist' (162); writing like this is simple, he declares, 'almost anyone can do it' (163); 'its presumption to depth is precisely what reveals it to be the crust it is' (164). It is the refusal of vitality that outraged the new generation.

In an editorial for *Encore*, Vanessa Redgrave, Judy Wright and Diana Harker repeated the charge against those who would 'deny the potency of words as a means of communication', alleging that Beckett may soon announce 'that there really isn't anything to communicate anyway. His next play will likely be all dumbshow'.[5] (Nearly right; *Act Without Words* was the one *after* next.) Kenneth Allsop showed how such continental scepticism was believed to have been transcended by claiming 'first that [Beckett] is in his technique an obsolete writer and second that his stand-point is a surprisingly orthodox one in the environment of the fifties' (1958, 37). Bill Hopkins, in *Declaration*, submits that Beckett makes 'a mockery of attempt, accomplishment and great-ness' (1957, 137). Charles Marowitz, reviewing Esslin's *The Theatre of the Absurd* (1962), a book which itself entrenched these divisions by draining these plays of any political radicalism, declared that ever since *Waiting for Godot*, the Absurd 'has been under fire [...] and is now reaching that delicate juncture at which even its staunchest supporters are beginning to defect' (1962, 57). The next thirty years would see many prominent British drama-tists scorn Absurdist ideas (Brenton 1976, 58; Bond 1980; Wesker 1994, 146). By the end of 1959, Tynan is able to note the lingering influence of Ionesco on N.F. Simpson and Beckett on Pinter, but 'otherwise', he concludes with an atomic piece of geographical nihilism, 'France is nowhere' (1967, 13).

Obliterating the French was designed to suppress questions which would undermine the naive realist strain of new British playwriting, while also demonstrating the superiority of native talent. The uniting of thought and feeling is part of the analysis diagnosing Britain's decline, which sees the rise of Europe as a threat to Britain's national identity, which was meant to be preserved in all its glory despite, or even because of, the disappear-ance of imperial status. A symptom of this is the easy way that these writers bat away any suggestion that they have been influ-enced from abroad. Doris Lessing, in *Declaration*, criticised Camus, Sartre, Genet and Beckett (1957, 19). Amis proudly disavowed any knowledge of 'Barbusse, Sartre, Camus, Kierkegaard, Nietzsche, Dostoevsky, George Fox, Blake, Sri Ramakrishna, George Gurdjieff, T.E. Hulme...' (quoted, Allsop 1958, 55), which functions both to trivialise philosophy, and to distance Amis from Colin Wilson, whose *The Outsider* (1956) was spattered with quotes from all these writers. Osborne scorned those who advocated 'a dollop of the gynaecological metaphysic of Simone de Beauvoir, a trilogy from Sartre and a slice of melo-drama from Camus' (1991a, 11). In his first volume of autobiography he admitted having read Locke, Berkeley, Hume and Nietzsche (1981a, 164), and was later '"into" the impene-trable brown rice of Heidegger, Kierkegaard, Jaspers and, of course, Sartre' (171). The confused rhetoric – being 'into' some-thing 'impenetrable' – manifests the violence of his historical rereading.

Brecht in Britain

The influence that Osborne most wilfully disclaims is Brecht. His autobiography fondly recalls formative days at the music hall; he adds, 'Twenty years later it was this shaky fragment of theatrical memory that was to nudge me towards *The Entertainer*; not, as I was told authoritatively by others, the influence of Bertolt Brecht' (1991a, 27). Reflecting on the 1956 Court production of *The Good Woman of Setzuan*, in which he acted, he contends that 'language, custom, national temperament, training, or lack of it, even physical appearance seemed to doom the effort'; Brecht was simply incompatible with the British 'national temperament' (28).

Despite Osborne's hostility, Brecht seemed to have made his mark in the mid-to-late fifties. Despite a few radio and amateur productions, performances of Brecht's work had been sparse before the war. A couple of theoretical writings appeared in *Left Review*; the films of *The Threepenny Opera* and *Kuhle Wampe* were given film club showings, and his *Threepenny Novel* was published in 1937 as *Penny for the Poor* (Jacobs and Ohlsen 1977, 23–33). In the forties, his poems and writings continued to be published in left-wing journals, along with a number of essays on his work,[6] and there were productions by German emigré club theatre companies in London (Noble 1948, 55). But by the end of the decade, people like Herbert Marshall who tried to interest producers and actors in the plays met with ignorance and indifference. The Edinburgh Festival committee turned down the Berliner Ensemble's *Threepenny Opera* as 'quite unknown' to them (Jacobs and Ohlsen 1977, 35); when Ronald Duncan mentioned Brecht to 'Binkie' Beaumont, he had never heard of him (Duncan 1968, 108); Willett's proposal of a short monograph on Brecht for a series on European thought was rejected because the series was only for 'the better known figures' (1984, 13), and when *New Theatre* published an essay of Brecht's and invited responses from certain theatre practitioners, John Gielgud described the article as 'obscure, pretentious and humourless' and speculated, 'Mr Brecht presumably writes his own scripts, and it might be interesting to see a performance of one of them'.[7]

It was in the mid fifties that Brecht's plays first began to receive serious attention. Joan Littlewood, who, through Ewan MacColl, had been acquainted with Brecht's work since the thirties, directed and (reluctantly) acted the lead in *Mother Courage* at the Taw and Torridge Festival in 1955. This was set up by Oscar Lewenstein, who also produced Sam Wanamaker's *Threepenny Opera* at the Royal Court Theatre in 1956. There was a lengthy appraisal of Brecht's work by John Willett in the *Times Literary Supplement* in the spring, anticipating the summer visit of the Berliner Ensemble to London, and a production of *The Caucasian Chalk Circle* at RADA in July. The English Stage Company performed *The Good Woman of Setzuan* later in the year, and Unity *The Exception and the Rule*. All this Brechtiana was amplified by the sustained campaign of Kenneth Tynan in the *Observer*. As Martin Esslin has noted, his constant use of Brecht as a reference point, almost regardless of what he was reviewing, echoed Shaw's championing of Ibsen in the late 1890s, and had the same effect of bringing the playwright into common discourse (1970, 85).

But it was not the same Brecht, the cerebral theorist disdained by the forties. Tynan's review of *The Good Woman of Setzuan* found that:

> at every turn emotion floods through that celebrated dam, the 'alienation-effect'. More and more one sees Brecht as a man whose feelings were so violent that he needed a theory to curb them. Human sympathy, time and again, smashes his self-imposed dyke.
>
> (1964, 231)

Christopher McCullough has noted Tynan's reading of Brecht as 'a romantic irrationalist, producer of theatrical emotions so intense as to swamp his own self-imposed theoretical constraints' (1992, 126). Peter Brook argues similarly when he claims that 'I found that however much he tried to break any belief in the reality of what happened on stage, the more he did, the more I entered whole-heartedly into the illusion' (1988, 42).

The reason for this is simple: 'writers do not write according to theories', explained Alan Ross; 'if they do they usually write badly' (1960, 9). Brook had been even blunter: 'in the theatre any theory is apt to be a disaster' (1950, 782). Adler urges similarly that 'Didacticism is dramatically justifiable wherever it is made clear that we are listening to the voice of the author' (1961, 30). In other words, the complexities of a Marxist aesthetic are to be subsumed beneath the Leavisite notion of an author's authentic voice. This sense is reinforced by commentators' tell-tale use of the word 'vital' to describe his work (cf. Grindea and Ferry 1956, 3; Devine 1956, 15).

Even in the writings of Brecht's most prominent supporters, theory, that arid conceptualising that Europeans are so prone to, is systematically ignored, suppressed and trivialised. 'I have read,' announces Tynan, 'a great deal about Brecht's theory of acting, the famous *Verfremdungseffekt*, or "alienation effect". What it boils down to in practice is something extremely simple' (1964, 239). This tone is extremely common in British commentaries on Brecht: J.C. Trewin writes that Brecht's 'complicated demands [...] can be fined down – freed from jargon – to call for simpler staging and acting less theatrically emotional' (1965, 27). John Fernald tells us, 'For the English interpreter the Brecht theories boil down to this [...]' (1956, 14). He also suggests that the theories are a quite superfluous imposition between text and production, since 'the treatment of a Brecht play follows quite naturally from a perusal of his scripts, and any of our good English theatre-artists – the least intellectual artists in the world – can make a good job of most of them' (13). Not only does this depressing conviction, if taken seriously, imply that Brecht need never have put theoretical pen to paper but also that we would never need to put his plays on, since their production could be 'naturally' inferred from reading the printed page.

What these comments add up to is to imply that Brecht was, in a sense, already pretty British. As Arden writes, far from being

> very novel and revolutionary, I immediately recognized what he was talking about. I did not know much about Brecht's theories then: I suspected, as I still do suspect, that he had few that had not been held intuitively by the Elizabethans.
>
> (1960, 13)

Hobson agrees: 'most of Brecht's ideas, of course, apart from his silly little placards, must have come as no surprise to our lighter stage, just as they would have come as no surprise to Shakespeare' (1959, 15). These writers, by constructing a Brecht whose priorities are emotional, personal, intuitive, practical and British, are constructing a Brecht who in his new incarnation begins rather to resemble John Osborne. Of course, Brecht was extremely critical of those who saw ideology to the exclusion of anything else in his work (e.g. 1993, 429), but, as John Willett says, 'nobody is all that much of an Anglo-Saxon empiricist whose theoretical writings can occupy six or seven volumes' (1984, 23).

What *really* appealed about Brecht can perhaps be best judged by Tynan's account of the Berliner Ensemble at the 1956 Paris Festival: 'My first impression,' he recalls, 'was of petrified amazement at the amount of money involved' (1964, 239). In the hiatus between the passing of the *National Theatre Act* at the end of the forties and the eventual release of the money in the early sixties, a constant pressure was needed to ensure that the promise was not forgotten. The Berliner Ensemble, as Esslin points out, was an ideal example of what could be done with sufficient state backing (1970, 85–86). In this sense, Brecht was not so much an example to follow as a prestigious beacon to outshine.

As with so much about the Royal Court, this has all been retrospectively re-written. The early plans and press releases for the English Stage Company give equal weight to its interest in presenting new British and European work (Lewenstein 1994, 10).[8] Yet it was soon written about as if it had only ever been interested in domestic writing. Robert Hewison even construes Devine's view of French drama as a useful stop-gap; until more Osbornes came along 'the first season [...] had to have a judicious stiffening of import and translation' (1988, 166).

These cultural rivalries also explain the exclusion of Poetic Drama from Royal Court policy. There was a close association between the Poetic Drama movement and European drama. Ronald Duncan had translated Cocteau's *The Eagle Has Two Heads* (1946) and *The Typewriter* (1950); Donagh MacDonagh adapted Anouilh's *Roméo et Jeanette* as *Fading Mansion* (1949); Christopher Hassall collaborated on *The Devil's General* (1953); Fry offered *Ring Round the Moon* (1950) and *The Lark* (1955) both from Anouilh, and *Tiger at the Gates* (1955) and *Duel of Angels* (1959) both from Giraudoux. John Whiting, also branded an emaciatedly intellectual playwright, and who had been incriminatingly 'discovered' by Fry, translated Obey's *Sacrifice to the Winds* (1955) and Anouilh's *Madame de...* and *Traveller Without Luggage* (1959). But more than that, the Poetic Dramatists shared with these writers a fantasised, non-naturalistic playfulness which set great store by speculation and paradox. Fry, in particular, habitually foregrounds the semiotic qualities of language in a way that defers representation in favour of spiralling verbal abundance.

Duncan's involvement with the Royal Court began in 1953 when he co-founded the Taw and Torridge Festival and began to consider the possibility of a company which would eventually become an important strand of the English Stage Company. Eliot, Fry and Whiting were early supporters, and Cocteau promised a new play (Duncan 1968, 371, 374). Lewenstein recalls that 'Ronnie was interested in Eliot, Whiting, Fry and Ustinov', adding diplomatically, 'George Devine, Tony and I were less than enthusiastic about these' (1994, 15). Osborne recalls Devine's somewhat less diplomatic verdict on Fry, Ustinov and Whiting: 'They're all absolute shit' (1991a, 7). Duncan suggests that submissions from these playwrights were screened out and that even when Eliot publicly voiced an interest in writing for the Court, he was never approached with a commission (1968, 379–380). This became even pettier: Whiting claimed that when he was briefly a theatre critic, the Court habitually gave him the worst seats in the house (1966, 46).

The deliberateness of this policy may be judged by the treatment of Duncan's own work. He submitted two plays for the first season, which Devine suggested be cut into a double bill. It opened a week after *Look Back in Anger*, played to 18 per cent houses and was taken off after eight performances. Duncan believed it was 'outright sabotage' but Wardle argues that 'Duncan's allegations of sabotage are flatly contradicted by Duncan's own friends who saw Devine after the opening, close to tears and bitterly reproaching himself for having "ruined Ronnie's plays"' (1978, 182–183). Again Osborne's recollection is a little different. A performer in the company at the time, he suggests that Devine directed the plays 'with the unconcealed intention of killing them off as soon as possible' and that he and Tony Richardson turned them into 'a triumphantly unpresentable evening' (1991a, 16): 'Duncan watched helplessly as his unactable double-bill [...] was rolled back unceremoniously like a stack of dusty rugs at a department store. It was a small but cruel revenge on Verse Theatre and Higher Thought' (26). Those final words are a telling indication of what the defeat of Poetic Drama signified.

When Ivor Brown bemoaned the lack of public money for 'demonstrations of our acting and productive talent' (1956, 2), he was marking a wound to national dignity. The Royal Court restored that dignity. Kingston noted, 'Without the Royal Court serious theatre might well be something we would still have to travel to Paris for' (1960, 19). Another writer remarks, 'The new English dramatists got their chance because English national pride was aroused by the success of Osborne's first play' (Wellwarth 1965, 223). French drama was not merely replaced but chased off, as can be seen from this extraordinary *Encore* editorial from 1959:

> As an influence, France is not what it used to be. Gone are the days when serious theatre anywhere revolved around the work of Sartre, Anouilh, Camus, Giraudoux and Cocteau. There are the newer voices, of course. But Beckett and Ionesco have had their success in England as grotesque jokers rather than as serious writers; Genet has been dismissed with genteel horror; Adamov has only just penetrated the sound barrier; writers like Schéhadé and Vinaver, not at all. And our own rebel group of younger writers – Osborne, Wesker, Pinter, Arden, Delaney – are driving off healthily on native lines of their own: which is just as it should be.[9]

The triumphant tone of barely-disguised nationalist glee reflects the defeat of what the New Wave had come to think of as treasonable forces at home. The New Wave had to eliminate Gallicism within British theatre partly to restore prestige, but also to retrieve the compromised vitality of the early Empire's buccaneering individualists. French theatre represented a danger to British drama both because it appeared to be outshining British theatre, and because it seemed to be raising problems for the very project the New Wave had set itself. While it may initially seem a minor and inevitable part of the revolution in British theatre, the repatriation of French theatre may be, on closer inspection, key to understanding further its theatrical and dramaturgical priorities, while also pointing up the dubious imperial nostalgia that animated them. But it remains true that the autonomy of British theatre was constituted unavoidably in relation with its cultural other. This paradox is tacitly acknowledged in the exchange from *Déjàvu* that I quoted at the head of this chapter. Jimmy Porter's disdain for that emasculated French play, *La Paix du Dimanche*, contains a hidden irony. *La Paix du Dimanche* was the French title of *Look Back in Anger*.

If French theatre was a symptom of this enervated cultural malaise, this inability to reconcile inside and out, what was the fundamental cause of it? There's a clue in Devine's praise for the Berliner Ensemble:

under its red neon sign, the atmosphere of the theatre is quiet and informal. The group appears to function in a natural and unneurotic manner, and by West End standards the kind of theatre they believe in seems carefree and dedicated, but without polish.

(1956, 14–15)

We've met most of these tropes before; the concern for quietness, informality, a suspicion of superficial 'polish'. But a key word is 'unneurotic'. This word pointed, in the fifties, to a phenomenon that runs underneath the entire revolution in British drama, challenging and troubling it at every turn, and it is the subject of my last two chapters: homosexuality.

6

SOMETHING (UN)SPOKEN

Quoting, queers, and the fear of theatre

> Through the footlights, the actor could only dimly trace the elegantly tailored outline of the theatre manager. The dark lines of his suit made him almost invisible, his presence only indicated by the soft glow of his cigarette.
>
> 'Go ahead', said the seated figure. 'What do you have for us?' The actor announced a speech and began.
>
> As he finished, he looked up again. There was a long silence before Binkie Beaumont leant into the light to ask, 'Are you *queer?*'
>
> The actor blushed and stammered. 'No – no I'm not', he said. '*But it won't show from the front*'.
>
> (Mythical theatrical anecdote, c. 1950)

Standardly, it is said that homosexuality in the forties and fifties was silent. Nowhere is this silence more evident than in theatre history, which has consigned this period to the dark ages of gay theatre, a time when the law and self-oppression conspired to keep homosexuality firmly closeted, hidden away from the public gaze.

Kaier Curtin's '*We Can Always Call Them Bulgarians*' refers to the group of 'closeted' playwrights of the immediate post-war period, but notes that none of their plays 'contained characters that identified these playwrights' lifestyles, at least as far as the public could ascertain' (1987, 251). John Clum, in *Acting Gay*, records that 'the gay playwright's unspoken compact with producers and audiences entailed keeping his homosexuality offstage or presenting homosexuality in a coded manner so that heterosexuals in the audience needn't notice it' (1994, xv). His point is underscored by his not finding any British plays dealing with homosexuality between 1933's *The Green Bay Tree* and 1956's *Look Back in Anger*. Such histories characteristically cite

155

the sixties as the moment when the closet door began to be inched open, and, as the veils of stereotype and ideology came off, the true contours of homosexuality become more and more sharply visible.

Several questionable assumptions structure this account: a belief in homosexuality as an ahistorical identity, of history as a simple narrative of liberation, of theatrical representation as a fixed set of signs that pre-exist their reception. A lot of work has been done recently to challenge these premises. What has proved particularly productive about this work is that it has enormously broadened the field of lesbian and gay studies, rendering visible traces of the energy deployed around sexuality in areas which have hitherto seemed impervious to sexual-political analysis. As Andrew Parker writes, it has opened the potential for 'a reading that could map the (de)structuring effects of eroticism even – or especially – in works whose subjects seem utterly unsexy' (1991, 31). The work of Foucault and others has been influential in proposing that the nineteenth-century reconstruction of sexuality was a keystone in transforming political and personal life, and is thus bound up with interactions that go far beyond what is usually conceived of as 'sexual'. As Eve Sedgwick has argued,

> homo/heterosexual definition has been a presiding master term of the past century, one that has the same, primary importance for all modern Western identity and social organisation (and not merely for homosexual identity and culture) as do the more traditionally visible cruxes of gender, class and race.
>
> (1990, 11)

While the Wolfenden Report and the Sexual Offences Act undeniably wrought crucial social changes, after Foucault we should be very suspicious of claiming that homosexuality was 'repressed' beforehand, or that its theatre can be written off as one big closet. In fact, homosexuality in the forties and fifties, far from being nowhere, seemed to many to be everywhere.

A police matter

The war years saw an expansion in the number of pubs, clubs and cafés where homosexual men could meet. The clubs, mainly in London, Brighton and Blackpool (Westwood 1960, 72), had the appearance and style of gentlemen's clubs. One of them, with its soft pink illumination (Gardiner 1992, 17), was surely the inspiration for Rodney Ackland's *The Pink Room* (1952), later rewritten and retitled *Absolute Hell*. Certain pubs, like the Salisbury in St Martin's Lane, were associated with gay[1] men and lesbians, though different pubs were chosen for brief periods, the new clientele moving on to avoid the threat of prosecution (Westwood 1960, 72). The *Sunday Pictorial*'s notorious series of articles, 'Evil Men', denounced a 'dirty café off Shaftesbury-avenue [*sic*], where dozens of the most blatant perverts meet, calling each other by girls' names openly' (Warth 1952, II, 12). Nearby stood the Long Bar in Piccadilly Circus, numbering Emlyn Williams amongst its regulars (Harding 1993, 61). Rodney Garland, in his novel *The Heart in Exile*, wrote that 'the "underground" [...] in wartime London came as near the surface as perhaps it had ever come in the course of English history' (1953, 41).

The 'prevalence' of homosexuality was shockingly revealed by the 1948 *Kinsey Report*, and its famous figures of 10, 25, and 37 per cent (Kinsey *et al.* 1948, 650–651). The report's 0–6 scale made visible histories that had been ignored in previous surveys, appearing to give the impression of a sudden glimpse into a huge hidden domain of invisible perversion, and encouraging a desire to root it all out, to discriminate the genuine heterosexual from the sham.

In the introductory volume of his *History of Sexuality*, Foucault observed that 'in the eighteenth century, sex became a "police" matter' (1979, 24). In the nineteen fifties, the police took on this responsibility with new enthusiasm. Labour's right-wing Home Secretary, Herbert Morrison, and the staunchly Catholic Director of Public Prosecutions, Theobald Matthew, cracked down on homosexuality in the mid forties. In the early fifties, the defection of Burgess and Maclean had given a political urgency to this search, as had the American government's concurrent purge on 'Homosexuals and other Sex Perverts' as part of the McCarthy investigations. In October 1953 it was reported that a plan to 'smash homosexuality in London' was being prepared by the Tory Home Secretary David Maxwell-Fyfe (Wildeblood 1957, 50). In December, he told the Commons that 'homosexuals in general are exhibitionists and proselytisers and are a danger to others, especially the young'.[2] The new Police Commissioner, John Nott-Bower, went about his task with alacrity. There were several high-profile prosecutions for homosexual offences, including those of Lord Montagu, Rupert Croft-Cooke, Michael Pitt-Rivers and Peter Wildeblood. The forties had seen a fourfold increase in arrests for homosexual offences, and in the following five years this rose by half as much again, from 4,416 in 1950 to 6,644 in 1955, amounting to nearly a 600 per cent growth between 1940 and 1955 ('Wolfenden Report', 130). Eugene Savitsch observed in 1958 that 'the search for Mata Hari has been replaced by a search for the homosexual' (1).

More generally, the forties saw an increase in public discussion of homosexuality. Frank Pearce's survey of British newspaper coverage notes that before 1950 there was barely any reference to homosexuality in the press (1981, 306), but from the fifties onwards reporting was widespread. Scare stories like 'Evil Men' were accompanied by a stream of reports of the arrests. In November 1953 an issue of the *News of the World* which welcomed the initiative of the Home Secretary and London magistrates to 'plan an anti-vice drive in the capital' reported at least twenty prosecutions for homosexual offences.[3]

A recurrent theme in the fifties was that homosexuality was increasing. The suggestion was made in the House of Commons by a speaker for the Home Office.[4] Many writers found it hard to imagine that these inflated figures could be due to what H. Montgomery Hyde politely calls 'an excess of zeal' (1970, 213). Viscount Hailsham saw 'no evidence of any change in the detection rate for homosexual offences' (1955, 21). The Wolfenden committee agreed, finding it 'improbable that the increase in the number of offences recorded as known to the police can be explained entirely by greater police activity', even denying the existence of a witch-hunt at all ('Wolfenden Report' 1957, 20, 48). Despite the eloquent testimony of Wildeblood and others, the use of entrapment was firmly denied.[5] The *Sunday Pictorial* quoted statistics to suggest that known homosexuals in Britain numbered one million, and rising (Warth 1952, I, 6). The Wolfenden Report professed to know that only 1 in 30,000 homosexual offences came to the attention of the police (18*n*), which, based on the 1955 figure, implied almost 200 million unrecorded homosexual offences. Whether there was any real increase is probably impossible to ascertain. But the vast growth in arrests, the Kinsey findings and the new coverage of homosexual offences in the press mutually fed off each other to create a widespread fear that homosexuality was on the up.

Maxwell-Fyfe was not alone in his assertion that homosexuals habitually seek to draw others into their twilight worlds; Viscount Hailsham records that 'initiation [...] by older homosexuals whilst the personality is still pliable' accounts for the great rise in homosexual practices, adding that 'homosexuality is a proselytising religion' (1955, 22). For the Viscount, the dangers were apocalyptic, since homosexuality was 'contagious, incurable and self-perpetuating' (24) and its converts formed a 'potentially widely expansible secret society of addicts' (27). 'Evil Men' also suggested that homosexuals passed on their conditions by corrupting youths, and that this condition was 'irreversible' (Warth 1952, I, 6).

Many reasons were proffered to explain this alarming rise. The Wolfenden Report blamed the 'loosening of former moral standards', the 'broken families and prolonged separation of the sexes' in the war, and the general social instability (20). The British Medical Association (BMA) offered emotional immaturity, seduction, imitation, sexual segregation, a defective home life, cultural aspiration, and depravity (1955, 13–15), and, more predictably, the rise of the Welfare State (9), which it had bitterly opposed.

One commonly-suggested cause was sexual segregation; that in a single-sex environment people may often turn, temporarily, to homosexual 'outlets' (e.g. 'Wolfenden Report', 11; Savitsch 1958, 15). 'Evil Men' denounced homosexuality in the army (Warth 1952, I, 6), and in prisons, describing Borstals as 'veritable nurseries for this sort of vice' (1952, II, 12). One writer claimed that prisons are places where homosexuality 'thrives in its most evil and intense form' and that single-sex schooling 'seems designed to increase it' (Martin 1953, 508). J. Tudor Rees rates the value of imprisoning homosexuals as high 'as to hope to rehabilitate a chronic alcoholic by giving him [*sic*] occupational therapy in a brewery' (1955, 6) and cites a police officer to suggest that there are those who would 'commit an offence for the express purpose of being sent to such a place. A life sentence to be served there would to them be a paradise' (8).

Most of these institutions were used as the basis of a play which addressed the perils of sexual deviance; prison (*Now Barrabas...*); the priesthood (*Serious Charge*); school (*The Children's Hour, The Hidden Years, Tea and Sympathy, Quaint Honour*); sports teams (*Cat on a Hot Tin Roof*); the army (*Third Person*); the navy (*One More River*). Throwaway remarks are made about scoutmasters in *A Taste of Honey* (Delaney 1959, 73), the Army in *The Long and the Short and the Tall* (Hall

1961, 73) and the Navy in *No Concern of Mine* (Kingston 1959, 14).

The West End vice

The theatre, although not single-sexed by any means, was habitually described as encouraging homosexuality, almost of itself. Clifford Allen discussing the army, remarked, 'If homosexuality does not break out overtly (and it usually does) it appears disguised under the aspect of men dressing up as women in concerts and plays and so on' (1958, 45). The drag revues performed within individual barracks were so popular that towards the end of the war they began to be exported; the first was *We Were in the Forces* in 1944, but a succession of highly successful shows were produced in the ten years after the war, including *Soldiers in Skirts*, *Forces Showboat*, *Misleading Ladies*, *Boys will be Girls*, and *Forces in Petticoats*. As the (often heterosexual) ex-servicemen became bored of performing, their parts were apparently taken by gay men (Kirk and Heath 1984, 15–18; Baker 1968, 182).

These seemed to be seductive sites for homosexuality in the forties. Osborne recalls seeing a photograph of 'Rattigan, dressed in a *tutu*, carrying a wand, accompanied by a line of aircraftsmen, during which Terry had sung his own show-stopper, "I'm just about the oldest fairy in the business. I'm quite the oldest fairy that you've ever seen"' (1981a, 223). Ian McKellen describes the actor Robert Eddison's wartime experience in a drag concert: 'After the show, the Petty Officer breathed heavily, what Robert always considered the best notice he ever had: "You know, Eddison, I never knew you were so fucking lovely!"'[6]

The association between homosexuality and theatre was wider than drag. Commentator after commentator insists on the crucial role of the theatre in the homosexual lifestyle. Donald West is apparently critical of the association of male homosexuality 'in the public mind with Bohemian artistic and theatrical circles' (1955, 21), but also insists that at what he described darkly as 'fashionable' parties, 'conversational virtuosity, a frothy wit, and an ability to gossip knowledgeably about the theatre are assets second only to the possession of a trim figure and pretty face' (31). Yoti Lane, in his book, *The Psychology of the Actor*, argues that a homosexual is drawn to the theatre because it offers him power and authority which he [*sic*] would fear to fight for in real life. He can, as far as his audiences are concerned, appear to be a potent and fascinating lover in romantic roles which his immature emotional development would prevent his undertaking in the outside world. Also he is in an environment where a love of fantasy, and a delight in dressing up, is approved.

(1959, 50)

The author of *The Invert and his Social Adjustment*, suggests that the theatre exerts 'a peculiar fascination' for homosexual men ('Anomaly' 1928, 124). The same sentiment is voiced by Rodney Garland, who describes the host of a *very* 'fashionable' party: 'Everard seemed to have a good sense of theatre even in his private life' (1953, 225).

While we should be cautious about accepting any essential link between homosexuality and theatre, both of which are far too historically mercurial ever to be yoked together like this, the theatre did seem to be a beacon for gay men. It habits and mannerisms offered a density of signs and structures through which to experience and explore an identity. The gay slang Polari was fuelled partly by theatrical slang, and was very popular in the theatre (Farnham and Marshall 1989, 52; Lucas 1994, Ch. 5). Those London cafés, clubs and bars were mainly clustered around Shaftesbury Avenue, two well-known cottages were named after a theatrical costumiers and a nearby theatre (Hyde 1970, 206, 211), and in the rear stalls area of many London theatres there was a deep, dimly-lit area between the seats and the back wall, which was often used as a miniature cruising ground (Gardiner 1992, 17; Allen 1958, 29).[7] When, in a case-study, West refers to a man who 'went to work in theatrical circles, and slowly developed a definite preference for relations with other men', the syntax seems to propose a causal link between the two moves (1955, 88; see also Westwood 1960, 57–58).

If the theatre, then, offered the promise of a relatively tolerant space for homosexuals to work, and provided opportunities to meet, talk and have sex, it also came be thought of as an 'attribute' by which people might be identified as gay. Gaskill recalls that in the mid fifties, the words 'gay' and 'theatrical' 'were almost synonymous' (1988, 10). During Wildeblood's trial it was suggested darkly that he had lured the airmen, Reynolds and McNally, to see *Dial M for Murder*; this dissolute mixing of class territories seemed proof positive that seduction was afoot.

The purge on vice that swept the capital targeted national figures, including theatre workers: Cecil Beaton and Benjamin Britten were rumoured to be on the hit list (Tynan 1988, 118). One of the first figures to be 'outed' by the police was John Gielgud, arrested on 21 October 1953 in Dudmaston Mews, Chelsea for 'persistently importuning'. He had given a false name and occupation and was fined £10, but his appearance in court happened to be witnessed by reporter and his arrest headlined the Evening Standard that day.[8] Some years later, when John Cranko was arrested on the same charge, John Deane Potter in the *Daily Express* noted that he 'is the latest on the list of famous stage names who have been found guilty of this squalid behaviour' and notes that this 'has become known as the West End vice' (Potter 1959, 8).

Potter uses the occasion to launch an offensive against homosexuals in the theatre, who have 'spun their web through the West End today until it is a simmering scandal. I say they should be driven from their positions of theatrical power'. He takes issue with two aspects of the queer influence, their *personal* power and their *professional* power; the first of these charges accuses homosexuals in the theatre of actively denying heterosexuals employment. This statistically improbable accusation is, of course, hard to discriminate from the bar-room grouching of failed actors (e.g. Heather 1972, 73). Tied to this is the suggestion that gay producers operated a casting couch. Potter describes how an aspiring young actor will 'not have to travel far along the corridors of the West End back-stage to meet the smooth, unspoken proposition'. Kenneth Hurren, many years later, recalled 'unofficial "auditions" at the London house in Lord North Street, where Binkie [Beaumont] held court reclining in pastel pyjamas in black silk bed sheets' (1977, 157). These accusations may or may not be correct, but they are not noticeably balanced by similar accusations which could be made against men like Charles Cochran, who was well-known for the diligent personal interest he took in selecting the starlets for his spectacular legshows. The second charge is that this queer conspiracy is working 'to foist upon the public a false set of values'. The idea that beneath an apparently *normal* play lurks an actually *queer* one is a complex suggestion to which I shall return later.

Yoti Lane, in *The Psychology of the Actor*, suggests that:

it is only during the past thirty years that the homosexual has obtained such a strong foothold in the theatre. A number of older players with whom I have discussed this point all agree that thirty years ago a company was unlikely to have more than one homosexual.

(1959, 50)

Now, he suggests, homosexuals may not even be a minority in the theatre (54) and cites one young actor as saying, 'When I go into a company I find it safest to assume that every male there is a homosexual until I have proof that he is not. I count myself lucky if I find there is one normal man among them' (51). Lane records that 'as a result of a particularly publicised scandal [probably Gielgud's fine], there was a rumour that homosexuals were to be banned from the theatre' (51) and another suggestion that Equity should refuse membership to homosexuals (58). So widespread was homosexuality believed to be that this raised the spectre of theatregoers having to endure a decade of fifty-year-old Romeos, and the proposal was dropped.

These claims are, of course, exaggerated. But one should not dismiss them outright. Gay men *were* powerful in the British theatre of the forties and fifties. After all, a list that includes Terence Rattigan, Noël Coward, Ivor Novello, Rodney Ackland, John Gielgud, Max Adrian, Wynyard Browne, Michael Benthall, Cecil Beaton, Laurence Olivier, Robin Maugham, Melville Gillham, Frith Banbury, Emlyn Williams, Alan Webb, Loudon Sainthill, Eric Porter, Eric Portman, Michael MacLiammóir, Hilton Edwards, Frankie Howerd, Paul Dehn, John Van Druten, Alec MacCowan, Laurence Harvey, Richard Wattis, Kenneth Williams, Vivian Ellis, Peter Bull, R. C. Sherriff, Richard Buckle, Esmé Percy, John Cranko, Somerset Maugham, Binkie Beaumont, Benjamin Britten, Philip King, Peter Shaffer, James Agate, T.C. Worsley, Charles Laughton, Alfred Lunt, Denholm Elliott, Rupert Doone, Michael Redgrave, Robert Helpmann, Sandy Wilson, Oliver Messel and Alan Melville is not just a list of homosexual or bisexual men; it is a roll-call of one generation in British Theatre.[9]

The linguistic pervert

To understand the anxieties that the theatre generated, and the reason why the general homosexual panic should have been directed so concentratedly there, we need to return to what the

New Wave identified as the general crisis in British culture in the decade after the war. The failure of feeling and the excess of technique that they saw undermining national identity and good intentions found a particular focus in a charge of emotional repression. As a speaker from the floor at a symposium at the Royal Court remarked, the previous theatrical generation were guilty of a 'fear of anything emotional'.[10]

Certainly, a recurrent motif in mid-century plays was the avoidance of emotional display. A couple of examples will illustrate the point. Near the beginning of *His Excellency* (1950) by Dorothy and Campbell Christie, we watch the following sequence:

[LADY KIRKMAN] *is turned slightly away from* CHARLES, *and cries quietly. It is no more than a sniff and two or three tears into a small handkerchief, and she does her best to calm herself. After a few moments she dries her eyes, puts her handkerchief in her bag and turns to* CHARLES.
Lady Kirkman: I'm sorry, Charles.

(1951, 1–2)

In Huxley's *The Gioconda Smile* (1948), Janet makes a similar attempt to hide her feelings: 'JANET looks at him for a moment without speaking; then suddenly turns away and, covering her face, begins to sob uncontrollably' (1948, 32). In Alan Melville's *Castle in the Air* (1949), Mrs Dunne quizzes the Earl of Locharne's secretary, a young woman known as 'Boss' Trent:

Mrs Dunne: You're in love with him, aren't you?
Boss: (*in a level voice*). Yes.
Mrs Dunne: Is he in love with you?
Boss: (*in the same level voice*). No.

(1951, 48)

If characters do not effectively police their own emotions, there are always others who will. In Noël Coward's '*Peace in Our Time*' (1947), a married couple say goodbye to their friends. The scene threatens to dissolve into tears:

Nora: Good luck to you both – always. (*She dabs her eyes*)
Fred: Now then, Nora – none of that.

(1958, 228)

Another frequent motif is for a character to hide their emotions until they are left alone on stage. At the end of Act Two of Peter Ustinov's *The Indifferent Shepherd* (1948), Hilary finally acknowledges that she knows Henry loves her, and makes him an offer:

Hilary: [...] Would you like to kiss me?
Henry doesn't move. After a pause, HILARY *goes quietly out, on tiptoe, expressionless.* [...] HENRY *rises impetuously.*
Henry: (*heartbroken, to the empty room*). Yes, I'd like to kiss you.
He turns his face to the wall, full of shame and anguish.
(1950b, 285)

Other playwrights built such emotional restraint into the choreography of much larger sequences. In Denis Cannan's *Captain Carvallo* (first performed in 1950), a young woman, Smilja, has agreed to play along with a faked romantic assignation with the Captain, and has played her part well. However, she has also fallen in love with him, and at the end of this witty, cynical play, he returns to the war, and, in an unexpected moment of unacknowledged grief, she is left in her kitchen, crying. Similarly, in his lamentably unrevived *Misery Me!* (first performed in 1955), a woman used by a man to make his lover jealous fails to admit that she actually loves him.

Rattigan built much of his theatrical craft around these moments. *Love in Idleness* (1944) has an exemplary scene; the play centres upon a woman whose son, Michael, intensely dislikes her new lover, John. At the end of Act Two, the son tells his mother to choose between them. She decides her loyalty is with her son and tells John that she is leaving him. Just at that moment their party guests arrive and the two lovers slip elegantly into their formal rôles of host and hostess, barely mentioning the appalling decision she has had to make. The emotions in the scene are there to be imagined by the audience and are given a terrible intensity by the smooth efficiency with which they take on their public rôles (Rattigan 1953, I, 322–325). In *After the Dance* (1939), at the end of another cocktail party, Joan commits suicide, and we observe every stage of her decline, without her once articulating what is on her mind (cf. 1995, xxvii–xxviii). In *Table Number Seven* (one of the two plays that comprise 1954's *Separate Tables*), Major Pollock is desperate that no one from the guest house in which he is staying discovers that he has been fined for groping women in a cinema; when the residents find out, there are moves, led by the imperious Mrs Railton-Bell, to have him removed. But in a tacit revolt against her judgement, Major Pollock is allowed to take up his usual seat at breakfast: 'A decorous silence [...] reigns once more, and the dining-room of the Beauregard Private Hotel no longer gives any sign of the battle that has just been fought and won between its four, bare walls' (1953, III, 195).

This is why these writers have been censured by gay critics. The emotional repression in these plays 'reflects the internalized homophobia of the playwright' (Clum 1994, xvii) and thus they 'dramatize and maintain the closet' (85). Such scenes could well be cited in support of such a view.

Except that the reverse is true. In each of these cases, what we actually have presented before us *is* emotion, emotion which is perhaps immediately hidden, but in the moments when tears are dabbed away, when characters are tongue-tied with grief, or are left alone on stage with their feelings, *we* are given clear signs of emotion. Indeed, a writer like Rattigan built his craft around showing emotions apparently 'beneath' the calm surface. As one character says in Huxley's *The Gioconda Smile*, people often 'make no obvious effort to express themselves. And yet you're aware of depths and volumes and psychological spaces' (12). In 1949, J.C. Trewin writes of 'the modern fashion for plays which depend for their success on the *display*, and for their development on the *analysis*, of emotion' (15, my emphases).

This structure of giving *and* withholding, revealing *and* concealing, of suggesting that beneath a normal surface, there may be *something else*, opens up a space between text and subtext and continually troubles the relation between what is said and what is unsaid. In *Castle in the Air*, the very levelness of Trent's voice, the very *absence* of emotion indicates its presence. This emotional code has considerable affinities with the mid-century figuration of homosexuality. Theatrical anecdotes are an intriguing discursive form because, myth-like, they evade the circuit of truth and falsehood. As such they are a usefully performative means of thinking homosexuality in the forties and fifties. The anecdote at the head of this chapter is instructive because, quite apart from the theatrical inversion that forces someone to apologise for being heterosexual, it identifies very precisely one of the peculiar features of sexuality: *it doesn't show from the front.*

This quirk of homosexuality offers grave difficulties for anyone who would try to identify and discuss it. In their submission to the

Wolfenden committee, the Church Information Board, as a preliminary, insist that 'homosexuality is not in any sense a kind of *conduct*. It is a term used to denote a *condition* in male or female' (1954, 7). Conduct, for the Board, is a kind of mimetic activity, a means through which one *represents* one's identity to the world. As Eugene Savitsch states: 'in genuine homosexuality the physical acts are the outcome of an inherent condition' (1958, 16). This proposes a stable pair of categories, homosexual and heterosexual, who are naturally visible through their respective practices. However, the Board unhappily discover that there is a third term; the *pervert*. According to the Board, 'The *pervert* is not a homosexual, but a heterosexual who engages in homosexual practices' (1954, 7). Derrick Sherwin Bailey, who organised the Anglican report to the committee, amplifies this point: 'indulgence in homosexual acts is, in fact, no more than an indication that the subject *may be* an invert – just as a capacity for heterosexual acts is no proof that the subject is not an invert' (1956, 26). So what the pervert perverts is representation; the pervert wreaks havoc with the unity of the signifier-conduct and the signified-identity; crucially, this pervert is a *linguistic* pervert.

In fact, if perversion is, in this instance, to act in a way counter to one's *real* self, then homosexuals were thought almost always to be perverts. Homosexuality was often characterised by lying and deceit, the artistic sensibility and 'gay' lifestyle hiding their true selves. Donald West describes a glittering homosexual party and the fabulous creatures that inhabit it, before adding sharply that 'their relationships are brittle and fickle and beneath the protective social gloss many are frustrated and unhappy' (1955, 31). This motif reappears in his description of a 'drama queen' as 'a fastidious, mannered *poseur*' (52). Stanley Heather recalls one homosexual's musical ability as a 'veneer [...over] a nature avidly vicious, vain and utterly debased' (1972, 73). In *Third Person* (1951), two homosexuals comment on each other: Felix argues that 'underneath [Kip's] guileless boyishness lies something malignant' (Rosenthal 1952, 389) and Kip suggests that what drives men like Felix to suicide is 'the false fronts on their lives' (399).

This production of a façade of apparent 'normality' – 'passing' – is another kind of deception, and therefore another kind of perversion, one which multiplied the hermeneutic panic inspired by the Kinsey reports. Many writers alert their readers that they may wrongly picture lesbians as mannish and gay men as effeminate; 'that is why,' argued 'Evil Men', 'people, so often, remain in ignorance of their danger' (Warth 1952, I, 6). For many commentators, the deceptiveness of homosexuality lies in not appearing homosexual at all. Savitsch cautions that 'in external appearance he [*sic*] may not differ at all from an average individual' (1958, 43). Westwood insists that 'the largest majority [*sic*] of homosexuals are microscopically indistinguishable from the other men in the community' (1952, 44). In *Beyond the Fringe* (1960) this is playfully exploited in the sketch, 'Bollard', in which four queens meet to record an advert; at the climax of the sketch, the camp *badinage* about the previous night's revels is dropped as they intone in *basso* voices, 'Bollard! a *man's* cigarette' (Bennett, *et al.* 1987, 29–30).

The anonymous author of *The Invert and his Social Adjustment* gave a comprehensive description of what passing involved, including 'don't be too meticulous in the matter of your own clothes, or effect extremes in colour or cut; don't wear conspicuous rings, watches, cuff-links, or other jewellery; don't allow your voice or intonation to display feminine inflection – cultivate a masculine tone and method of expression' ('Anomaly' 1928, 135–136). But such advice presents a further twist to the concept of perversion. It offers heterosexuality as a set of behavioural codes which can be deployed by homosexuals.

This parasitism is exploited in *Tea and Sympathy*, which had a high-profile British premiere in 1957. Al is trying to explain that Tom 'does act sort of queer' (Anderson 1955, 46). Laura retorts that if he continues spreading these rumours, she may spread some about him

Laura: [...] once I got them believing it, you'd be surprised how quickly your – manly virtues would be changed into suspicious characteristics.

AL *has been standing with his hands on his hips.* LAURA *looks pointedly at this stance.* AL *thrusts his hands down to his side, and then behind his back.*

Al: Mrs. Reynolds, I got a chance to be captain of the baseball team next year.

(47)

It seems that all sexualised acts are prey to iterability (in Derrida's sense); they are all capable of being detached from the bodies from which they are usually thought to issue, and then issued from unusual ones. And if either 'heterosexual' acts or 'homosexual' acts can be issued by straight or queer, then this iterability must be thought to be the condition of 'ordinary' sexual performances. This – what we might call, after J.L. Austin – sexual *infelicity* is, of course, precisely what the Church Information Board described as perversion. And if there is no necessary link between identity and behaviour, homosexuality begins to be the condition of all sexuality, and we are all perverts.

Perversely, then, the very desire to seek out and identify homosexuality opens up the discrepancy between body and action, identity and behaviour. Homosexuality begins by being situated as the abnormal, discrepant form of behaviour, a conduct that perverts ordinary behaviour. However, the more these writers try to mark its secondary status, its supplementary character, the more it seems to threaten the very stability of heterosexuality itself.

In Beverley Cross's *One More River* (1958), the bored, frustrated crew of a ship mutiny against the tyrannical Captain Sewell and organise an *ad hoc* trial for what they believe to be his murder of a young cabin boy; their accusation imputes homosexual desires to the Captain. They recall seeing him with a young boy, whom we later discover is actually his son. But adrift on the sea, cut off from most of the stabilising connections of land, the Captain finds it impossible to 'prove' his heterosexuality. The failure of the attempt to define homosexuality begins to chip away at the self-evident stability of heterosexuality. Even the August office of the Lord Chamberlain felt these reverberations; a plaintive memo discussing *South* remarks, 'most people have gone mad on the subject [of homosexuality] – surely it *is* possible to be friends with a man – or, indeed, attracted by him – without ripping off one's trousers? Physically or mentally'.[11]

The problematics opened up by homosexuality are, therefore, by no means restricted to the sexual domain proper, but are in fact bound up with concerns we have already met in previous chapters: the stability and constancy of our speech acts, the dislocation of feeling and expression, the disunity between inside and out. As Andrew Parker argues, 'sexual orientation – in troubling any simple continuity between outer appearance and inner identity – remains [...] capable of generating the most wrenching interpretive anxieties' (1991, 29). It is this interpretive crisis that I now want to trace in relation to the alleged invisibility of homosexuality in mid-century theatre.

The glass closet

All this panic intensified the search for a foolproof method of detecting the homosexual. A common method was to isolate a set of attributes by which one might unequivocally identify homosexuality. I've already suggested that being interested in the theatre was itself reckoned to be a bit of a giveaway, but there were many more. The list is eclectic and often bizarre, but its diversity reflects a variety of assumptions about what homosexuality *was*: the BMA takes a physiological stance, offering 'delayed puberty, subnormal growth of facial and pubic hair, appearance younger than age,' amongst others (1955, 29). West cites 'small stature, excess fat, wide hips, smooth skin, a feminine distribution of pubic hair, narrow shoulders, a boyish face, luxuriant hair' (1955, 22). Another offers 'a predisposition for the colour green' (Neustatter 1955, 80). Wearing suede shoes, being unable to whistle, and having an arm span greater than one's height were also adduced.

In *Now Barrabas...* (1947) by William Douglas Home, the sexuality of one character, Richards, is indicated by a kind of attribute shorthand. He is a chorus boy and ballet dancer (1947, 22), thinks women are cruel (32), he has 'very long hair elaborately arranged, [and] theatrical gestures' (5), cries when upset (65), and comes from a broken home (32). He admires tough men, beards and airmen (56, 6, 34). The other inmates call him 'Polly' and the author calls him 'precious' (5).

Philip King's play, *Serious Charge* (1955), concerns the effects of a malicious accusation of homosexuality. An unmarried vicar, Howard Phillips, lives in a small village. The maid, Eva, is having an affair with Larry Thompson, a local boy. But another girl has been made pregnant by him; when she sees Eva and Howard together one night she recoils and is knocked down by a car. Howard summons Larry and accuses him of responsibility for her death. In retaliation Larry starts remarking how suspicious it looks 'a young lad up here in the Vicarage with you alone' (1956, 39). He hears Hester, a friend of Howard's mother entering, and fakes sounds of a struggle. Hester believes Larry's lie and the accusation spreads through the town. Howard receives hate-mail and his windows are broken. In the final act, Larry is in Hester's cottage, delighting in the mischief he has caused. When Hester discovers Larry trying to steal money from her, he threatens to lie about her, too. She calls Howard, who appears with some of the villagers, and Larry is forced to confess that his accusation is false.

But *is* the accusation false? There is a play of attributes and codes that makes it very difficult to come to any final conclusion. Howard lives with his mother, a dominant figure, with whom he has an easy, slightly campy relationship (rather like Louise and Clive's relationship in *Five Finger Exercise*). The play opens with Hester admiring the decoration of the vicarage: 'so – artistic – if you know what I mean. What you might call a real woman's room' (1956, 1), before being told that it was Howard who had decorated. Hester comments, 'One would never think it – meeting him. One usually thinks of artistic men as being rather – well, you know what I mean' (3). And when Howard is discussing Thompson, he rather incongruously refers to 'your golden hair, your angelic face' (35). In the fifties, an absent father, an appreciation of male beauty, and a flair for interior design intimate accusations of their own.

But these signs of homosexuality do not emanate from Thompson; they overflow the narrative and suggest the vicar's homosexuality quite separately from the charge made against him. The narrative certainly suggests that Thompson's accusation is malicious, but it does not insist that it is false. Further, the heterosexuality in the play is uniformly presented as cruel and violent; from Thompson's rejection of his pregnant girlfriend, to Hester's decision to believe the lie, which seems motivated by Howard's rejection of her own advances. Even the end of the play does not close the issue. The violent antipathy that Howard has encountered is dwelt upon; a particularly ironic off-stage effect has a group of carol singers throw stones at the windscreen of his car. And instead of finding a vicarly compassion for his persecutors, Howard discovers that he cannot forgive: 'what I *feel* is a deadly hatred that has grown up inside me' (72). His mother recognises that some of the mud will stick; and indeed, the play of codes and attributes cannot be contained by the narrative, which opens the play to a queer reading in which the mud does stick, and the vehemence of the ending remains as a pointed denunciation of heterosexual society.

This reading is not entirely without precedent. Some of the reviewers suggested that Howard could or *should* be gay.[12] The Lord Chamberlain's office received an anonymous letter raging at the licence, which respectfully suggests that plays on the subject of inversion are attended in the main by those who are themselves perverts or near-perverts. The author of this play is himself a well-known homosexual whose life is spent amongst men of the same type, and the [...] play's argument is open to the gravest suspicion [...] A work which seriously examined the problem of the corruption of the young by men of this class, if written by a serious-minded man who was himself above suspicion, might conceivably have a not altogether pernicious effect (though even this is open to doubt).[13]

Even read in the more conventional manner (cf. de Jongh 1992, 66), as a play about a *false* accusation, the play undermines the unreliability of attribute theories. After all, that male homosexuals showed artistic flair, tended to be close to their mothers and occupy professions like the priesthood was not simply the folk wisdom of the *Sunday Pictorial*. If the apparent argument of the play is true, and these traits do not precisely locate homosexuals in their clutches, then this set of attributes is false, and another more reliable list should be found. But if Larry has by chance *correctly* accused Howard Phillips, then there may be grounds for continuing with their use. In order to assess the reliability of these attributes we need to know whether Howard Phillips is queer or not. (The play, of course, cannot give us a final answer.) But this means that attribute theories are unverifiable, since they have to be verified by precisely the knowledge that the theory is meant to generate. Based on the various attributes mentioned already I could 'prove' myself to be both heterosexual and homosexual.

This semiotic ambiguity, with its simultaneous revelation and concealment, is exploited even more fully in the development of queer codes. The general hostility to homosexuality necessitated a method by which gay men could identify one other without being spotted; this took the form of recognised signals and code words. Westwood describes how this worked:

When two men are both trying to find out if the other is homosexual, certain words and phrases, which would go unnoticed in another context, are used almost as if they were code words [...] one man makes a move; if the other

172

man is homosexual he will respond in a certain way; if he
is not, the remark will go unnoticed.

(1960, 35)

The word 'gay' was one such word. West pictures the scene:

> entry into this camaraderie is a matter of visiting the right
> places in the right clothes and knowing the right conver-
> sational gambits and *doubles entendres*. A newcomer puts
> on just the shadow of a meaning look, remarks with just a
> tinge of the accepted inflexion, 'Isn't it *gay* in here?' and,
> if he is a presentable young man, he is lonely no more.
>
> (1955, 28)

The gay slang, Polari, produced an alternative vocabulary (*riah*, *lallies*, *bona*, *trolly*, *vada*, *eek*, etc.), used both in gay bars and in the theatre. Again these words were designed to be semi-hidden since they would only be picked up by those in the know. 'Evil Men' tried to disrupt this mechanism by glossing the meaning of terms like *slap*, *dragging up*, *send up*, *camp*, *steamer*, *skipper* (Warth 1952, I, II). Westwood provides an (un)helpful glossary of 'the Homosexual Vernacular' at the end of his book (1960, 207–208).

However, many of the codes were more difficult to define, and evaded the attempts of 'Evil Men' and others to make them more generally detectable. Westwood asked 127 gay men how they could spot another homosexual; most of the signals are rather intangible, and none of the codes on their own would amount to very much. This is clear from the sign identified by the largest number of interviewees: the eyes. 'Homosexuals were said to have "liquid eyes", "a sadness of the eyes", "a hunted look", "searching eyes – almost like a snake's eyes", "sharing eyes" ' (84), all of which are matters of interpretation, rather than strictly detectable attributes. The same is true of another of Westwood's interviewees who calls this signalling 'a sort of code – a homo-sexual-flavoured conversation' (85). The metaphorical vagueness of 'flavour' is telling, because the way that these codes worked was simultaneously to disclose and to conceal the speaker's homo-sexuality. If challenged, the speaker can always produce an *alibi*; after all, Noël Coward could be using 'gay' in all those songs quite 'innocently' and one could just be asking another man for a light.

This indefinable, diffuse, half-hidden identity is quite different from the notion of 'being closeted'. Sedgwick, in *Epistemology of the Closet*, calls this structure the *glass closet*; 'the glass closet can license insult [...] it can also license far warmer relations, but (and) relations whose potential for exploitiveness is built into the optics of the asymmetrical, the specularized, and the inexplicit' (1990, 80). Her notion of the glass closet is pessimistic, but we could perhaps give it the kind of valuation Sinfield accords the similar structure of the 'open secret' (1990, 119). The value of these terms is to insist that the contemporary geometry of the 'closet' cannot be read uncomplicatedly back beyond the Wolfenden Report. The glass closet shows but denies final access, gives an appearance but keeps a distance. The closet, which has been so rigorously employed to maintain strictly binary in/out, shame/pride relations, is not a transhistorical figure, and an image like this one suggests a mediation of those binaries, places the closet, as it were, under erasure. The mechanisms of coding and passing allowed homosexuals to be both in and out of the closet.

To criticise authors of the period for shirking homosexual representation in their work is inappropriate. For one thing, the Lord Chamberlain would not have it. But secondly, as we have seen, the West End's signifying practices, through ambiguous structures like the star system, allowed a variety of possible meanings to pass through the fourth wall: a structure which itself reproduces the form of the glass closet, or Sinfield's open secret (1990, 115). These writers transcended representation to construct a homosexuality that was both present and not-present on the stage. To claim, like de Jongh, that a writer like Rattigan 'funked it' (1992, 58) ignores the hinted homosexuality of Tony and David in *First Episode* (1933), the Major in *Follow My Leader* (1940) who is blackmailed over an incident in Baghdad ('After all', he explains, 'a chap's only human, and it was a deuced hot night –' (Rattigan and Maurice 1939, I, 31)), the suspiciously polymorphous servicemen of *While the Sun Shines* (1943), Alexander the Great and T.E. Lawrence from *Adventure Story* (1949) and *Ross* (1960), Mr Miller in *The Deep Blue Sea* (1952), the schoolboys in *Cause Célèbre* (1977), and several others. In none of these cases could one definitively say that these characters were queer, but nor could one say they weren't.

An interesting example of the anxieties raised by this is the all-woman performance. George Taylor tackles this point in *Writing for the Stage*, when he notes that in writing a play for an all-female cast, 'the ingenuity of the dramatist lies in inventing situations in which the male sex have participated, and in which it is not necessary for them to appear in the flesh' (1947, 23). Falkland Cary's *Practical Playwriting* is less circumspect about this need for a touch of manhood: 'you are up against a tough proposition. Your love scene is ruled out. You have to steer between the twin perils of a suggestion of sexual perversion and the eunuchoid unreality of reported-speech love' (1945, 39). One book, expressly designed for women's theatre groups, considers the question of women playing men's parts; 'Women', the authors decide, 'should *not* do so' (Graham-Campbell and Lambe 1960, 22). Their advice is 'shun [...] any pretence at a serious treatment of a romantic situation; the better it is played the more it is likely to be distasteful [...] In general, avoid modern dress' (23). What is distressing about a love scene performed well? Perhaps in the kind of good performance they mean, it would be impossible to be sure that the two women involved did not mean what they were doing. Whether the scene was *actually* lesbian or straight would be thrown into scandalous question.

The combination of fourth wall and the glass closet offered a dangerously queer seductiveness. In *Tea and Sympathy* suspicions about Tom are heightened when it is learned that he is playing Lady Teazle in the school play (Anderson 1955, 37). Roger Gellert's *Quaint Honour* (1958) is set in a public school in which homosexuality is rife. Throughout the play the heterosexual characters refer nervously to theatrical activity; Park, the Head of House is trying to initiate a crackdown on the crushes but finds it hard to discover who is involved: 'I'm not sure about Bennett, sir. I thought he overdid the love interest in the House play rather much', he worries (1985, 19). Later, Park advises Tully, the queer House Prefect, who is casting the school play, that a proposed cast member 'enjoyed being looked at too much' and that in the case of another 'too many people enjoy looking at him' (26). And when Tully accepts the challenge of seducing the awkward and bookish Hamilton, success is assured by his manipulation of the fictional frames that surround the audition and acting process (27–33).

Quaint Honour also provides several clear examples of the glass closet in operation. Near the beginning of the play, Turner and Hamilton are in the Housemaster's office, when Tully and Park appear. They cross in the doorway and 'TURNER, as he draws abreast, gives an infinitesimal leer, to which TULLY responds with a threatening motion, also infinitesimal' (18). This minute code, unnoticed by the straights in the room, is only perceptible by the audience, who are thus situated as homosexual in the relations of the code. This privileged (though ambiguous) audience position also operates to create resonances and double meanings that subvert the authoritarian structures of the school that the play is (apparently) presenting. Hamilton and Turner are there to listen to a startlingly incompetent piece of sex education. The reluctance of Hallowes, the Housemaster, to get down to specifics opens up space for the boys to reinterpret the intended meaning of the speech. His claim that the proper use of the penis is the 'final expression of love between a man and a woman [...] the consummation of love' (15) opens up the problem of identifying when one is in love:

Turner: (*hesitating, with tremendous seriousness*) Sir, what I don't see is – well, I don't really see how you can *tell* when it's love, sir. I mean, does it affect your...body differently? I mean, it would be useful to know, sir.

(15)

Turner's affectation of 'tremendous seriousness' is a typical strategy of the glass closet. And the combined indirection of Hallowes and Turner produces a number of stray *double entendres* when the Housemaster comes to discuss romantic friendships between boys. Despite his insistence that 'what *is* wrong is for any sort of...physical contact to come of it', he immediately says, 'It's a temptation that you must put right behind you' (16). This inadvertent advocacy of anal sex is repeated moments later when he advises 'you must value very strongly the friendship and unselfishness in it, and utterly turn your back on anything which could spoil it' (16). Later, as Hamilton appears in Tully's room for his audition/seduction, Park, the rigorously heterosexual Head of House, remarks, 'this may be the very boy you need' (26). The codes, the indirection and the passing create extra registers of meaning that signal out through the fourth wall.

This was how plays often managed to get by the Lord Chamberlain, because *double entendres* always have an alibi, and can function without anyone's obvious intention. Sandy Wilson's *Valmouth* (1958) is filled with suggestions of sexual deviance; the Lord Chamberlain picked up on a couple of them, insisting on omitting 'a dubious passage of the priest and the footman' and sternly noting that 'the lines about massage between a black villainess and a lustful old woman are not tolerable'.[14] Despite this, a lot more got through, including 'Niri-Esther', an extraordinary song between those 'pals together on the ocean' (1985, 34), Captain Jack Thoroughfare and Lieutenant Jack Whorwood, in which Dick opines, 'though a sweetheart's divine / There is always a time / When it's fine to have a friend' (35). Dick also delights in Jack's presence, 'Oh Jack! It's good of you to come home with me. You have been a real chum – as Patroclus was to Achilles and even more' (34). This sentiment, and the curious association between homosexuality and luxuriant hair, is echoed by Jack's mother, who blithely tells Jack, 'I adore your hair – and so does Dick [...] My boy is very fond of you', to which Jack replies, 'And I'm very attached to him' (41). The Lord Chamberlain's recommendation was that *Valmouth* undergo 'extensive revision [and] deodorisation'.[15]

The metaphor of 'odour', like 'flavour', suggests the diffuse site of sexuality in these pieces, which troubled the censor's simplistic prohibition on homosexual *representation*. In *Valmouth*, the Cardinal is reported as having gone to a fancy dress ball dressed as Sappho (43); the barely comprehensible inversions of the image do not fall within the proscribed area, and so it has to stay in. Alan Melville's Biblical epic on the David and Bathsheba story, *Jonathan* (1948), initially included David's climactic line 'I sinned with Jonathan'. The reader's report doubts 'if any suggestion of perversion is intended, but the words are ambiguous, and should I think, be cut or altered'.[16] A note of agreement by the assistant comptroller reads, 'There is plenty of suggestion elsewhere which might lose its point if the suggested line were removed'.[17] When Oscar Lewenstein sent Genet's *The Maids* for licensing, the reader was clearly disturbed by this 'horrible, deeply decadent and morbid play' but found it hard to pin down his intuition; of one passage he comments, 'Might be harmless, but not in this, I think' and of another, 'I suspect this, though I do not understand it fully'. Finally he admits that 'I am cowardly enough to welcome the definite indications of Lesbianism which simplify my task'.[18] However, they still felt that perversion was not restricted to specific characters or events, and that its effects were endemic. The assistant comptroller commented that 'I can only hope his prospective producer won't want to know if it can be licensed after alteration'.[19] A second version of the play, without the more obvious references to lesbianism, still left the Office uncomfortable: 'all indications of lesbian relations between the mistress and her two maids have been removed [...] Nevertheless the play remains, as I originally called it, horrible, deeply decadent and morbid'.[20]

This unplaceable homosexuality works through indirection, encoding, irony, ambiguity, and *double entendre*. Stating without stating, it gave rise to the same panicked suspicion as the Kinsey findings and the prevalence scares. An audience member, hearing that *Third Person* was to receive a West End production wrote to the Lord Chamberlain in disgust:

> It's hard for me, as a laywoman, to say exactly *why* but although the words seemed all right in their way there was a curious undercurrent of evil about the whole work [...] It isn't what is said but what is unsaid that I feel is dangerous.[21]

Exploring mid-century theatre with a receptiveness to this double-coding can transform its apparent landscape. For example, *Plays and Players* emerges as a pre-eminently queer publication. Its coverage and support of plays which concerned homosexuality was second to none; it campaigned for foreign plays on the subject to be produced in Britain.[22] But more than this, their coverage and advertising implies, when taken *in toto*, a large gay male readership. Alongside a photograph of Ralph Meeker (fig. 6.1), then starring in Inge's *Picnic on Broadway*, an article notes, 'Meeker's naked upper extremities are more or less continually on display. Fortunately he possesses the kind of physical development that would make any male feel proud'.[23] Such photographs appear throughout the early years of its publication; one issue features a snapshot captioned 'How Press Agents Keep Fit', describing how 'Eric Braun spends much of his time in the gymnasium, and cycles all over the country to attend first nights'. The article is illustrated by the robust Mr Braun in classic 'physique' pose.[24] The magazine also carried a column from the first issue entitled 'Theatre Correspondents'; ostensibly this was a column designed to find companions and pen-pals for theatre trips. However, most of the correspondents were bachelors hoping to meet other bachelors.[25]

Their advertising is also strong evidence of a perceived queer readership. One advert reads 'Pictures (naturally) by TOM HUSTLER Photographer'.[26] The combination of the name and the hint in 'naturally' implies physique photography. A small holiday advertisement urges its readers to 'GO GAY in Romantic

178

Figures 6.1–6.6 Plays and Players; an imagined gay readership?

Majorca'.[27] Another issue offers by mail order a book entitled *Eros Kalos*, a compendium of 'Greek Love [...] inspired by the beauty of boys rather than that of women', with illustrations chosen for 'their racy originality and audacity'.[28] And later there is an announcement of 'EROS, an anthology of homoerotic friend-ship. *Sent under plain cover*'.[29] More curiously, an advert ostensibly for a free-lance domestic gardening adviser offers a picture of a muscular young man and insists (with what seems to me an indefinable series of erotic promises), 'Raymond would like to / Supply your flowers / plant your window boxes / organise your floral decor / ask for him at / House of Flowers' (fig. 6.5).[30] More specifically, from 1954 onwards, 'Vince' advertised his range of menswear in the magazine. 'Vince' had been a 'physique'

179

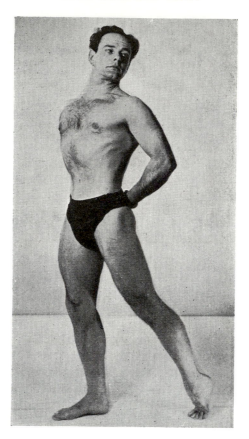

photographer but restrictions on what could be sent through the
Royal Mail moved him into semi-nude shots, and he began
redesigning commercially available underwear to show off his
models' bodies. These were so successful that he went into mail
order and eventually opened his own menswear shop (Smith 1994,
64). He is also credited with having popularised the modern clone
look, and an ur-clone, with plaid shirt and moustache, adorns one
of his *Plays and Players* advertisements (fig. 6.3).[31]

Travers Otway's *The Hidden Years* (1947) concerns the
'forbidden friendship' between Digby and Martineau, an older
and a younger boy at a public school. The play's title and argument claims such relationships are an open secret. Whether it is a
good or bad thing seems difficult for the teachers to decide; one
comments, 'it's unsettling. You never know where you are with it'
(1948, 113). A second explains to Reverend Dowson, 'It's all so

damn disturbing...Sorry padre. But it's so unsettling [...] And I don't like being unsettled' (116). At one point, the relationship is discovered by the sporty heterosexual teacher, Johnstone. He bursts into their room: 'So this is what has been going on. I thought as much when *I saw you making signs* to Martineau this morning in chapel, and then to-night I discover you both missing' (88, my emphasis). That his rage should focus on their *signs* itself signals the troubling implications of this sophisticated semiosis for our thinking about the audience and the integrity of the public sphere.

The Girls' Friendly Society

In *The Angry Decade*, Kenneth Allsop criticises the 'private languages' of the previous generation (1958, 25), and the phrase recalls many commentators' insistence that homosexuals were so efficient at signalling to each other that it could be done beneath a straight person's nose. Savitsch speaks of an 'incredible radar' which allows one gay man to spot another 'like a homing pigeon, flying to its destination with mathematical precision' (1958, 40). But this fear of private languages was given particular emphasis when considering theatre audiences.

Anxieties fastened upon certain forms of audience laughter. An

Evening Standard article criticised the 'sex-sniggers, tawdriness and violence' in a 'sniggery, pettily-vulgar farce'.[32] When the *Daily Mail* reviewed *Valmouth*, it wearily dubbed it 'brittle, sniggering fun'. *The Times* elaborated it as 'a good private joke which the sophisticated will chuckle over appreciatively'.[33] Sniggers and chuckles suggest kinds of laughter that are half-hidden, semi-private laughs, which compare unfavourably with a full-throated and honest laugh, in which everyone may join. Crucially, this

suggests that the anxieties I discussed in Chapter 4 about the *noise* of the audience may be sexually inflected.

Underlying this uneasiness is the fear of a queer subculture. Potter's tirade in the *Daily Express* speaks of a 'secret brotherhood'. West suggests that homosexuals 'make themselves understood by the use of a slang that is almost a Masonic code' (1955, 28–29). The Progressive League, Viscount Hailsham and Derrick Sherwin Bailey all make use of the term 'freemasonry' (1955, 4; 1955, 31; 1956, 84). And in these secret circles, more sniggering takes place. West warns that these societies may encourage 'a sense of self-importance derived from belonging to an "underworld" group, and the enjoyment of laughing behind society's back' (1955, 31). The Church Information Board also believes that the law is encouraging this sense of community (1954, 22), in which, as Bailey writes, 'feelings are exacerbated and sympathy becomes a kind of desperate camaraderie in the face of social ostracism and legal oppression' (1956, 34).

One might imagine that the revulsion of many of these writers towards their distasteful subjects might applaud anything which kept it off the streets, but Bailey articulates an altogether more serious fear: 'not only may it serve to attract others to homosexual indulgences, but if not judiciously handled it could foster a self-conscious and aggrieved minority which might prove a dangerous focus for social or political disaffection' (84). The Union of Ethical Societies observed that the law 'tends in the community to create a minority group whose attitude may become one of generalised anti-social behaviour' (1955, 2). An anonymous interviewee told Westwood: 'the everlasting shadow of the law – Oh I know there's nothing I can do about it and I don't worry and fret. But sometimes I just get very, very angry' (1960, 57).

This underscores the concerns about theatre audiences sniggering. Potter finds peculiarly exasperating that most homosexuals 'are not tortured misfits. They do not want psychiatric treatment or cures. They live complacently in their own remote world, with its shrill enthusiasms'. But this world is not remote enough for Potter, who believes it to wield through the theatre enormous and insidious power. 'What is often received with trills of praise – by the closed West End set – remains puzzling to the normal mind of the average theatregoer who is unaware of the lace-like intricacies of the decor or the obscure oddities of the plot' (Potter 1959, 8).

Priestley expressed his views in different tones but his perspective is the same. In 1947 he called for a Theatre that attracts to itself plenty of virile men and deeply feminine women, and is something better than an exhibition of sexual oddities and perversions. We need, in fact, more psychological maleness and femaleness, and a good deal less sexiness. We want a Theatre that is not a mere shop-window for pretty young women on the make and posturing introverts.

(1947a, 53)

'Posturing introverts' was a loose term in his own rather sketchily-developed psychological theory, but it is not hard to hear in it a reverberation of the word 'invert'. In 1953, he returned to this theme:

There are some aesthetic enterprises that are hardly likely to succeed without some assistance from the Inverts' Block – called by a sardonic friend of mine 'the Girls' Friendly Society' – which enthusiastically gives its praise and patronage to whatever is decorative, 'amusing,' 'good theatre,' witty in the right way, and likely to make heterosexual relationships look ridiculous: all of which is probably the stiff price we are paying in London for our stupid laws against inversion.

(516)

Four years later, Priestley denounced the hostility to homosexuals, on the basis that it inspires them to believe themselves 'members of a great secret society, of a superior persecuted minority' and thus it is their persecutors who 'will now make sure that the homosexual influence in our cultural life will at least be as strong as ever' (quoted, Westwood 1960, 190).

Priestley's disarming bluffness does not do justice to the full extent of the suspicion and fear engendered by this private theatrical language. The scale of the anxiety is better seen in the response to the performance of a drag revue, *We're No Ladies*, given only five performances at the Twentieth Century Theatre, Westbourne Grove, London.

This was the second time that Terry Dennis and Phil Starr, two drag performers, had hired the theatre, previously distributing tickets amongst friends. This new show was to be a public performance and, since there was also dramatic material in the show, it had to be licensed by the Lord Chamberlain. The reader, Charles

Heriot, took exception to a pun on the name Beucharov ('I don't know why you don't Beucharov now')[34] and recommended 'Cut the chamber-pot gag and the outrageous story about the duck', but otherwise felt that 'this is an all-male revue, and, of course, the jokes are all female, with a lot of *travestie* but nothing immediately discernible as homosexual'.[35] Further material was submitted and certain jokes substituted or modified. The show opened on 4 February 1958.

Trouble began when a reporter from the ever-vigilant *Sunday Pictorial* contacted the Lord Chamberlain's office to say that they had received complaints. His Lordship had also received a letter from a Mr Bennett: this unlucky innocent had supposed that the revue would be 'quite harmless, something like the Army camp shows, vulgar, brash but very funny and nostalgic to some of us'.[36] Imagine his horror when he found it to be 'a vehicle for the basest perversion – a smutty badly performed homosexual orgy, in which the "converted" audience joins'. Invoking now familiar fears of *coterie* laughter, he lambasts 'this deplorable homosexual filth, in which the most sacred and lovely affections of men and women are mocked and debased as they all laugh at their private jokes'. Oddly, Mr Bennett returned after the interval (having already witnessed some pretty queer goings-on), because he argues,

> That these men exist and that they work their evil on each other we all know. But to stand and sing the 'National Anthem' in both 'soprano' and normal male voices, grimacing all the time at friends in the audience, is an insult to a gracious lady and great position, and an affront to English people.

Fearing the effect on young people, he exhorts 'It is a travesty of entertainment with which your ancient and highly respected office should concern itself soon and with firmness'.

Mr Bennett's use of the terms 'parody' and 'travesty' indicates already a sense that this show is using a slyly infelicitous register in order to insinuate its coded message. Two letters sent to the LCC (who licensed the theatre) display striking indecision about whether this piece was obvious or covert in its register: one letter deploys a telling oxymoron to insist that 'the whole performance was *openly suggestive* of homosexuality';[37] the other begins by denouncing its openness, in the 'the blatant and undisguised perversion which is displayed', before positing somewhat more insidious activity, by expressing a hope that someone may 'clean up this nest of homosexuality in our midst'.[38]

In response, on 6 February, the Lord Chamberlain's office dispatched Rudolf Hill to report on whether the performance had been changed from the one licensed. As a result we have a uniquely detailed record of an illegal drag performance from the late fifties.[39] Hill's task was to report on the piece itself, which was the concern of St James's Palace, and on the conduct of the theatre, which was a matter for the County Council. As Dennis and Starr might have said, Hill impressively exceeds his briefs.

Hill found that, for the most part, the letter of the text was adhered to, although such deviations as there were – and owing to the darkness of the theatre, he could not write them all down – made a considerable difference to the tenor of the show. Many of the deviations are the interpolation of lengthy sexual jokes, some (as often in drag) at the expense of women; some of them are simply pantomime jokes, one of which involved taking a swig of gin and discovering it to be cat's piss. Others do seem to rely on a momentary acknowledgement that there are gay men beneath the frocks, as when one of the leads touches his hair and remarks 'I've just washed it in OMO'; at another moment, in a scene entitled 'Le Parisien Fashion Parade', a 'woman' is measuring another 'woman' for a dress fitting;

The VENDEUSE *after measuring the* WIFE *and finding her 12' x 12' x 12' measures her hips again to check.*
Wife: She likes doing this bit.
Vendeuse: (having measured hips) '12' *(and then putting the tape measure vertically between wife's legs and across her stomach)* '12'.
Wife: That's not in the script.

In another unscripted moment, one of the leads remarks: 'I've been married three times to a [?], a doctor and a sailor. I've been had on the flannel, on the panel and up the channel'. There is a reference to the size of the orchestra's instruments, various references to male prostitution ('She went out with a Pole and came back in with a Czech'), and a character announces their entrance with the words 'I'm coming – I'm coming on the stage'.

Very little of this material could be described as unambiguously homosexual, but the use of *double entendre* and the undecidability produced by the performers' oscillation between 'male' and 'female' identities begin to have a peculiar effect on Mr Hill. For one thing, he begins to see sexual innuendo where there is none. At one point, he records, a performer walked through the auditorium with electrically-lit earrings, one of which went out, to which the performer quipped, 'I've got a bad connection'. Surely, the sexual shading of 'connection' is rather remote.

Hill's hermeneutic panic is shown most clearly in a concern which is well beyond his stated remit: the audience. The first item that Hill remarks is a piece of dialogue *and its response* from a two-part item, 'Gipsy Encampment' and 'Romany Queens':[40]

Man: Is this the Gypsy Encampment?
Hag: It's camp all right!

Hill adds, 'Loud laughter from whole audience'. In an item entitled 'We're no Ladies 1926', a character appeared called Olga Campovski; Hill remarks 'we passed this, but the audience didn't'. Neither the Lord Chamberlain's jurisdiction nor Hill's brief covered audience behaviour, since no law prohibits the enjoyment of sexual puns, yet at the end of his report, Hill transfers his scrutiny from stage to auditorium:

> Next the audience – I naturally looked at those present with some care. There was one almost certain homosexual but apart from him the company present all looked most respectable and there were many accompanied by wives or girl-friends who obviously had no perverted interest in the proceedings. I listened, and certainly in my vicinity there was no questionable conversation. I saw no undesirables making themselves conspicuous during the interval.

Hill's evidence, while perhaps hampered by his desire to avoid appearing to importune, suggests that there was no queer constituency in evidence. But homosexuality being perverted in its (non)appearances, this did not deter him. He submits three counter-arguments to the apparent absence of homosexuals from the audience:

1   The introductory remark 'This is Camp all right' which is specialised actors' slang for a homosexual gathering [*sic*] was greeted with a roar of laughter from the whole audi-

ence, who must thus be more familiar with the phrase-
ology of the perverted than appeared.

2   Although the show was a mediocre revue/variety entertainment, the hall was full (Seats 4 to 6/-) and the
audience was quite enthusiastic.

3   One could sense that there was a rapport between audience and stage – in some cases Christian names were
known, e.g. shouts of 'Bravo Wally' at some piece of
acting. Either those present had been to many shows of
this sort or they met the actors socially or anti-socially
elsewhere.

Here we have a very extreme example of the ways in which
fears about private jokes and coterie audiences intersect with fears
of a queer community. Hill himself admits 'it is possible to specu-
late a great deal on the implication of this'. But speculation is all
that the performance left available to him, and it is instructive to
see in which direction it runs.

He departs once again from a strict interpretation of his task to
consider the performers themselves. He notes that 'apart from one
or two questionable gestures, the actors' conduct on the stage was
simply that of women [...] there were no "cissy" gestures or
attempts to impose a male personality on that of the womanly
one'. However, he still asserts that while 'some of the actors
approximated to the dame type, others were pathologically effeminate'. At the end of the report, he concedes that:

I can offer no concrete evidence of the Twentieth
Century Theatre becoming a focal point for pederasts. At
the same time my impression as to the habits of some of
the actors, whilst not given here, is pretty firmly formed
in my mind.

The following evening, Hill had a meeting with Phil Starr and
went through the deviations from the script with him.[41] He also
informed him of Mr Bennett's complaint about the singing of the
National Anthem (slyly listed in the programme as 'The Queen'),
suggesting that Starr discontinue its being sung by female imper-
sonators, vaguely threatening that although he 'had no authority
to make him do it, [...if] there were any breach of the peace, there
was action which the Lord Chamberlain was bound to take'.
Instead he proposed, 'why not just have the orchestra play and

stand to attention yourselves without singing'. Starr agreed to this rather unentertaining suggestion. Perhaps realising that his speculations on the audience had even less force, Hill did not mention them. However, the meeting has given him food for thought and new questions have presented themselves:

a   How do they suddenly command such a large and enthusiastic audience?
b   The show was very well dressed – how do they find the money, Mr Phil Starr, one of the managers, did not impress me as being a man of wealth.
    If anything further comes in from them it might be worth asking the police if there are any records of association with any undesirable club.

Hill's new thoughts, together with his suspicions about both performers and audience, add up to a new and extraordinary conviction. The show was funded by male prostitution, and the audience was largely made up of rent boys and their clients.

The whole episode is punctuated by a terror of covert homosexual communities. Of course, as he confesses, 'we can't refuse to licence a piece on the grounds that it may be performed by pansies'.[42] However, Norman Gwatkin makes the anxiety clear when he reports to the London County Council that while no direct legal redress is possible, 'the increase in homosexuality could give such performances a new implication [...] his Lordship is not altogether satisfied that the piece was being received purely on its dramatic merits'.[43] The Lord Chamberlain's reply on behalf of the LCC to the original complainants sinisterly reassures them that he was aware of 'the dangers that may accompany such performances, and obviously they will be subjected to surveillance if they are repeated'.[44]

The traditional image of homosexuality in the forties and fifties as closeted, hidden and silent fails to recognise that it was actually throwing into question the boundaries between secrecy and openness, knowable and unknowable, visible and invisible, private and public, lies and honesty, intention and expression, performance and reception, interpretation and misinterpretation. It will already have been spotted that these were precisely what the New Wave felt were responsible for the crisis in British culture and identity; indeed, the whole revolution in British theatre can be seen as responding to the linguistic perversity of a homosexuality which seemed on the point of constituting itself as an oppositional subculture, destabilising the vital unities which seemed the foundation of a strong national identity. I shall now examine the detail of the New Wave's confrontation with the theatrical queer.

7

SISTER MARY DISCIPLINE

Growing up straight at the Royal Court

> Look Back in Anger [...] that is what I call a proper piece
> of theatre, ladies and gentlemen. It's in black and white,
> lots of ironing and absolutely no musical numbers.'
>
> (Neil Bartlett, *Night After Night*, 21)

It has been suggested that homosexual representation broadly benefited from the new honesty of the fifties. Nicholas de Jongh, for
example, suggests that in *Look Back in Anger* 'a full-scale tirade
was delivered against the ruling establishment and its social and
sexual conformities' (1992, 52). The revolution of 1956, then,
actually meant a new realism in sexual matters, and thus prompted
a great leap forward in the development of gay theatre, allowing it
to become more and more truthful in its presentation of homosexuality. Yet this claim involves a particular contradiction.

The new realism of 1956 was prompted and shaped by a desire
to revitalise British culture, a culture now shouldering the burden
of embodying national supremacy as one of its real bases, its
Empire, rapidly declined. The ills of that culture were said to be
the increasing disengagement of thought from feeling, the inner
from the outer, the fragmentation of a confident public sphere into
competing semi-public, semi-private interpretive realms.

And this was precisely the anxiety prompted by homosexuality.
Far from being invisible, homosexuality seemed to be everywhere,
driving a wedge between meaning and expression, destabilising
the security of our national and cultural identity. The greatest fear
was that this was all creating the conditions for an aggrieved and
politicised queer community, founded not on honesty and identity
but subversion and difference. Curiously, the West End, so often
seen as deeply conformist, was seen by many as a hotbed of
subversion and resistance.

Historically, then, there is nothing neutral about the project of representing homosexuality openly and honestly, at a time when the most alarming feature of homosexuality seemed to be its ability to unsettle the possibility of openness and honesty. We have already seen the infelicities that assailed previous attempts to capture and represent homosexuality by its supposed 'attributes'. It remains to be shown how something that so playfully undermined identity, representation and utterance could be subjected to representation.

The key to this lies in the mid-century use of psychoanalysis. In the first volume of *The History of Sexuality*, Foucault charts a nineteenth-century move in the regulation of sexuality from the Church to psychology. By the forties and fifties, the prominence of psychoanalysis in Europe and America is remarkable. Lord Ammon noted in 1954, 'In my youth they used to call things of this sort sin; now they call it complexes' (quoted, Rees and Usill 1955, 214).

Psychoanalysis and homosexuality

Almost everything written in the fifties which attempted to address homosexuality, whether sociological, psychological, legal, theological or physiological, makes use directly or indirectly of psychoanalytical concepts.[1] Mid-century psychoanalysis claimed it could solve the 'problem' of homosexuality. Firstly, it claimed to be able to effect a cure. It is worth noting that Freud was highly sceptical that it could be 'cured'. In one case study, he cautions the parents of a young lesbian that his treatment might reveal that parental prohibition was her main problem, and that a cure might simply mean that she 'goes [her] own way all the more decidedly' (1979, 375). He also notes that, since the developmental model of sexuality proposes an originary polymorphousness, it is most unlikely that treatment could effect a full transition from homosexuality (the repression of one possible object choice) to heterosexuality (the repression of a different object choice). Nor, of course, would the *opposite* move be likely to succeed; although, Freud notes mildly, 'the latter is never attempted' (376).

It was the second claim that made it particularly inviting. While other methodologies tended to sink in the hermeneutic quicksand of linguistic perversion, psychoanalysis offered an explanatory model of homosexuality *and* a way of talking about it without getting your hands dirty. In doing so, it provided important conceptual tropes that recur well beyond the realm of psychiatry proper.

Psychoanalysis employed a developmental model to explain the old question, what *causes* homosexuality? Jerome Neu, in an excellent essay on the psychoanalytic theory of perversion, reminds us that Freud's model of psychosexual development offers a number of ways of negotiating the Oedipal phase. One of Freud's major contentions was that a great many aspects of our lives are governed by sexual aims, even (or perhaps especially) those which do not seem remotely sexual. But, as Neu points out, while this makes 'clear why the sexual perversions count as sexual, it becomes unclear why they are perverse' (1991, 181).

The key is whether perversions are to be thought of as 'defective'. Freud saw perversions as:

> sexual activities which either (*a*) *extend*, in an anatomical sense, beyond the regions of the body that are designed for sexual union, or (*b*) *linger* over the intermediate relations to the sexual object which should normally be traversed rapidly on the path towards the final sexual aim.
>
> (Freud 1977, 62)

Neu points out various problems with this explanation, but argued that they can be resolved once we see that perversion is, for Freud, a *cultural* term, suggesting an activity which departs from the *social* norm of reproduction (1991, 190). Neu concludes that perversion is not to be seen as identical with 'defectiveness' (given the reproductive potential of 'defective' acts like incest and rape) and that perversion is a morally neutral concept (194). In his case study of a lesbian, Freud remarks that her father's view of her as 'vicious, as degenerate, or as mentally afflicted' finds no support in psychoanalysis (1979, 373).

Perversion is not a morally neutral concept for those writing in the fifties. Reproduction is not considered a *social* norm, but a biological destiny. Without revealing its sources, the BMA discloses that the 'proper use of sex' and its 'primary purpose' is reproduction (1955, 9). Viscount Hailsham dismisses the argument that homosexuality should be no more condemned than adultery or fornication on the basis that at least these latter practices involve the use of 'complementary physical organs' (1955, 25). This sentiment finds its way into Hallowes's maladroit sex education lecture in *Quaint Honour*, when he tells his young charges that a woman's body is 'designed to fit perfectly with a man's body. You could say that she's concave where he's convex; or, if you like, she's the lock and he's the key' (15).

This normative explanation has a sharp effect on the developmental model. It makes it possible to discriminate between good and bad negotiations of the Oedipal phase. Chesser asserts that homosexuality is a symptom of 'failure in early development' (1958, 51). Donald West suggests that 'however one tries to smooth the path of *normal* development, so that more and more can attain *full* stature, a few will always run into *difficulties* and find solace in this *half-way* adjustment' (1955, 128, my emphases).

Achieving a correct sexuality therefore involves waving a firm goodbye to infantile homosexual desires. In Freud's terms, this is an error of chronology; since homosexuality and heterosexuality are products of the Oedipal phase, it makes little sense to define a pre-Oedipal child's desires as homosexual. However, guaranteed by nature, homosexuality's proper place is now exclusively in the pre-Oedipal state, and as a result is drained from any other location within the scheme, creating an entirely normative model of psycho-sexual development.

It now becomes possible to describe homosexuality as infantile, retarded, immature, regressive and childish. It can hardly be stressed enough how pervasive this notion is. The BMA describes the various phases through which the child passes before it reaches 'normal heterosexual maturity' and infers that to be a homosexual in adulthood 'therefore represents some immaturity of development' (1955, 11). Clifford Allen diagnoses 'some form of immaturity and lack of emotional development' (1958, 34). Caprio regrets that 'no matter how talented or brilliant some lesbians may be, their emotional life is childish and immature' (1952, 9). Eustace Chesser puts it bluntly: 'the invert has not grown up' (1959, 48).

This theory allows one to elaborate various possible *causes* for homosexuality, particularly the parenting error of a dominant mother and a weak father. Clifford Allen minces Freud's words to argue that a boy must 'mould his personality on his father and "learn to be a man" from contact with him' (1958, 65). If the boy is ill-starred enough to have an 'insufficiently sexed father', homosexuality may result (49). Westwood cautions mothers against 'over-protection – monopolizing, sentimental, over-considerate maltreatment that warps the boy's normal development and wrecks his chances of a normal happy life' (1952, 157–158). He blames the apparent homosexual boom on the wartime absence of male role models (1960, 65).

This fabric of diagnostic concepts finds itself clearly woven into all attempts to put homosexuality on stage: Howard Phillips, in *Serious Charge*, has a dominant mother and a maid whom, it is said, 'spoils and mollycoddles Howard', and Howard, to his shame, 'loves it – wallows in it, in fact' (King 1956, 2). In Otway's *The Hidden Years*, Martineau's father was killed in the war (1948, 47); in *Look on Tempests* (1960), Philip Sinclair's homosexuality is explained by the twin misfortunes of a dominating mother and a weak father, the latter having 'even fainted once', says Philip's mother, 'when I was having my ears pierced' (Henry 1960, I, 27). In *Third Person*, Kip Ames's dogged Oedipalism leads him to pretend that his father is dead, and that he was raised by his mother (Rosenthal 1952, 398). In Rattigan's *Separate Tables*, the subtextual homosexuality of Major Pollock is hinted through his affinity with Sibyl, a girl with a dominant mother and a dead father. Clive Harrington in Shaffer's *Five Finger Exercise* (1958) is nervous of his father and easy-going with his mother (12), whose dominance is inscribed in the very walls of the house, the décor of which 'almost aggressively expresses Mrs Harrington's personality' (9).

But there is a potential danger in this analysis. The ways of the id seem perilously akin to those of the queer; hiding, passing, subverting the boundary between the latent and manifest. Alarmingly, homosexuality may be detected within apparent heterosexuals. Eustace Chesser suggests that for a man to be attracted to a woman in jeans rather than a 'full skirt' is a symptom of repressed homosexuality (1959, 87; see also Davis 1950, II, 24).

But how can these writers face the facts about something which so notoriously problematised the boundaries of the visible and invisible, the false and the true? How does psychoanalysis escape what Chesser calls 'the collapse of rationality when sex is brought into open review' (1958, 25)? These accounts are always accompanied by the calm assertion of the importance of being objective, realistic and sensible. Eustace Chesser hopes that once people's 'blind, unreasoning prejudices' ebb away, those 'perplexed and uncommitted members of the public [may be able] to keep their heads in the storm and reach a balanced decision' (1958, 9).

Clifford Allen pits 'sensible' understanding against 'emotional bias and unreasonable prejudices' (1958, 11–12). The Progressive League note with concern that the law fosters 'an unbalanced and unhealthy atmosphere' when what is needed is a 'sane and educative' discussion (1955, 3). Gordon Westwood hopes that 'complete detachment' may thwart 'blind prejudices and extreme emotional reaction' (1952, 20). Rees and Usill aim 'to set out quite objectively' the generalities of the problem (1955, vii), which 'must be faced openly and realistically' (xii).

This may seem uncontentious but these writers have a specific sense of what it is to be irrational, prejudiced and biased about homosexuality. And that is to be homosexual. The forces of repression and denial suggest to every writer that someone's vehement hostility to homosexuality is 'a desperate repudiation of their own homosexual tendencies' (Westwood 1952, 105). For Clifford Allen, 'those nations which have suppressed homosexuality, abuse it and hate it, [are] thus revealing an inner longing for it' (1958, 20). They 'project onto a scapegoat what they themselves would unconsciously like to do' (Chesser 1959, 132); 'In most men's hearts, if not overtly, the sins they so shrilly condemn have already been committed' (1958, 22). There is a difference between a homosexual and someone who violently opposes homosexuality, but for these writers the distinction is superficial; both states are produced by an inadequate repression of homosexual instincts at the Oedipal stage. It is a way of blaming queers for everything.[2]

But if violent opposition to homosexuality renders one incapable of objectivity, it should not be inferred that homosexuals are any better. Gordon Westwood explains the tendentious knowledge produced by the queer community:

> men or women who are not homosexual very rarely gain entry into these circles with the result that the attitudes of the group, which sometimes may be biased or distorted, have no possibility of correction. One contact described the group atmosphere as 'cosy', and this word conveys the self-protection factor, and the absence of outside streams of thought that would prove healthy and cathartic.
>
> (1960, 185)

A lack of rationality is even a sign of homosexuality: Rose Sinclair, in *Look on Tempests*, went to the ballet with her husband:

I became irritated by his excitement over the performance of one of the male dancers. I teased him about it – eventually saying 'No wonder people think you're "queer".' He was so *unreasonably* angry that – for the first time – I began to suspect it was true.

(Henry 1960, I, 30)

Plays are peppered with these figures, upon whom, by their very apoplectic hostility to homosexuality, suspicion is cast: Medworth in *Now Barrabas...* thinks that the effeminate Richards has 'an evil influence' (Home 1947, 62), but is seen expounding the virtues of boy-love (36). In *Tea and Sympathy*, Laura is married to Tom's housemaster, who has been trying to have the boy expelled; she rounds on her husband: 'Did it ever occur to you that you persecute in Tom, that boy up there, you persecute in him the thing you fear in yourself?' (1955, 84). Michel in *The Immoralist* (1954) has fled to North Africa with a new bride. He is soon horrified to hear of a nearby community comprising only 'beautiful men' (Goetz and Goetz 1954, 61). Worse yet, a young Arab boy begins dancing sensuously for him. 'Stop that!' he cries. 'Stop that, immediately!' (65).

Rationality, objectivity and honesty are thus constituted as eminently heterosexual virtues. If the hatred of homosexuality and homosexuality itself are the result of too much and too little repression, only those who have undergone *just enough* repression – heterosexuals – can have sufficient soundness of mind to be rational about homosexuality. The frequent appearance of the word 'balance' as a term of praise for a report or a play indicates not simply attention to all points of view, but that it is heterosexual in origin.

This is not to suggest that homosexuality should be supported by the happy rationalist. It is only *irrational* prejudice that is condemned. One submission to the Wolfenden Committee described various attitudes to homosexuality, and finds in favour of the 'more or less neutral' few who have 'genial contempt for the pansy' (1957, 10). The Union of Ethical Societies proposes that any 'normal' person feels 'distaste [...] for this conduct' (1955, 2); Chesser suggests that objectivity is perfectly commensurate with disgust and proposes a neat analogy with a surgeon who may well shrink with revulsion from some particularly gruesome operation (1958, 28).

It is fairly evident that psychoanalysis is being pressed into service of a conservative sexual politics. Commentators who warn mothers not to dominate and fathers not to take a back seat are advocating the restitution of very archaic gender roles. But further, this approach serves to pathologise the queer community. The BMA believe that 'association only with members of the same sex' is an immature condition (1955, 11), and thus requires Chesser's scalpel. Lesbianism is used as an accusation with which to undercut (rather than reinforce) a political position: amongst women, suggests one writer, a 'fundamentally aggressive attitude towards the male sex is a symptom of homosexuality' (Chesser 1959, 100). Caprio goes further to argue that some girls 'develop a false psychology that it is a handicap to be a woman and attempt to overcompensate for their feelings of inferiority by striving for masculine aggressiveness and power' (1952, 7). Such uses of psychoanalysis are detectable in the theatre: Lesley Storm's *Black Chiffon* (1949) shows a husband making use of a psychoanalyst's diagnosis to reassert his dominance in the household.

It is crucial to note here that 'realist' tropes that punctuate this discourse have nothing to do with wishing to acknowledge the presence of a social group; the aim is to eradicate what is seen. Celia Kitzinger has noted such rhetorical devices in scientific accounts of homosexuality: 'light is continually being shed, candles lit, dark cupboards opened, and blankets or cloaks of ignorance removed to reveal homosexuals as they really are' (1987, 25). One of the central concerns evoked by homosexuality, as I have argued, is precisely that it refused to occupy a socially intelligible space, neither firmly in the dark cupboard, under the cloak, nor fully 'out' of these spaces either. The function of this genial enlightenment is in fact to reinforce the boundaries between light and dark, to prevent homosexuals exploiting the 'glamour of "forbidden fruit"' (BMA 1955, 38).

The 'forbidden fruit' argument suggests that homosexuality has increased precisely because of its half-hidden, furtive and proscribed character – as Walter suggests in *Five Finger Exercise*, 'Some things grow more when they are not talked about' (Shaffer 1958, 82) – and that to remove this liminality from homosexuality would reduce its attractiveness. 'The subject [must] be discussed openly and without embarrassment', cautions Westwood. 'The secrecy and shame that surrounds the subject at present gives it the aura of forbidden fruit which is unwise and unhealthy' (1952, 173). Frank Caprio tells us that 'we are finally emerging from that darkness of sex blindness, inspired by the conviction that

"Ignorance is the mother of vice"' (1952, viii). 'Evil Men'
concurred:

> as a start it is necessary to turn the searchlight of publicity
> onto these abnormalities [...] End ignorance, and, at once,
> a new situation exists in which the vice can be controlled
> [...] Bringing the horrors of the situation out into the
> open is the first necessary step to getting control.
>
> (Warth 1952, I, 15)

Joan Henry's *Look on Tempests* is marked throughout by this
motif. Philip Sinclair is a married man who has been arrested for a
homosexual offence. His mother, Mrs Vincent, is disgusted by the
suggestion and refuses to believe it; she finds the need even to
discuss the subject otiose: 'It seems to me,' she says, 'that some
things are best faced in private' (1960, I, 30). Rose, Philip's wife, is
the opposite and calmly watches all the trial proceedings. The play
fully supports Rose's position and slowly each character learns the
importance of facing the facts; the Barrister, who admits to being
revolted, accepts that justice demands facing these things openly
(30) and suggests that Philip admit his guilt (31). And when Mrs
Vincent is persuaded to go to court, she has a revelation: 'Could it
be that "circumstances" that "life" [...] have handed me a pair of
spectacles which, until now, I've always been too vain to use?' (II,
30). And by embracing her erstwhile rival, Rose, she promises not
to (s)mother her son. It is suggested, though half-heartedly denied
by Clive, that a newer approach may prevent homosexuality in the
future. The play urges that we all look on tempests.

Mid-century psychoanalysis saw homosexuality as childish and
immature. Seeking solidarity in communities was pathological,
while excessive hostility to the subject was corrupted by the same
source. Only the objective-heterosexual analyst could evade the
heuristic horrors attending homosexuality and represent it
honestly and realistically. In this separation between the speaker
and homosexuality, the latter was constituted as something which
could be spoken *about*, and as such its effects *within* communication were brought firmly under control.

The Lord Chamberlain and the Wolfenden Report

One of the decisive battles in the liberationist narrative of homosexuality and theatre is that between theatre workers and the Lord

Chamberlain. The official approach to homosexual representation before 1958 was very simple: His Lordship would not permit it. In Maxwell Anderson's *The Bad Seed* (1955), there is a gay character called Emory and 'there is, in consequence, some slight badinage about homosexuality, which, since the subject cannot be treated seriously on the English stage, can still less be joked about'.[3] It is cut. In a British version of the Poulenc/Appollinaire opera, *Tiresias* (1958), a single lesbian reference is omitted.[4] In the first version of Jeremy Kingston's *No Concern of Mine* (1958), a small number of references to the homosexuality of certain characters is blue-pencilled.[5] In 1940, a play was submitted to the Lord Chamberlain entitled *Queer People*. So horrific was this piece that the Director of Public Prosecutions was alerted.[6] A further list of plays, including *The Children's Hour, Tea and Sympathy, The Immoralist, South, The Catalyst* and *A Lonesome Road*, which 'mainly & unmistakeably [...] concern themselves with the subject'[7] and where judicious cutting was impossible, were banned in their entirety. The depths of his disdain can be measured by the fact that when *Suddenly Last Summer* (1958) was submitted for licensing, the reader noted, 'There was a great fuss in New York about the references to cannibalism at the end of this play, but the Lord Chamberlain will find more objectionable the indications that the dead man was a homosexual'.[8]

It is usual to imagine the battles with the Lord Chamberlain as one between radicals and conservatives. It is certainly the case that his decisions were becoming increasingly and aggravatingly arbitrary.[9] But the calls for him to pass plays with homosexual subjects were no more motivated by a permissive desire for homosexual representation than those psychoanalysts were by liberal pluralism. The demands for honest representation were, paradoxically, aimed at stamping homosexuality out.

The problems with censorship begin to emerge where the homosexual element is not sufficiently contained to be eradicated by the censor's blue pencil. In the original version of Osborne and Creighton's *Personal Enemy* (1955), two brothers, Don (fighting in Korea) and Arnie Constant, have fallen under the influence of Ward Perry, a librarian in Langley Springs, USA. A state investigator arrives to inform the family that Don has converted to Communism and is refusing to return home. He also intimates that Don, Arnie and Ward are homosexual. The Lord Chamberlain observed the associated accusations of homosexuality and communism, and judged 'the perverted element [...] to

201

be a gratuitous addition'.[10] As a consequence, he insisted on striking references to it. One very extended sequence included the sneering accusation that boys like Arnie are unsafe with 'people like you around, *Mister* Perry' (Osborne and Creighton II.ii.4), the description of Don and Arnie as 'tainted', the revelation that Perry had recently been to a psychiatrist, and the suggestion that he therefore has 'an unhealthy mind' (5). Earlier in the play we discover that Ward has given Don and Arnie books inscribed 'with love from Ward' (I.20), which the investigator clearly sees as intimating homosexuality (II.ii.5). At one point, Arnie's sister, Caryl, says to Ward, 'Listen – glamour boy – I have a little news to lay at your doorstep, too. I have witnesses who would be willing to be called who have seen you at the drug stores with your arm round Arnie's shoulder' (II.ii.7); at another Arnie rails at his mother: 'Aren't you proud of me, your son, a pervert?' and is goaded into shouting at his mother, 'Yes! Yes! Yes! It's true! Is that what you want? It's true – anything you want to believe' (II.ii.11). These and a few other lines are cut.

But has homosexuality been removed from this play? Once again a difficulty emerges because of the way in which homosexuality unfolds through coding and hints. It is impossible for the Lord Chamberlain to excise every possible homosexual reference, since the play hangs, as so many of them did, on the very notion of suspicion, hint, the reading of ambivalent signs. To remove, for example, the fact that Ward Perry gives both brothers a copy of *Leaves of Grass* would be absurd – surely the Lord Chamberlain could not ban all references to Walt Whitman? So the reference stays. Many other suggestions, whose meanings cannot be pinned down, remain in the play; Caryl suggests that 'it's usually these so-called cultured men who are a bit cracked somewhere' (II.ii.8); on Ward Perry's first appearance the stage direction suggests that 'He is about 34, slim, fair, neatly dressed in a dark suit, well laundered white shirt and bow tie. He has an air of quiet dignity at all times' (II.ii.3); at one point Mrs Constant observed that Arnie's 'hair is so soft. Like a girl's' (II.i.5); and Arnie's parents fall neatly into the weak father/strong mother paradigm. It is the cumulative effect of codes like this that constitute the traces of homosexuality in these plays.

I have already noted that fears were engendered by the realisation that not all homosexuals were effeminate or wore drag, and that there was a much larger, but quite undetectable number of queers who 'passed'. In Rodney Ackland's *The Pink Room*, the reader's report notes that 'the film director, Maurice, is an "auntie" with a common little secretary-chauffeur called Cyril, with whom he is always quarrelling. There is a lesbian literary lady, Ruby, and her hearty WREN friend, known as Bill'. Although these characters 'are treated extremely delicately' they are nonetheless 'obviously perverted';[11] the licence was eventually issued on the understanding that ' "Clatworthy" [is] not to be played as a "pansy" [and] the character "Bill" not to be played as a lesbian'.[12] When a rewritten version of *Third Person* was submitted, the reader noted approvingly that 'the homosexual element has been soft-pedalled', though a 'PS' to the report suggests that 'Kip must not be played pansy-fashion'.[13] This is included in the licence, which demands – rather more formally – that the part of Kip should not be played 'in an effeminate manner'.[14] The Lord Chamberlain remarked later, 'It is true that there was a big disparity in their ages, but there was much more ambiguity in the theme. Indeed, it was quite possible for the audience not to spot the homosexual possibilities. I remember going to it with a clean-minded sailor and his wife, and it never occurred to them for one instant'.[15] But as we have seen, it is precisely this fear that homosexuality can manifest itself beneath the noses of unsuspecting straights that caused so much agitation.

The result of all this was to exacerbate the anxieties around homosexuality. By leaving only the most ambiguous codes, by insisting that gay characters be transformed into straight ones, by removing signs of effeminacy, he strengthened the glass closet, heightened the linguistic perversions. Clifford Allen scornfully noted of the Lord Chamberlain, 'It is impossible to persuade the officials to pass a play which discusses homosexuality *in a serious manner*, although jokes which refer to it are permitted' (1958, 9, my emphasis). Serious theatre, founded on a set of felicitous speech acts, was being impaired by St James's Palace. It is a measure of the influence of psychoanalysis that the Lord Chamberlain was felt to be encouraging homosexuality and that to lift his ban would help prevent its spread.

Another crisis centred on the Lord Chamberlain's traditional blind eye to *bona fide* club theatres. Any theatre which operated a strict member-only policy could stage unlicensed plays. Homosexuality, therefore, could only be staged in a theatre club. And this multiplied fears about the queer community. I have already cited the correspondent who believed that mainly homosexuals attend plays about homosexuality, and R.J. Hill's terrifying evening in the Twentieth Century. Other observers can be found speculating that the club theatres are being attended for reasons which are not 'purely' aesthetic: J.C. Trewin worried in the mid fifties that 'the regrettable thing is that, as a rule, a ban acts as an advertisement; one that calls up playgoers with the wrong kind of curiosity'.[16]

Anxieties about the relation between the private and public were exaggerated by one of the boldest challenges to the Lord Chamberlain made during the fifties: the New Watergate Theatre Club. Three successful American plays, *A View from the Bridge*, *Cat on a Hot Tin Roof*, and *Tea and Sympathy*, would have been impossible to stage publicly before 1958, because of their homosexual elements. In spring 1956, *Plays and Players* reports that Graham Campbell-Williams, the director of the Arts Theatre Club was looking for a larger theatre to stage the plays under club conditions.[17] But he failed to win the rights, which instead went to 'Binkie' Beaumont and Donald Albery, and in the Autumn, it was reported that the West End's Comedy Theatre was to be converted into a theatre club, the New Watergate.[18]

Making the eight-hundred-seat Comedy into a club meant that all members had to fill in a membership form and pay a fee at least twenty four hours before a performance. That this arbitrary act could transform a large public building into a private space was felt to place further in question the distinction between private and public. As *Plays and Players* put it, 'it is not easy to convince visitors of the logic of our British way of life in these matters. They find it impossible to understand how the public has ceased to be the public by signing a club membership card'.[19]

The widespread ridicule of this 'extravagant pantomime'[20] stimulated further calls for the abolition of theatre censorship. Richard Findlater saw the New Watergate Theatre Club as part of a 'new resistance movement [...] against the direction of English drama from St James's Palace'.[21] The Lord Chamberlain's office themselves recognised the threat that this posed. St Vincent Troubridge wrote in a letter to a colleague in April 1957:

> It seems to me that our venerable institution of the Revels is under stronger attack at the moment than at any time since Percy Smith's Bill ten or twelve years ago, though perhaps it will last my remaining five years out. It's the constantly recurring provocation of that damned Comedy.[22]

And in a meeting between the Lord Chamberlain and the Home Secretary, R.A. Butler, the Earl of Scarbrough confided that 'the New Watergate Theatre Club [...] had created a position in which the law and the censorship was becoming rather farcical' (quoted, Johnston 1990, 212).

The stakes were extremely high and both sides were prepared to exceed the traditional limits of their influence. At the end of 1956, the assistant comptroller met with Beaumont and Albery, who were considering setting up another West End theatre as a club. Gwatkin predicted 'only two possible results of that action, either the logical end of the censorship or the end of the Private Theatre Club'.[23] In a subsequent memo, Gwatkin suggests that if a second theatre were placed under the New Watergate umbrella then the licences of both theatres might be withdrawn.[24]

This crisis in the censor's ability to protect the definitions of public and private is paralleled in the law relating directly to homosexual offences. One unexpected side-effect of the police's anti-vice campaign was that the spheres it was designed to protect were being damaged. In March 1954, concerns were raised over underhand methods which had been used to procure evidence and secure convictions of Wildeblood, Pitt-Rivers and Lord Montagu, including the doctoring of a passport, the use of a 'conspiracy' charge, searches without a warrant, and the immunity offered to the two airmen who turned – what was ironically called – 'Queen's Evidence' against Wildeblood, Pitt-Rivers and Montagu.[25] Within a month, it was announced in Parliament that a committee would be established to investigate the law pertaining to homosexual offences and prostitution. And in July 1954, John Wolfenden was appointed to chair it.

While the Wolfenden Committee's recommendations did propose releasing certain activities from the criminal list, it would be wrong to perceive the function of this document as pure liberalisation. In September 1957, after three years of deliberation, the committee recommended that 'homosexual behaviour between consenting adults in private should no longer be a criminal offence' (25). But, as Jeffrey Weeks has argued, the report was in fact designed such that 'the legal penalties for *public* displays of sexuality could be strengthened' (1989, 243). Indeed, in the committee sessions in which the wording of the *Sexual Offences Bill* 1967 was debated, a great deal of time was spent trying to clarify the position of such liminal spaces as public toilets, private rooms on merchant ships, oil rigs, orgies in private houses, and even, at one irresistible moment, the Houses of Parliament them-selves.[26]

The report also tackles the sexual infelicities which had been undoing the pursuit of sexuality. The report notes all the problems involved in precisely identifying and quantifying homosexual activity (11) and therefore rejects the various distinctions between latent and manifest, invert and pervert, acknowledging the confusions they open up (13, 17). Instead, they propose to sweep these aside by simply acknowledging acts and resituating identity as private and beyond the law. Thus the infelicities produced by the identity/action division were annulled.

One of the arguments for reform maintained that the law as it stood assisted the blackmailer, since their victims could hardly go to the police for fear of arrest. The report's decision to recommend legalising certain private acts would help lessen this danger; in the long run reform may make it possible for gay men actively to declare their sexuality (40). By consigning homosexuality to the private, interior realm of *identity*, while simultaneously preparing the ground for individual homosexuals to identify themselves, the committee was shoring up the distinction between private and public, and by default constituting the public realm as hetero-sexual. This is particularly apparent in discussions about preserving the public against indecency, *as if* the public will be uniformly heterosexual and disapproving.

As a corollary to this, it is worth noting a shift in the meaning of the phrase 'coming out'. In one of the few studies of this concept from the fifties, Evelyn Hooker notes that it signifies only an entry into a homosexual subculture (1956, 221). The contemporary meaning of 'coming out' is generally to announce yourself to heterosexuals (workmates, parents, family, groups that one can rarely *assume* to be homosexual), and itself indicates that one is crossing a barrier between private (homosexual) and public (heterosexual) worlds. This also corresponds to the psychoanalytic model whereby the only objective and open position is hetero-sexual. In combination, these two discourses suggest that homosexuality can only be considered truthfully and realistically represented when it (re)presents itself to heterosexuals.

As such, the report initiated an ethic of truth-telling within homosexuality. The contract implicit in the Wolfenden recommendations is the same as one proposed by the BMA in its submission to the Committee: 'it is hoped that, with a less prejudiced approach to the subject, homosexuals themselves will volunteer information and be willing to undergo treatment' (1955, 49–50). The Wolfenden Committee's master-stroke was to find a way of extending control over homosexuality, by encouraging queers to organise their semantic economies into clear identities, which could then be represented to the now heterosexual public world.

Faint traces of this move were prefigured theatrically in a most unexpected place. The premiere in June 1954 of Julian Slade and Dorothy Reynolds's musical *Salad Days* followed hard on the police crackdown of the previous winter, the much publicised trials, and the announcement of the Wolfenden Committee. The plot concerns the discovery in a park of a magic piano which has the power to make people sing and dance. Such intense physical experiences in a public park cause the government grave concern, especially the killjoy Minister for Pleasure and Pastimes, who enlists the help of press and public to track down the source of this disorder. In 'We're Looking for a Piano', these eager vigilantes jostle lyrically to express their impatient desire to hunt for the piano (which, they excitedly declare, is 'not any old piano / But one that makes you gay!'). The crowd disapprove of its disruption of the public realm:

> Its owners are requested
> To appear and be arrested,
> For it makes the park congested
> When it draws so large a crowd.

The problem with their quest is the strangely simultaneous appearance and disappearance of the piano: 'It's come, it's gone, it's out of sight / This piano's most elusive'. This adds to their urgency to be realistic and face the truth of the situation, a move which is not necessarily a prelude to punishment:

> They may decide to be benign,
> But first it would be wise to
> Be sure they're able to define
> The crime they close their eyes to.[27]

Amusingly, it may be *Salad Days* itself, as much as its magic piano, that is smuggling dissident pleasures into the public realm.

Two months after the Wolfenden Committee reported, during the belated parliamentary debate, Anthony Greenwood, for the Government, remarked, 'I should be more prepared to retain the

status quo if I felt that the present law made any effective contribution to preventing homosexual practices or deterring those who
indulge in them'.[28] The Report was a preventive and deterrent
measure. In the nine years after the Sexual Offences Act, the
number of convictions for indecency between men quadrupled
(Weeks 1989, 275).

Towards a mature theatre

The demand for changes in the laws on censorship and some
private sexual acts were both seen as a means of limitation,
control and prevention. This new ethic of preventive honesty can
be traced in the critical response to the theatre.

The Arts Theatre was one of the longest running and best
known club theatres in London. What is less often remarked is
that from the late forties to the late fifties it presented a series of
plays concerning homosexuality which would rival most theatres
before or since: *Vicious Circle* (1946), *Third Person* (1951), *Two
Loves I Have...* (1952), *The Immoralist* (1954), *South* (1955),
The Children's Hour (1956), *The Balcony* (1957), *A Lonesome
Road* (1957), *The Catalyst* (1958), *Quaint Honour* (1958), and
Garden District [*Something Unspoken/Suddenly Last Summer*]
(1958). Since it was a club theatre, this prompted the usual
worries about coteries and their codes, but more interesting is the
way in which critics framed their encouragement and appreciation
of the Arts Theatre's efforts. For it is here that we see the traces of
legal and psychoanalytic discourses which aim to use representation as prevention.

Many of the reviews praise these plays in terms of their seriousness and honesty. Cecil Wilson called *The Children's Hour* 'a good
play that treats its problem with a delicate and compassionate
candour'.[29] Of *The Catalyst*, Philip Hope-Wallace decided that it
managed to 'deal seriously at heart, and with some truth, with the
subject of sex'. *The Times* found it 'unusually frank' and the
Observer 'the first serious English play about sex for many
years'.[30] The *Daily Telegraph* thought that *Quaint Honour* was
'honestly and unusually outspoken' and finds that this is because
'it is all written straightforwardly without a leer or a snigger, and
it is all realistic'. J.C. Trewin found it 'honest'. Kenneth Tynan
hailed it full-throatedly as 'the most honest and informative play
about homosexuality that has yet been performed'.[31]

Within Tynan's remark lies an implication that this play is

speaking to heterosexuals: who else would need to be informed? It is symptomatic of the new division opened up between the objective heterosexual observer and the homosexual *subject matter*. Several critics refer directly to more 'scientific' or 'objective' texts to validate these plays: Maurice Wiltshire in the *Daily Mail* called *Third Person*, 'the Kinsey Report in dramatic form';[32] the Trewins referred to *Quaint Honour* as 'almost a footnote to the Wolfenden report' (1986, 62). And frequently commentators appeal to psychology to suggest the objectivity of the representation. Darlington's review of *Third Person* in the *Daily Telegraph* describes Kip as 'a quite remarkably unpleasant specimen from a psychiatrist's case-book'.[33]

The psychoanalytic distinction between objective analyst and irrational, immature homosexual is reproduced in reviews like *The Times*'s of *Third Person*: 'this American play treats states of mind which, however regarded, are unhealthy, with sincerity, insight and dramatic force'.[34] Standardly, the objectivity and realism of the play is contrasted with the 'unhealthy', 'psychopathic', 'neurotic' characters.[35] When *Plays and Players* reviewed *South*, its admiration was of its (heterosexual) objectivity: 'even though the play deals with the reactions of a homosexual, it is handled with [...] adult perception and fine feeling'.[36] When *Third Person* was nearing the end of its successful run, Emile Littler applied to the Lord Chamberlain to allow a transfer to a West End (i.e. public) theatre; he pleaded for 'sympathetic consideration' in the cause of 'serious adult drama'.[37] After a heavily amended script was passed, the production at the Criterion was advertised as 'an adult play' (Trewin and Trewin 1986, 42).

What such realistic representations are ushering is an adult theatre. Milton Shulman used the announcement of the New Watergate project and a revival of *The Children's Hour* at the Arts to take up the cudgels: 'The Lord Chamberlain is being besieged by a campaign designed to force him into the admission that the theatre is an adult art form'.[38] *Punch* used the same occasion to criticise the Lord Chamberlain with another metaphor of infantility, predicting that these plays 'will knock a much bigger hole in the nursery wall which still absurdly protects us'.[39] *Plays and Players* summed up this line of attack against the tyrant of St James's Palace:

is it any wonder that our stage remains infantile when these important subjects are barred? Does it not explain why the intellectual level of the ordinary West End offering is that of an audience of the mental age of twelve – and a retarded twelve at that?'[40]

Kenneth Tynan argued that 'censorship has so brusquely retarded the theatrical treatment of sex that it is still, to our shame, in its infancy. *The Immoralist*', he claimed, 'is a stumble towards maturity'.[41] And perhaps showing that heterosexuality operates just as precisely through codes and signals, this argument proposes something quite perverse: to represent homosexuals on stage is a sign of a healthily heterosexual theatre.

The shift of mood through the decade is clear. Critics in the early part of the decade either thunder against the 'nauseous matter' and 'repulsive odour' of the plays, or simply do not mention homosexuality at all.[42] But only a few years later, when *A Lonesome Road* was produced, critics complained that the play was too hesitant; the *Daily Mail* opined that 'the authors have approached their subject honestly, and, if anything, a little too discreetly'. The *Daily Telegraph* felt that the play ran on 'without ever really touching on the homosexual problem'. Tynan in the *Observer* admired some aspects of the play, 'but how many blushes and evasions, how many sudden rages and hints of unnatural bachelorhood, are required before the nature of his crime is made explicit?'; and the *Tatler* feared that 'at all essential moments the shadow of the Lord Chamberlain has prevented the protagonists from communicating with the audience except by unexplained emotional silences'.[43] When Terence Rattigan's *Variation on a Theme* was produced in 1958, the critics rounded on the play insisting that it declare its secret homosexuality immediately. Tynan in the *Observer* suggested that Rattigan had pandered to his audience's prejudices by hiding the play's 'real' subject, a charge also taken up by Alan Brien in the *Spectator* and Gerard Fay in the *Manchester Guardian*; Harold Hobson's review in the *Sunday Times* was headed with the question, 'Are things what they seem?' (Young 1986, 147; de Jongh 1992, 56).

The success of this ethical shift, from glass closet to truth-telling, was crowned when, as intended, homosexual men took it up. Angus Wilson and Roger Gellert wrote articles at the tail end of this period and both are organised around precisely this affirmation of maturity and self-disclosure. The title of Angus Wilson's article 'The Theatre Faces the World: Morality' hints at an emergence of private discourse into the public realm. Wilson is dismissive of plays like *Serious Charge* on the grounds that either the emotions represented were not mature enough or that the plays were not honest enough: 'it is not arguable surely that if it is to be presented it should not be truthfully or in adult form' (1959, 187). He also excoriates the 'transvestite plays': 'most playgoers can remember excellent plays in these last years that were clearly conceived in homosexual terms and presented in heterosexual ones. There is little doubt, I think, that they were the poorer for the transformation' (1959, 186; see also Gellert 1961, 32).

Roger Gellert's essay is similar to Wilson's, in its careful navigation of the homosexual into public life. His own aetiology of homosexuality shows a dependence on psychoanalysis: 'the queer thing about "queers" is not that they are homosexually aware but that they are heterosexually crippled' (1961, 30). He revealingly accuses the 'problem play' of emotional irrationality, and says: 'I hope we can go on from there and let some unsentimental light in on the tangle of irrational fears and preconceptions' (38). He takes up Wilson's plea that the comic side of homosexuality be stressed. But neither man thinks this comedy is justifiable as entertainment; comedy is important as part of *showing all sides* of homosexuality: 'above all, what we need on the subject is not emotion so much as knowledge and reason. The funniest and most moving thing in the world, really, is truth' (39; see also Wilson 1959, 188).

Philip King's two fifties plays about homosexuality, *Serious Charge* and *A Lonesome Road* (written with Robin Maugham) show evidence of this progression. The first play is structured around hints, semi-disclosure, a possible queerness beneath the apparently false charge; in the second play, the homosexuality of Martin Smith, the protagonist, is admitted (though not, as I have indicated, quickly or firmly enough for the critics). The play revolves around his attempts to hide it and his agent's determination not to let the truth come out. When a young man, in love with him, commits suicide, Martin Smith insists that he must put deception behind him: 'I'll never pretend again as long as I live' (71).

These discursive forces secured their victory on 6 November 1958, when the Lord Chamberlain announced that the representation of homosexuals would henceforth be permitted by his office. All commentators use the moment to reinforce the prevailing discourses: Cecil Wilson, in the *Daily Mail*, applauds the fact that 'after a long and stubborn opposition' his office has reflected 'the realistic new official approach to the subject'. (The government had just announced a debate on the Wolfenden recommendations). He welcomes 'this new broad-minded step by a Court official whose views on what playgoers should or should not see have hitherto seemed to belong to some remote Puritan age'.[44]

His familiar dark/light opposition, also captured in his description of the 'enlightened new times', is echoed in Kenneth Allsop's delight that we would now be able to see, 'both the warm, enriching relationship between a man and a woman, and the off-centre shadowy complexities that torment millions of people'. Allsop also applauds the 'new honesty', an attitude he describes as 'scrupulous and serious' and, in a familiar series of attributes, 'more adult, more sophisticated, more tolerant, more rational. It is a climate in which sex is being shorn of the leer and the snigger'. The end of the snigger marks the stifling of the queer community which Allsop warns is not a symptom

> of maturity but of neurotic infantilism. If we wish to preserve and extend the new standard of what is proper knowledge for grown-up citizens, who can face the facts of life without being coddled in cosy ignorance, we must be rigorous about what we reject.

Allsop's rhetoric suggests that newly liberated taboo topics are being brought before the gaze of heterosexuals, only to be the more rigorously condemned.[45]

There were limits to this freedom, all in keeping with the strategy of preventive honesty. The Lord Chamberlain insisted that only 'sincere and serious' plays would be permitted, and in which 'references to the subject are necessary to the plot' and where the dialogue is not 'salacious or offensive'.[46] He later set out the parameters of offensiveness in more detail, insisting that 'embraces between homosexuals will not be allowed', and, more mysteriously, that 'plays violently homosexual will not be passed' (quoted, Johnston 1990, 172). These boundaries indicate the construction of a homosexuality in the process of emergence; plays which flaunted or celebrated homosexuality were still not to be allowed. The stipulation that homosexuality be necessary to the plot may be seen as an attempt to confine the queer to the *subject* of a play rather than a force within the whole structure of performance.

The chair of the Theatres National Committee, Charles Killick, welcomes it as 'a progressive step'.[47] And the same view was expressed by another who described the policy shift as 'marvellous and a big step in the right direction [...allowing] us to do any foreign plays on the subject which we ought to see under conditions which are not hypocritical'. This celebrant is George Devine, himself at the heart of other radical changes in British theatrical production, and so it is to the Royal Court and the English Stage Company that I now turn.

Freedom from camp

I should now be clear why the sense of cultural parasitism that I outlined in Chapter 1 was so particularly felt in the theatre, whose very modes of production and reception were inimical to the vitalisation of British culture. Those broad cultural anxieties were focused around and heightened by the anxieties around homosexuality.

It will be recalled that emotional honesty was very important to this new generation. From Osborne's 'lessons in feeling', through Jellicoe's aim 'to get through to the audience, to involve them, to make them feel' (1958, 26), and Anderson's recollection of the Court style deriving from 'complete purity of feeling' (1957, 43), and offering an 'emotionally open' acting style (1981, 145), these writers and directors poured scorn on the emotional 'repression' of the previous era, what Osborne described as the 'British Way of Feeling' (1957b, 9). Osborne identified the originality of *Look Back in Anger* as 'honesty. I tried to write it in a language in which it was possible only to tell the truth' (1993, viii).

It is not merely speculation to suggest that this honesty was sexually marked. In the film of *Look Back in Anger*, Osborne has Jimmy and Cliff break into Helena's rehearsal. We see only a tiny fragment of the play – *The Forgotten Heart* – but as its title suggests it is a pastiche of a West End melodrama. Jimmy is especially revolted by the play, blazing, '*Who wrote this filthy thing?*'. He answers his own question, recalling sarcastically, 'Oh yes, yes I remember, "a penetrating examination of love and personal relationships". The bloke who wrote that was never in a woman's bedroom; not even his mother's when she found out the truth about him'.[48] Here the falseness of the theatrical era is explicitly linked with homosexuality, an exterior masking a different interior. Emotional dishonesty involves keeping your heart 'concealed, like Rattigan's and Coward's' (Osborne 1981a, 271). The vast project of limiting the parasitic effects of performativity is rooted in the urge to flush out the theatrical queer.

Its effects are found everywhere. In *Roots*, as I have argued, we see a concentrated attempt to upend the relations of language, creating direct links between world and word, thought and feeling, belief and expression. Amongst her shattering revelations about art, knowledge and politics, Beatie brings another:

Beatie: [...] Sometimes he hurt me but then, slowly, he'd build the bridge up *for* me – and then we'd make love! (*Innocently continues her meal.*)
Jenny: You'd what, did you say?
Beatie: Make love. Love in the afternoon gal. Ever had it? It's the only time *for* it. Go out or entertain in the evenings; sleep at night, study, work, and chores in the mornings; but love – alert and fresh, when you got most energy – love in the afternoon.

(1964, 90)

The lusty appetite of Ronnie and Beatie for work, knowledge and art is crowned by an equal enthusiasm for spontaneous sex, to be discussed 'innocently' with no artificial restraint. Later on, Beatie is in the bath when Mrs Bryant tries to tell her that the local pub landlord, Jimmy Skelton, has been arrested 'for accosting some man in the village' (124), and not for the first time. But this is gossip, about something which has happened before, and relates to the insincerities of homosexuality. The play juxtaposes Mrs Bryant's repetition of a repetition of a repetition with the immediateness and sensual fullness of Beatie's bath: 'OOOhh, Mother it's hot [...] ooh – it's lovely. The water's so soft Mother [...] these bath cubes smell beautiful. I could stay here all day' (124–125).

Osborne and Devine's first meeting, in August 1955, on the houseboat that Osborne shared with Anthony Creighton, marks a clear moment where the heterosexual agenda of the Court was established.

I let slip that I had more or less admired *The Browning Version*. Realizing my error, I hedged that I had no high opinion of *Separate Tables*. Before I had time to compound my blunder on *The Deep Blue Sea*, he cut me short about the patent inadequacies of homosexual

214

plays masquerading as plays about straight men and women.

(1991a, 9)

This impatience at transvestite playmaking was part of a general policy at the Court. Devine felt 'that the blight of buggery, which then dominated the theatre in all its frivolity, could be kept down decently by a direct appeal to *seriousness and good intentions* from his own crack corps of heterosexual writers, directors and actors' (10, my emphasis). As Osborne succinctly sums up: 'the implication was unmistakeable. In the newly-formed, middle-class-liberal English Stage Company, principles would be applied [...] No fancy salaries and the nod that queer folk were not to be considered, certainly not as officer material' (8).

On one level, the plan laughably failed, as a brief survey of almost every director of the ESC's first three seasons will show. But these directors held the same views as Gellert and Wilson, and with even greater earnestness. The theatre was a serious place, not to be compromised by homosexual frippery. Dexter was sacked after he and Gaskill were found cuddling in Gaskill's office, Richardson piously describing him as a bad influence (Gaskill 1988, 24). As Lindsay Anderson recalls, writing about the Court in general: 'Its freedom from "camp" was total. Perhaps this was the strong university influence; certainly it was a reflection of the personality of George Devine' (1981, 144; see also Osborne 1994, 86). This edict was applied with rigour; apparently they even found the Berliner Ensemble too camp (Gaskill 1988, 13). Wesker writes of John Dexter, whose later queening is legendary, that 'part of him hated theatrical camp' (1994, 505). Not quite enough, however, to stop him giving Osborne the superbly apt nickname, 'Sister Mary Discipline' (Osborne 1991a, 97).

This freedom from camp is most immediately obvious in the visual mood of the staging at the Court. Potter's tirade in the *Daily Express* against the West End suggested that 'the lace-like intricacies of the decor' were covertly depicting an inverted moral universe. The Court's decor was not lace-like or intricate. Lindsay Anderson's characterisation of the Royal Court's 'aesthetic' was that 'we pursue beauty without extravagance and knowledge without effeminacy' (1981, 148). In place of the lavish settings of gay designers Oliver Messel and Cecil Beaton, the Court dressed down. Osborne recalls that at the time drabness was considered very male and flamboyance rather 'cissy' (1981a, 123). And this is felt in the brick walls of *The Kitchen*, the dustbins on stage in *The Entertainer* and *Fin de Partie*, the attic-room with its bare walls and sloping ceiling in *Look Back in Anger*, and the monochromatic austerity of the permanent surround. In the place of what Eric Bentley called British Theatre's 'rococo effeminacy' (quoted, Hartley 1956, 7), the Court offered sombre virility.

The Court's famously aggressive attitude to the audience is also marked sexually by a desire to impede the circulation of secret meanings around the auditorium. The dream of directness, of disambiguity, is responding to the fear of a queer community. Osborne was quick to clamp down on any attempt to revive such rereadings; in the first volume of his *Collected Plays*, he strikes his usual stance, railing at the 'fanciful inventions', 'speculative and disordered hindsight', the 'crass misconceptions' which critics have developed around *Look Back in Anger* (1993, vii). He lists various of these, but his final example is 'the American-Freudian view of Jimmy and Cliff as lovers [which] is still irresistible to academics and feminists alike' (xiii). He returns to the theme in the introduction to *Déjàvu*, observing that 'wearisome theories about [Jimmy's] sadism, anti-feminism, even closet homosexuality are still peddled to gullible students by dubious and partisan "academics"' (1993, 279). And in his autobiography he is aggrieved that this kind of 'absurdity' is 'meted out to this day in dumb textbooks imposed upon children for their A-levels' (1991a, 8).

This is not to say that the New Wave were trying to keep homosexuality off the stage; Devine applauded when the Lord Chamberlain lifted the ban. But the conditions of this representation were to construct the self-tagging, *individual* homosexual, conducting him or herself with honesty, openness and clarity. In *A Taste of Honey* (1958), Delaney includes a homosexual character, Geoffrey Ingham. Jo suspects that his landlady may have thrown him out because of his homosexuality: 'Come on, the truth. Who did she find you with? Your girl friend? It wasn't a man, was it?' (1959, 47). Geof denies this suggestion, but Jo pursues the point.

Jo: Look, I've got a nice comfortable couch, I've even got some sheets. You can stay here if you'll tell me what you do. Go on, I've always wanted to know about people like you. [...] I won't snigger, honest I won't. [...]

Geof: I don't go in for sensational confessions.

Jo: I want to know what you do. I want to know why you
do it. Tell me or get out.

(48)

The conditions of Geof's presence are that he stay and explain
his sexuality, that he 'confess'. Jo promises not to snigger (this is
an adult response), and, in a striking echo of a psychoanalytic
session, even asks him to lie on the couch.

But what is there to confess? Very little; Geof is a very strange
homosexual. For much of the play he seems more interested in
trying to start a relationship with Jo (57–58). He is certainly cut
off from the queer community, and thus has little to counter his
descriptions as a 'pansified little freak' (63), a 'bloody little pansy'
(79), an old woman (79), 'that queer' (80). In a famous exchange,
the two of them stress their exclusivity from such broad group-
ings:

Jo: [...] I'm an extraordinary person. There's only one of me
like there's only one of you.
Geof: We're unique!
Jo: Young.
Geof: Unrivalled!
Jo: Smashing!
Geof: We're bloody marvellous!

(50–51)

Exhilarating though this moment may be, it is a profoundly
apolitical sequence, which re-enacts the emergence of individual
sexual identities, and their severance from communities of political struggle.

The limit on this new representation is made clear by stern
prohibitions against 'flaunting' and community politics. Osborne
has written of 'the then prevailing theatrical love that mercifully
dared not speak its name and which now cannot be restrained
from shrieking itself silly' (1994, 61; see also 1991a, 10). The first
edition of *Déjàvu* includes a characteristic diatribe levelled against
the gay community: 'I think perhaps Oscar Fingal O'Flahertie
Wills might have found Reading less offensive than rapturous
membership of something calling itself a community. Better to
suffer in Athens than glory in Thebes' (1991b, 61), and the entire
play is punctuated with sniping asides at homosexuality (e.g.
1993, 291–292, 297, 310, 332). Kingsley Amis notes, 'I object to

sexual abnormality in itself no more than I object to non-prosely-
tizing Roman Catholicism or vegetarianism, but I do feel a little
overwhelmed when a great thing is made of it' (1957, 10).

These plays never make a great thing of homosexuality. *Chips
With Everything* (1962) and *Inadmissible Evidence* contain homosexual characters, but they are minor and seem unlikely to disturb
the focus of these plays on their heterosexual protagonists. The
queer's tame presence, indeed his or her definable *presence* itself,
indicates the mature heterosexuality of these stages. In certain
plays based on personal experience, like Wesker's *The Kitchen*, the
homosexuals in the source situation have been silently excised (cf.
Wesker 1994, 326, 333–334). In *Look Back in Anger*, the queer
Webster – based on Dexter, whom Osborne knew from the Derby
Playhouse – is kept off stage. Cliff, almost certainly based on
Anthony Creighton, seems to be heterosexual. The only New
Wave queers allowed on stage are like Geoffrey Ingham, shorn of
their subversive performativity – their *queerness*.

But while you can take the theatricality out of the queer, you
can't take the queer out of the theatre. The silencing of
Creighton's sexuality was reproduced in Osborne's first meeting
with Devine on his houseboat. As he rowed towards them,
Osborne insisted that Creighton stay in his cabin. 'I feared that,
fortified by gin, he would lurch in and, literally, queer my uneasy
pitch' (1991a, 8). What Osborne was really worried about is
unclear; Gaskill remembers that there was speculation that
Osborne and Creighton were lovers, but the intimation evaporates
from his book (1988, 12). Osborne admits 'people often assumed
that Anthony and I were lovers. This didn't bother me much but I
didn't want this kind of absurdity to cloud my early encounter and
cast new meanings upon the play' (1991a, 8). Tony Richardson
remembers that in the houseboat they had 'posters of Marlon
Brando in *The Wild One* and *Julius Caesar* and other American
muscled movie stars. All this made for instant speculation that
they were homosexual lovers'. But he puts our mind at rest. 'This
was never true of John – quite the opposite' (1993, 74).

Osborne was once invited to dinner by Noël Coward. At one
point, Coward seems to have asked him, 'How *queer* are you?'
What Osborne replied is unclear. In his autobiography he records
answering, 'Oh, about twenty per cent' (1991a, 271); in a review
of *The Noel Coward Diaries*, he recalls saying, 'Oh, about 30 per
cent' (1994, 59). The slippage is interesting, especially since after
Osborne's death, Creighton publicly stated that the two of them

were lovers (de Jongh 1995; Ellison 1995). Of course this cannot be proved, and printed excerpts from the letters do not so far seem decisive; but it would perhaps be a fitting irony if this particularly heterosexualising revolution of sincerity and good intentions were founded on a coded, infelicitous, slyly queer work.

It would be wrong to claim that Cliff and Jimmy are 'actually' lovers; there is, first of all, the obvious objection that these are fictional characters and thus are not 'actually' anything. Also, any definitive declaration of these characters' sexualities is a post-Wolfenden gesture which should be resisted. Finally, it denies the more crucial fact that these characters are precisely *not* lovers in the play. In fact, their relationship is tremulously non-sexual, in a way that is, to my mind, of greater interest than any nugatory conjecture about their off-stage lives. It is because of this that homosexuality threads through this play, structurally, as a kind of organiser of narrative, and thematically as an ongoing concern of the characters.

The values of the play, as Osborne describes them, are the same as the values of Jimmy Porter. The first stage direction describes Jimmy like this: 'He is a disconcerting mixture of sincerity and cheerful malice, [...] a combination which alienates the sensitive and insensitive alike. Blistering honesty, or apparent honesty, like his, makes few friends' (1993, 5). As I described in Chapter 1, Jimmy's honesty is produced through his emotional openness and his vitality: he is described (sometimes by his own words) as the only character who truly cares about life and other people, exemplified in his close attachment to Hugh's mum, and his grudging respect for Alison's father. Describing the slow death of his own father, he remarks, 'I was the only one who cared' (55). This culminates in his despair at there being no 'good, brave causes left' (83).

But Jimmy's anger is precariously intertwined with the homosexuality the new generation tried so hard to exile. The 'no brave causes' speech is often quoted, but usually without the last sentence: 'no, there's nothing left for it, me boy, but to let yourself be butchered by the women' (83). The problem this raises is that by having Jimmy express so decisively his dislike for women, Osborne binds him into a kind of homosociality which, Sedgwick (1992) has argued, is not decisively separated from homosexuality but intimately bound up with it as its dangerous other side. As Alan Sinfield puts it, 'effeminacy is not banished by manliness; it is its necessary corollary, present continually as the danger that manliness has to dispel' (1994, 62). The absence of brave causes is seen as something which emasculates men; tellingly, the only other reference to this idea is in the context of his sermon on homosexuality.

> I've just about had enough of this 'expense of spirit' lark, as far as women are concerned. Honestly, it's enough to make you become a scoutmaster or something, isn't it? Sometimes I almost envy old Gide and the Greek Chorus boys. Oh, I'm not saying that it mustn't be hell for them a lot of the time. But, at least, *they do seem to have a cause* – not a particularly good one, it's true. But plenty of them do seem to have a revolutionary fire about them, which is more than you can say for the rest of us.
>
> (1993, 32, my emphasis)

The only people who possess a cause are homosexuals; but Jimmy's desire for a masculine cause with which to fight off the carnivorous women must be carefully distinguished from homo-eroticism; he describes Webster, the offstage queer, in the following way.

> I dare say he suspects me because I refuse to treat him either as a clown or as a tragic hero. He's like a man with a strawberry mark – he keeps thrusting it in your face because he can't believe it doesn't interest or horrify you particularly. [...] As if I give a damn which way he likes his meat served up. I've got my own strawberry mark – only it's in a different place.
>
> (33)

There are three operations in this speech: one is the 'making visible' of homosexuality (captured in the 'strawberry mark' metaphor); the second is the familiar denial that it is anything sensational, and that mature heterosexuals can face it without sniggers or fear. The third is that Jimmy is forced to parallel himself with homosexuals, in order to represent his desire for a cause, but then must distinguish himself, since it is homosexuality which is part of the very emasculating force he is trying to flee. Intriguingly, Jimmy's costume for the first performances (shown here from the recast version, with Alec McCowan) recalls the 'Clone' look from 'Vince's' advertisement (p. 181).

This ambivalence is felt elsewhere. His great speech about enthusiasm is picked up when he describes the off-stage queer, Webster:

Alison: I thought you said he was the only person who spoke your language.
Jimmy: So he is. Different dialect but same language. I like him. He's got bite, edge, drive–
Alison: Enthusiasm.
Jimmy: You've got it. When he comes here, I begin to feel exhilarated. He doesn't like me, but he gives me something, which is more than I get from most people.

(14)

Homosexuality again seems to hold out the promise of everything that Jimmy wants, and this promise seems ambiguously sexual in its expression.

In fact, by trying to construct a profoundly masculine sensibility, Jimmy/Osborne is forced into creating, through the enforced absence of women in these bonds, potentially homoerotic connections, which begin to trouble the play. The language in which he expresses his hope is intriguingly homoerotic in resonance: he calls for 'a kind of – burning virility of mind and spirit that looks for something as powerful as itself' (93). In another speech, 'real' love is described in conventionally masculine metaphors: 'It's no good trying to fool yourself about love. You can't fall into it like a soft job, without dirtying up your hands [...] It takes muscle and guts' (92). At another, a curious *double entendre* suggests an ambivalently homo/heteroerotic scene, when he envisages himself and Helena gazing at each other 'tenderly and lecherously in "The Builder's Arms"' (85).

More seriously, throughout the play, Jimmy's relationship with Cliff borders on flirtation. He tells Cliff, 'You're worth half a dozen Helenas to me or to anyone' (83) and twice invites Cliff to take his clothes off; once his trousers ('Take 'em off. And I'll kick your behind for you' (12) and later his shirt, torn in a manly tussle ('Well, what do you want to wear a shirt for? (*Rising*) A tough character like you' (81). At another point, the bonding seems to lurch into explicitly sexual activity, and Jimmy's response is violent:

Cliff:	Well, shall we dance?
	He pushes JIMMY *round the floor, who is past the mood for this kind of fooling.*
	Do you come here often?
Jimmy:	Only in the mating season. All right, all right, very funny.
	He tries to escape, but CLIFF *holds him like a vice.*
	Let me go.
Cliff:	Not until you've apologized for being nasty to everyone. Do you think bosoms will be in or out, this year?
Jimmy:	Your teeth will be out in a minute, if you don't let go!
	He makes a great effort to wrench himself free, but CLIFF *hangs on. They collapse to the floor C., below the table, struggling.* ALISON *carries on with her ironing. This is routine, but she is getting close to breaking point, all the same.* CLIFF *manages to break away, and finds himself in front of the ironing board.* JIMMY *springs up. They grapple.*

(22)

The railing anger that marks the entire play is something dependent upon, and violently opposed to, homosexuality.

The revitalisation of the theatre, the way it came to be seen as expressing 'once again' a certain Britishness, the consequent

redrawing of theatrical functions, the disempowering of the audience, all of these may be seen as reactions to a widespread
queering of the theatre in the forties and early fifties. The proliferation of meanings, the apparently secret coding, the hidden
audiences, the self-conscious fictionality of the stage discourse, all
heightened the parasitisms of culture and language detected by the
New Wave, the New Left, the Empire-loyalists, the Arts Council
and others. And they were also things which exacerbated fears of
a general queering of culture. So while the events of the mid fifties
could be seen as effecting a step forward for homosexual representation, it should also be recognised that representation created a
limited economy in which homosexuality was drained of much of
its subversiveness, of its queerness, in fact, of its theatricality.
Homosexuality, rather than simply being a theme, subject or topic
which could be introduced onto the stage, is more pertinently seen
in terms of a powerful range of structural effects which resonate
through the whole 'revolution' in British theatre.

AFTERWORD

Bernard: The crucial development in our theatre in nineteen fifty-
six was, as has been repeated and analysed ad nauseam:
Osborne's *Look Back in Anger.* (*Refers to notes card in
his hand.*) At the Royal Court theatre in London an
entire generation seemed to have found its own vehement, articulate expression in the character of Jimmy
Porter. *The interpreter comes one step forward and
repeats what he has said in Russian.*
(David Mercer, *After Haggerty,* in: *Plays One,* p. 290)

The anti-hero of David Mercer's *After Haggerty* (1970) is a
defeated and stale theatre critic, Bernard Link. Throughout the
play we see him touring various communist bloc countries,
attempting to lecture on British drama to increasingly unsympa-
thetic audiences. Mercer's vision of cultural and political aridity is
partly embodied in the vapidity of Bernard's desiccated, hackneyed
account of recent theatre history.

Mercer was writing at a time when fashions in British theatre
seemed to have turned yet again, with a new wave of countercul-
tural theatre groups, influenced by the physical and experimental
work coming out of the United States and northern Europe,
following a new touring circuit of arts centres, theatre labs and
polytechnics. Yet despite Mercer's evident boredom with the
clichés of 1956, his play is mildly satirical at the expense of
companies like New York's Living Theatre, and the excoriating
rhetoric of his play is more reminiscent of Osborne than of his
contemporaries.

It is emblematic of how the Royal Court's revolution had
become part of the foundations of British theatre practice.
Speaking after Tony Richardson's death, Bill Gaskill commented

that 'Look Back in Anger was a historic production [...] Within weeks it was understood as such'.[1] Indeed, 8 May 1956 seems to have inscribed itself on the British theatrical imagination, and despite changes, innovations and developments in theatre practice, much of what happens in the theatre still takes place in the shadow of that decisive premiere. Plays like Sarah Kane's *Blasted* (1995), Jez Butterworth's *Mojo* (1995) or Patrick Marber's *Closer* (1997) find themselves tiresomely held up against Osborne's 'breakthrough'. David Hare, in a platform lecture at the National Theatre, criticises the new generation for failing to produce a rallying cry like *Look Back in Anger* (1997, 14). Peter Ansorge, in *From Liverpool to Los Angeles*, calls for a defiantly oppositional theatre on Osborne's model (1997, 140). Yet the theatre to which these people appeal seems no better understood than it is by Bernard Link, standing uncomfortably before his Moscow audience.

During the 1990s, the work of that generation has been inching towards reassessment, helped by books like Charles Duff's *The Lost Summer* (1995), Maggie Gale's *West End Women* (1996) and Sean O'Connor's *Straight Acting* (1998). In the last few years, there have been revivals of mid-century plays by Enid Bagnold, Christopher Fry, James Bridie, Noël Coward, Daphne du Maurier, Dodie Smith, J.B. Priestley, and Rodney Ackland. The figure who has been most extensively re-examined is Terence Rattigan; there have been film, television or theatre productions of *French Without Tears*, *After the Dance*, *Flare Path*, *The Winslow Boy*, *Harlequinade*, *The Browning Version*, *The Deep Blue Sea*, *Separate Tables*, *In Praise of Love* and *Cause Célèbre*. David Mamet has directed a film of *The Winslow Boy* for release in 1999.

But even these productions take place against a certain memory of *Look Back in Anger*. It is striking how often contemporary critics commented on the power of these plays in comparison with *Look Back in Anger*, a play which, ironically, is itself rather out of theatrical favour. It is almost becoming a cliché to refer to mid-century British theatre as a 'lost' period, and figures like Rodney Ackland, like some literary version of an 'it' girl, is now pretty famous for not being famous. Yet inverting this hierarchy, as Derrida reminds us, is only the first step. Before we can say decisively that this lost era has been retrieved, we need to understand the curious dependence of the later period on the earlier, and the way we have read the earlier by the light of the later. The story of

British theatre in 1956 has been so often retold that its shape, its force, its power and meaning have been lost in the familiarity of the telling. If nothing else, there is a need to make the familiar unfamiliar.

NOTES

1 INTRODUCTION

1 e.g. Taylor 1963, 37; Wellwarth 1965, 222; Taylor 1971, 7; Gascoigne 1962, 196; Lumley 1972, 221; Nicoll 1976, 810; Edwards 1980, 10; Hewison 1988, 152.

2 In fact, the reason why Fry and others went to Hollywood was that they were no longer welcome. Fry's first play after 1956, *Curtmantle*, was produced in Holland and Vienna before the RSC decided to do it in London. And compared with his prodigious heights between 1948 and 1950, he subsequently wrote very little. As he recalls:

> I think one writes best when you feel that someone is waiting to receive it, that you have ears attending, as it were. One had rather ceased to feel that. [...] I think it was partly my own fault; I think I just gave up too easily, or something.
>
> (Fry 1992)

Rattigan similarly recalled: 'overnight almost, we were told we were old-fashioned and effete and corrupt and finished, and although I was a decade or two younger than Coward or Priestley I somehow accepted Tynan's verdict and went off to Hollywood to write film scripts'. Sheridan Morley, 'Rattigan at 65', *The Times*, 9 May 1977; Theatre Museum, London (TM) Personal File: Terence Rattigan.

3 'New Voices', *Plays and Players* vi, 1 (October 1958), p. 20.

1 'WHY SHOULD I CARE?'

1 *A Tribute to Ivor Novello* (2 CDs), LC 0464, EMI Music For Pleasure, 1993.

2 Anderson 1957 and *Encore* vi, 2 (March–April 1959), pp. 21–27.

3 That this is residually Leavisite may be detected in the organicist metaphors used to describe the working-class way of life: Williams talks of culture 'as an idea of the tending of *natural* growth' (1993). Hoggart describes life in a northern industrial town as having 'a kind of organic quality, closer and more varied relations between the social

groups' (Hoggart and Williams 1960, 26). As their work developed these tropes evaporated, yet the traces are at this point still evident.

2 THE NEW ELIZABETHANS

1 This name was adopted in April 1940; until then it had been operating as the *Committee* for the Encouragement of Music and Art. To avoid confusion, I have used the later name throughout.

2 'Use of Treasury Grant', *The Times*, 17 June 1940, p. 4.

3 'Music and the Arts', *The Times*, 15 June 1940, p. 7.

4 Indeed, it appears that anything which smacked of education was for Keynes an intrusion into properly artistic activity; one target of his scorn was the British Institute of Adult Education's 'Art for the People' project (Glasgow 1975, 268). As its director, W.E. Williams suggests, he objected to the 'guide lecturers' that accompanied the exhibitions (1971, 22). In 1943 CEMA, under Keynes, set up a touring exhibition scheme which implicitly rivalled Williams's; however, this one toured mainly to galleries rather than non-specialist sites (White 1975, 42).

5 At the Public Records Office, there is a large file dating from the late forties devoted to schemes to develop a national policy on 'the enjoyment of leisure' (Public Records Office (PRO) T 227/69).

6 'Organising the Audience', *Civic Entertainment* i, 2 (January–February 1949), p. 17.

7 *CEMA Bulletin* 27 (July 1942), p. 1.

8 Landstone denies that this was automatic, but his argument and language is evasive (1953, 36, 72–73). He cites in support of his claim the fact that there were exempt societies who were not associated with CEMA, but that is irrelevant to the proposition that CEMA association brought with it automatic exemption. He even admits 'I cannot think of any one company, Arts Council-recommended, that was refused exemption by the Customs' (73).

9 'The Truth About Tennents', iv, 91 (11 February 1950), pp. 4–5; Gordon Sandiston also notes the interdependence of many of these companies but denies that there is anything sinister about the set-up, and reserves criticism from the individual producing managers (1948, 57–58).

10 *Our Time* iv, 5 (December 1944), p. 3.

11 Collins 1947a, 1; Jackson 1946, 13; 'Professionals Will Regulate Entry', *New Theatre* iii, 2 (July 1946), p. 13.

12 Priestley 1947a, 31–32 and 1947b, 29–30; Dean 1945, 3; Johns 1945, 27–30; Ustinov 1950a, 62.

13 *Theatre Newsletter* i, 13 (4 January 1947), p. 9.

14 'Theatre in the Second Battle of Britain', *New Theatre* iii, 10 (March–April 1947), pp. 1–2; *Theatre Newsletter* i, 18 (22 March 1947), p. 1.

15 *New Theatre* iv, 8 (February 1948), p. 6–7.

16 'Now For The Real Work', *New Theatre* iv, 9 (March 1948), p. 1.

17 *Theatre Industry Journal* xxvi, 116 (April 1948), p. 69.

18 PRO T227/57, pp. 99–100.

19 'Entertainment Tax', *Theatre Industry Journal* xxvi, 116 (April 1948), pp. 57–62.

20 The Arts Council was asked for its views, and Ernest Pooley declared in favour of such a reduction (PRO T 171/395 E52, Letter [from treasury official] to C.H. Veale, 20 March 1948). Although they had previously acknowledged that tax reductions without rent control would only favour the theatre owners (PRO T 227/199, 19 August 1947), they were themselves rattled by the radicalism of the conference. When the plans were announced at the end of 1947, Mary Glasgow warned of 'far-reaching recommendations' being issued, and remarked, 'it might be useful for the Chancellor to receive the Council's recommendations before those of the conference' (PRO T 227/199, 9 October 1947).

21 'Progress-Fulfilment', *New Theatre* iv, 11 (May 1948), pp. 1–2.

22 'The Arts Council', *New Theatre* v, 1 (July 1948), p. 1.

23 cf. *Theatre Industry Journal* xxvi, 123 (November 1948), p. 200; *Civic Entertainment* i, 2 (January–February 1948), p. 14.

24 A treasury official notes that it might want to look at issues like rent control which 'are perhaps not those which we should want discussed' (PRO T 227/101, Hale to Proctor, 23 April 1948). Pooley suggests ignoring it and hoping it goes away (ibid. Pooley to Cripps, 27 May 1948). Cripps delayed, waiting for the findings of the Leasehold Committee, looking into business rents. The TMA strongly lobbied the committee, and their interim report in July 1949 (Cmnd. 7706) recommended exempting theatre buildings from rent control.

25 *Theatre World* xli, 247 (August 1945), p. 5.

26 *Theatre Today – A Miscellany* (No. 1), London: Saturn Press, 1948, p. 10.

27 'The National Theatre Bill', *Civic Entertainment* i, 2 (January–February 1949), p. 15.

28 Tennents were still technically in association with the Arts Council, though they never took up any of their guarantees-against-loss, and, having served their purpose, the connection was formally severed after the Festival.

29 Davies (1982) offers a good, if brief, account of the ABCA play unit, and Fawkes (1978, Chap. 8) adds some fascinating detail from the shows themselves recalled by participants and audience members. See also Willis 1991, 37–39, Chambers 1989, 203, Noble 1948, 95–97. For contemporary comments and reviews see: Stevens 1941 for the origins of ABCA; 'Notes and Comments', *Our Time* iv, 4 (November 1944), p. 3, for a stunned reaction to the first performances from the Play Unit; a review by Montagu Slater of their brief season at the Arts Theatre, can be found in *Our Time* v, 1 (August 1945), p. 20.

30 *Our Time* v, 12 (July 1946), p. 269.

31 John Andrews reviewed Theatre Workshop's *The Flying Doctor, Johnny Noble and Uranium 235* in *Theatre Newsletter* i, vi (5 October 1946), calling them 'probably the most interesting experimental theatre group in the country today' (11). Henry Adler

followed with an article on them in *Theatre Newsletter* i, 11–12 (14 December 1946), p. 12. In 'Theatre with a Method: Enterprise and Co-operation,' *Our Time* v, 12 (July 1946), pp. 258–259, W. Davidson discussed the same three plays plus Lorca's *Don Perlimpin*. Montagu Slater compared their work favourably with Theatre '46 in the same journal, vi, 6 (January 1947), p. 135. *New Theatre* iii, 1 (June 1946), pp. 20–21, has a favourable review of Theatre Workshop, and Frederick Piffard in 'New Themes for Old', *New Theatre* iii, 2 (July 1946), p. 17, endorsed their 'remarkable' work.

32 *The Stage*, 28 July 1955, p. 1.
33 Littlewood remembers it only as £100 (1994, 463).
34 'Eclipse,' *Plays and Players* viii, 3 (December 1960), p. 20.
35 *Encore* iii, 2 (Easter 1956), p. 30.
36 Groundling, 'A View from the Gods', *Encore* iii, 5 (June–July 1957), p. 4.

3 A WRITER'S THEATRE

1 *Illustrated London News*, 11 March 1939. All reviews and articles, unless otherwise stated, are from the Theatre Museum (TM) Production File (PF): *Johnson over Jordan* (1939).
2 *The Times*, 6 March 1939.
3 'Eclipse', *Plays and Players* viii, 3 (December 1960), p. 20.
4 *Theatre World* lii, 376 (May 1956), p. 26.
5 'No Medals', *Plays and Players* viii, 5 (February 1961), p. 20.
6 'Memories of the Theatre: A Double Lecture', *The Times*, 5 January 1954, p. 5.
7 'Creative Imagination and Acting: Sybil Thorndike's Lecture', *The Times* (9 January 1954), p.8.
8 Bentham himself was a life-long devotee of what he called Colour Music, the projection of coloured lights, often with the accompaniment of music. 'Just as the piano can forsake accompaniment for solo work, alone or with an orchestra, so one day we may expect solo lighting' (1950, 299). Strand had its own small theatre in which Bentham operated such events. On one occasion he even tried it without any musical accompaniment, but, by his own admission, 'the result was uncomfortable' (319).
9 'Making the World a Stage: Mr Devine on Illusion and Reality', *The Times*, 2 January 1954, p. 8.
10 *The Times*, 8 January 1954, p. 7.
11 *The Times*, 11 January 1954, p. 7.
12 'Theatrical Designs on View,' *The Listener* lviii, 1490 (17 October 1957), p. 599.
13 The only designer that had this kind of status at the early Court was Roger Furse, brought in for the calculatedly commercial *Look After Lulu* (1959).
14 Less flatteringly, Osborne recalls how she came to be known as Jocelyn Brown, because of the dull colour of most of her sets (1991a, 10).

4 OH FOR EMPTY SEATS

1 Noël Coward, *Blithe Spirit* Curtain speech, 16 June 1941. Copy at National Sound Archive.

2 John Sommerfield, '*Once a Criminal*' and '*Swinging the Gate*', 20 July 1940, Mass-Observation Archive (M-O A): Topic Collection (TC) Live Entertainment, Box 4 File E.

3 *Theatre World* xxxiii, 181 (February 1940), p. 29.

4 *Theatre World* xxxvii, 220 (May 1943), p. 28.

5 *Theatre World* xli, 240 (January 1945), p. 8.

6 A Mass Observation report on the Manchester premiere of *While the Sun Shines* records several rounds of applause for patriotic sentiments, M-O A: TC Live Entertainment, Box 3 File K. A report by an actress notes that in 'most places I have been to, I have got exit rounds. Not of course every night, nor every part, but quite a number'. D: BV5250. Theatre Report. 25 November 1947. M-O A: TC Films, Box 15 File I.

7 Beachcomber, cited in *Theatre Digest* 4 (1949), p. 161.

8 DR: 2984. Theatre and Cinema Report, 24 July 1948. M-O A: TC Films, Box 15 File I. (Diary entry, 21 July.)

9 DR: 2984. Film and Theatre Audiences, 16 September 1947. Ibid. (Diary Entry, 20 August.)

10 'Second Thoughts on First Nights', *Punch,* 23 April 1952. In: TM Miscellaneous File (MF): Audiences.

11 'Chocolates in the Theatre Annoy Dame Sybil', *Daily Telegraph,* 30 December 1952. In ibid.

12 'Should Audiences Eat Chocolates?' *Daily Mail,* 29 December 1953. In ibid.

13 *Plays and Players* i, 5 (February 1954), p. 3.

14 *Theatre World* lii, 376 (May 1956), p. 26.

15 'British Playwriting: Cause without a Rebel', *Encore* iii, 5 (June–July 1957), p. 17.

16 Tele-Obituary for Tony Richardson. *The Late Show,* 20 November 1991, BBC 2.

17 'Cheers from the Stalls' (15 May 1976), in TM MF: Audiences.

18 Osborne used the term himself in an interview on BBC's *Panorama,* 9 July 1956 (Ritchie 1988, 27). He claims its authorship in an interview for the Waterstones *Winter Catalogue,* 1991.

19 A copy of this leaflet is in TM PF: *Serjeant Musgrave's Dance* (1959).

20 See, for example, a letter from Harold Whitehead in *The Times,* 20 February 1954, p. 8.

21 e.g. 'There is nothing wrong with rock 'n' roll, there is only something wrong with it every day; three cheers for the whist drive and the football game, but God help the man who cannot enjoy something more' (Wesker 1958, 102). 'There's nothing wrong with football, only there's something wrong with *only* football. There's nothing wrong with rock 'n' rolling, only God preserve me from the girl that can do nothing else!' (Beatie quoting Ronnie, Wesker 1964, 89).

5 SOMETHING ENGLISH

1 *Plays and Players* iii, 2 (November 1955), p. 5.
2 Parmentier cites figures which suggest that a majority supported force in July but opposed it in October (1980, 435); Kyle shows that even early in the crisis, while many supported force, if backed by the United Nations and/or the United States, far smaller numbers supported unilateral action (1991, 226); Thomas cites polls from shortly after Anglo-French intervention, in which 37 per cent declared themselves in support of the action, and 44 per cent against, which certainly offered no public mandate for action (1967, 133).
3 David H. Shipman, *Spectator*, 15 November 1957, p. 643.
4 *Plays and Players* iii, 6 (March 1956), 3.
5 *Encore* iii, 2 (Easter 1956), p. 4.
6 Essays and poems by Brecht include 'A New Technique of Acting', trans. Eric Bentley, *New Theatre* v, 9 (March 1949), pp. 20–22. 'German War Primer', trans. Herbert Marshall, *Our Time* i, 11 (February 1942), pp. 7–9; 'The Soldiers Wife', trans. Honor Arundel, *Our Time* ii, 3 (June 1942), pp. 11–12. The *New Reasoner* carried two poems by Brecht in i, 3 (Winter 1957), pp. 55–56. Articles and chapters on Brecht included Bentley (1948 – an extract from *The Playwright as Thinker*); Peter De Mendelssohn (1950–1951). There was also a chapter on Epic Theatre in Gorelik's *New Theatres for Old* (1947, Ch. 9). Brecht's plays were only slowly published in English. By the end of the forties all that had appeared were the Gollancz edition of *The Private Life of the Master Race* and University of Minnesota's *Parables for the Theatre* (containing *Chalk Circle* and *Good Person*).
7 'Actors Reply to Brecht', *New Theatre* v, 10 (April 1949), p. 15.
8 e.g. *The Stage*, 28 July 1955, p. 1.
9 *Encore* vi, 4 (September–October, 59), p. 4.

6 SOMETHING (UN)SPOKEN

1 The word 'gay' crossed the Atlantic to Britain and became used widely in the forties. In America, it had become, suggests Cory, the most popular term used by homosexual men (1953, 107). The British Peter Wildeblood recalls first hearing the word in the 1940s and glosses it as 'an American euphemism for homosexual' (1957, 29). By the fifties, the term is referred to more widely, beyond the homosexual subculture (e.g. West 1955, 28–29). I shall also use the word 'queer', since it was also a widespread term of homosexual self-description.
2 *Hansard Parliamentary Debates*, Volume 521, 3 December 1953, London: HMSO, p. 1298.
3 *News of the World*, 1 November 1953, p. 6.
4 'Homosexuality (Treatment)', *Hansard Parliamentary Debates*, Vol. 526, 28 April 1954, London: HMSO, p. 1753.
5 *Hansard Parliamentary Debates*, Volume 548, 16 February 1956, London: HMSO, p. 2525, and 'Wolfenden Report', 1957, pp. 43–44.

6 Ian McKellen's address at Robert's Memorial Service, 8 April 1992, p. 3. In: TM Personal File: Robert Eddison.

7 Although hardly a rigorous survey, the published personal stories of gay men often involve pivotally theatrical encounters (Farnham and Marshall 1989, 17, 44, 59, 86, 96, 115, 130; Porter and Weeks 1991, 24, 56, 67, 74–75).

8 'Sir John Gielgud Fined', *Evening Standard*, 21 October 1953, p. 1. (Insisting on the 'Sir' is a plain piece of trouble-making.) It is worth remembering, however, that on his first stage appearance following the arrest, the audience gave him a standing ovation (Huggett 1989, 429–431).

9 A list could be made of lesbians in the theatre at the time, but it would probably be much shorter. This is largely to do with the relative marginality of women in the upper reaches of the theatre at any time, and also the different position of lesbians. There are two factors in this: since many lesbian sexual acts were not actually *illegal*, they did not inspire the outcry that met male homosexuality. Another reason derives from the fact that most writers of the period are convinced that women lacked any real sexual urge. The BMA's submission to the Wolfenden committee in 1955 noted that 'the promiscuous Lesbian, sometimes addicted to perverted physical practices, who delights in seducing and corrupting weaker members of her sex, is relatively rare' (18); Eustace Chesser suggested that women's sexuality was 'far more diffuse' than men's (1959, 93). It should be noted that this feeling was not universal; Frank Caprio warns of 'the naïve and ill-informed [...being] initiated into lesbian practices', and concludes that 'lesbianism is capable of influencing the stability of our social structure' (1952, viii), which – who knows? – may even be true.

But the combination of women's marginalisation in the theatre and the presumed modesty of their sexual appetites has meant that the information is far less available about which of the many women working in the theatre at the time were lesbian. A modest list might include Gwen Ffrangcon-Davis, Clemence Dane, Tallulah Bankhead, Lyn Fontanne, Daphne du Maurier and Caryl Jenner, but expanding this list and discussing the position of lesbians in British theatre of the time is more appropriately a task for someone else; nonetheless while I shall be focusing on male homosexuality, there are overlaps which it would be unduly pious for me to try to avoid.

10 'British Playwriting: Cause Without A Rebel', *Encore* iii, 5 (June–July 1957), p. 34.

11 Memo, Norman Gwatkin to Lord Chamberlain, 18 April 1955, British Library: Lord Chamberlain's Correspondence [LCCorr.] *South*. 1955/1791.

12 cf. *Observer*, 20 February 1955, *Tatler*, 16 March 1955, and *Daily Express*, 18 February 1955. In TM PF: *Serious Charge* (1955).

13 Letter, 'A. Mother' to the Lord Chamberlain, in LCCorr. *Serious Charge*, op. cit.

14 Reader's Report, St Vincent Troubridge, 21 January 1958, LCCorr. *Valmouth*. 1958/690.

15 St Vincent Troubridge, 21 January 1958, op cit.
16 Reader's Report, Geoffrey Dearmer, LCCorr. *Jonathan*. 1947/8718. In fact Melville has admitted to writing the play to have 'strong homosexual undertones' which would imply that 'David was kinky for Jonathan' (1970, 9).
17 Manuscript note [undated], Norman Gwatkin, ibid.
18 Reader's Report, St Vincent Troubridge, 1 January 1953, LCCorr. *The Maids*. 1953/191.
19 Manuscript note [unsigned and undated, though the handwriting looks like Norman Gwatkin's], ibid.
20 Reader's Report, St Vincent Troubridge, 20 February 1953, LCCorr. *The Maids* (second version). 1953/5250.
21 Letter, Mrs W. Wilson to the Lord Chamberlain; 23 November 1953, LCCorr. *Third Person*. 1951/3375.
22 e.g. 'Hopes for 1954', *Plays and Players* i, 3 (December 1953), p. 3, announced that it was looking forward to seeing *South* and *Tea and Sympathy*.
23 'New York's Matinee Idol', *Plays and Players* i, 1 (October 1953), p. 9.
24 David Raher, 'How Press Agents Keep Fit', *Plays and Players* i, 7 (April 1954), p. 17. In June of that year, the magazine printed a further two torso shots (23). This was commented on sardonically in a letter in the following issue (July 1954, p. 17).
25 e.g. *Plays and Players* ii, 9 (June 1955), p. 27. Of course, it would be impossible, and would spoil the fun, to prove that this was a gay ad. However, the fact that photographs are requested perhaps lends support to this view. In the case of an advert in which a 'YOUNG LONDON BACHELOR' wishes to meet similar for theatre trips and holidays (*Plays and Players* xi, 4 (January 1964), p. 51) it seems hard to imagine what other reason there might be for mention the marital status. But the glass closet always defers final proof.
26 *Plays and Players* x, 10 (July 1963), p. 30.
27 *Plays and Players* ix, 8 (May 1962), p. 39.
28 *Plays and Players* xi, 2 (November 1963), p. 51.
29 *Plays and Players* xi, 6 (March 1964), p. 51.
30 *Plays and Players* ix, 9 (June 1962), p. 51.
31 Vince's first advertisement is in *Plays and Players* ii, 3 (December 1954), p. 4, but he advertises throughout the decade. The homoeroticism of the images is another kind of 'glass closet' mechanism, since it is impossible to define whether an image is *of itself* homosexual; in one advertisement, he offers a more familiar encoding, when he roguishly announces the arrival of 'the latest French Bikini in Gay Striped Quick Dry Poplin', *Plays and Players* iv, 8 (May 1957), p. 36. The 'clone' advertisement is in *Plays and Players* ii, 6 (March 1955), p. 2. Another gay-identified clothes designer, Nicholas Perry, advertises towards the end of the fifties, his models often being bare-chested; e.g. *Plays and Players* iv, 3 (January 1957), p. 2 (fig. 6.4).
32 *Evening Standard*, 1 December 1951, in: TM MF: *Censorship*.

33 *Daily Mail*, 3 October 1958; *The Times*, 3 October 1958. TM PF: *Valmouth* (1958).

34 Letter, Norman Gwatkin to Phil Starr, 20 January 1958, LCCorr: *We're No Ladies*. 1958/667.

35 Reader's Report, C.D. Heriot, 17 January 1958, ibid.

36 Letter, H.C.R.A. Bennett to the Lord Chamberlain, 6 January 1958, ibid.

37 Letter, A.P.J. Rydekker to the LCC, 5 February 1958, ibid. [my emphasis.]

38 Letter, Brian Boss to the LCC, 6 February 1958, ibid.

39 Report, R.J. Hill, 7 February 1958, ibid. The report is brief and I shall not give page references. I have also clarified his erratic emphasis, layout and spelling.

40 Information (and spelling) taken from the programme, included with Hill's report, ibid.

41 This second report is attached to the original and is also dated 7 February 1958.

42 R.J. Hill, Manuscript note attached to his report, 7 February 1958, ibid.

43 Letter, Norman Gwatkin to the Clerk of the LCC, 10 February 1958, ibid.

44 Letter, Lord Chamberlain on behalf of the LCC to A.P.J. Rydekker, 12 February 1958, ibid.

7 SISTER MARY DISCIPLINE

1 See the submissions to the Wolfenden committee by the Institute for the Study and Treatment of Delinquency (5–7), the BMA (11) and the Church Information Board (11), also Derrick Sherwin Bailey's *Sexual Offenders and Social Punishment*, separately submitted to the committee (29). Wolfenden holds out against adopting the approach (11–12), but traces of it recur throughout the report (e.g. 13, 20, 26–27), and more intensively in Desmond Curran and Joseph Whitby's appended Medical Note (72–76).

  West (1955, 80–82), Eustace Chesser (1958, 51; 1959, Chapter 2), Allen (1958, 46), Caprio (1952, 110–120), Neustatter (1955, 75–76), and Westwood (1952, 29–43) all adopt quasi-Freudian positions. These are works of popular psychiatry. I am using them because they were widely read, and so played a significant role in shaping the public understanding of homosexuality. Nonetheless, Kenneth Lewes's history of *The Psychoanalytic Theory of Male Homosexuality* suggests that the more academic models expressed similar views (140–172).

2 Curiously, Nicholas de Jongh, in *Not in Front of the Audience*, uses the Jungian notion of 'Shadow Projection' – 'the device by which we unconsciously attribute to others those negative characteristics denied or repressed in ourselves' (7) – to explain revulsion against homosexuality, unaware, it seems, of its ideological embeddedness in the very debates with which he is engaging.

3 Reader's report, C.D. Heriot, 16 March 1955, LCCorr. *The Bad Seed*. 1955/7747.
4 Reader's report, C.D. Heriot, 17 March 1958, LCCorr. *Tiresias*. 1958/875.
5 Reader's report, St Vincent Troubridge, 28 September 1958, LCCorr. *No Concern of Mine*. 1958/1332.
6 See C.L. Gordon's Letter to Osbert Peake MP at the Home Office, 25 January 1940, and J.F. Henderson's Letter to the Director of Public Prosecutions, 22 February 1940, both pursuing prosecutions should *Queer People* be produced, even in a club theatre. LCCorr. *Queer People*. LR 1940.
7 Manuscript Note, Earl of Scarbrough, on Reader's report, C.D. Heriot, LCCorr. *A Lonesome Road*. 1959/1831.
8 Reader's report, St Vincent Troubridge, 29 May 1958, LCCorr. *Suddenly Last Summer*. 1958/1120.
9 For example, despite insisting on the cuts listed above, the Lord Chamberlain passed Agatha Christie's *The Mousetrap* in its entirety, which features a gay man and a lesbian. Their sexuality is never entirely explicit, but their coding is fairly obvious. Christopher Wren, as he is called, is a 'neurotic young man' with long hair who wears a 'woven artistic tie' and his first comments are on the interior décor (1954, 5). He also has a childish mind: 'I adore nursery rhymes, don't you? Always so tragic and *macabre*. That's why children like them' (9). At another point, 'He sings "Little Jack Horner" and chuckles to himself, giving the impression of being slightly unhinged mentally' (12). Miss Casewell, on the other hand, is 'a young woman of a manly type' (10); she speaks in a 'deep, manly voice', tends to laugh 'stridently' (11), and has a vigorous handshake (12). (And the play's resolution suggests Christie's belief in the genetic character of sexual deviance.) The reader's report refers to a 'mannish woman guest' and generally to the 'queer lot' staying at the guesthouse. But no action is taken to change these representations. Reader's report, C.D. Heriot, 17 September 1952, LCCorr. *The Mousetrap*. 1952/4570.
10 Manuscript Note, C.D. Heriot, 25 February 1955, on Reader's report, St Vincent Troubridge, 24 February 1955, LCCorr. *Personal Enemy*, 1955.
11 Reader's report, C.D. Heriot, 28 April 1952, LCCorr. *The Pink Room*. 1952/4196.
12 Licence, 15 May 1952, ibid.
13 Reader's report, C.D. Heriot, 20 November 1951, LCCorr. *Third Person*. 1951/3375.
14 Licence, 31 December 1951, ibid.
15 Memorandum, 'The Controller' to Lord Chamberlain, 30 September 1953, LCCorr. *South*. 1955/1791.
16 *Illustrated London News*, 6 October 1956, in TM PF: *The Children's Hour* (1956).
17 'Evading the Censor', *Plays and Players* iii, 7 (April 1956), p. 14.
18 'New Club Venture', *Plays and Players* iv, 1 (October 1956), p. 20.
19 'Alice in Theatreland', *Plays and Players* iv, 1 (October 1956), p. 4.

20 'Uncensored', *Plays and Players* vi, 3 (December 1958), p. 20.

21 Richard Findlater, 'Does Victoria *STILL* need the censor?' *Evening Standard*, 19 October 1956. In TM MF: Censorship.

22 St Vincent Troubridge to Norman W. Gwatkin, 30 April 1957, LCCorr. *The Entertainer*. 1957. The Bill referred to was the private member's *Censorship of Plays (Repeal Act) Bill* 1949, which, despite being carried on its second reading, never became law (Johnston 1990, 153–154).

23 Letter, Norman Gwatkin to Earl of Scarbrough, 25 October 1956, LCCorr. *Tea and Sympathy*. 1954.

24 Memo, Norman Gwatkin, 31 October 1956, ibid. The same threat is made in the 30 April 1957 letter, op cit.

25 Cf. Wildeblood 1957, 51–54; 'The Police and the Montagu Case,' *New Statesman and Nation* xlvii (10 April 1954), pp. 456–457; Hyde 1970, 216–225.

26 'Sexual Offences (No. 2) Bill. Standing Committee F', *Official Report*, 19 April 1967, HMSO.

27 *Salad Days* LC 6646 EMI Classics 1994.

28 'Homosexual Offences and Prostitution (Report)', *Hansard Parliamentary Debates*, Volume 596, 26 November 1958, HMSO, pp. 389–390.

29 *Daily Mail*, 20 September 1956. TM PF: *The Children's Hour* (1956).

30 Hope-Wallace, *The Times*, 26 March 1958; *Observer*, 30 March 1958. TM PF: *The Catalyst*.

31 *Daily Telegraph*, 2 May 1958; Trewin, *Illustrated London News*, 17 May 1958; Tynan, *Observer*, 4 May 1958. TM PF: *Quaint Honour*.

32 *Daily Mail*, 31 October 1951. TM PF: *Third Person*.

33 *Daily Telegraph*, 31 October 1951, ibid.

34 *The Times*, 31 October 1951, ibid.

35 Conway talks of the 'unhealthy influence' of this 'psychopathic young man', *Evening Standard*, 31 October 1951; Wiltshire, *Daily Mail*, 31 October 1951, Worsley, *New Statesman*, 17 November 1951, and the *Observer* all refer to him as a 'neurotic'. In ibid.

36 *Plays and Players* ii, 8 (May 1955), p. 16.

37 Letter, Emile Littler to Assistant Comptroller, 13 December 1951, LCCorr. 1951/3375.

38 Milton Shulman, 'The Prude Barrier Takes a Dent', *Evening Standard*, 20 September 1956, p. 7.

39 *Punch*, 29 September 1956. TM PF: *The Children's Hour* (1956).

40 'These are Taboo', *Plays and Players* ii, 5 (February 1955), p. 4.

41 *Observer*, 7 November 1954. TM PF: *The Immoralist*.

42 Review of *The Immoralist*, *Tatler*, 17 November 1954. In LCCorr. *The Immoralist*. 1958/1494. Darlington, *Daily Telegraph*, 9 November 1953. TM PF: *Serious Charge* (1953).

43 Wilson, *Daily Mail*, 29 August 1957; *Daily Telegraph*, 29 August 1957; Tynan, *Observer*, 1 September 1957; Gulley, *Tatler and Bystander*, 11 September 1957. TM PF: *A Lonesome Road*.

44 Cecil Wilson, 'Lord Blue Pencil Lifts Stage Ban', *Daily Mail*, 7 November 1958; TM MF: Censorship.
45 Kenneth Allsop, 'Suddenly...SEX without a snigger', *Daily Mail*, 26 November 1958, ibid.
46 Quoted, Cecil Wilson, 'Lord Blue Pencil...' op cit.
47 Quoted in 'Ban Ends On Plays About Homosexuals', *Daily Telegraph*, 7 November 1958. TM MF: Censorship.
48 *Look Back in Anger*. Woodfall Films, 1959. (My transcription.)

AFTERWORD

1 Tele-Obituary for Tony Richardson. *The Late Show*. 20 November 1991. BBC 2.

REFERENCES

Adler, Henry (1957) 'Bare Bones', *Encore* iv, 1 (September–October), pp. 21–25.

—— (1961) 'Brecht and After', *Drama* New Series, 63 (Winter), pp. 29–31.

Allen, Clifford (1958) *Homosexuality: Its Nature, Causation and Treatment*, London: Staples.

Allsop, Kenneth (1958) *The Angry Decade: A Survey of the Cultural Revolt of the Nineteen-Fifties*, London: Peter Owen.

Amis, Kingsley (1957) 'That Certain Revulsion', *Encore* iii, 5 (June–July), pp. 10–12.

Anderson, Lindsay (1957) 'Vital Theatre?' *Encore* iv, 2 (November–December), pp. 10–14.

—— (1958a) 'Art: Battleground or Playground', in *Artist, Critic & Teacher*, eds Alex Jacobs and Paddy Whannel, London: Joint Council for Education through Art, pp. 2–10.

—— (1958b) 'Letter', in Marowitz, *et al.* 1981, pp. 48–51.

—— (1981) 'The Court Style', in Findlater 1981, pp. 143–148.

Anderson, Perry (1965) 'The Left in the Fifties', *New Left Review* 29 (January–February), pp. 3–18.

Anderson, Robert (1955) *Tea and Sympathy*, London: Samuel French.

'Anomaly' (1928) *The Invert and his Social Adjustment*, London: Baillere, Tindall and Cox.

Ansorge, Peter (1997) *From Liverpool to Los Angeles: On Writing for Theatre, Film and Television*, London: Faber & Faber.

Arden, John (1960) 'A Thoroughly Romantic View', *London Magazine* vii, 7 (July), pp. 11–15.

—— (1966) *Serjeant Musgrave's Dance: an Un-historic Parable*, London: Methuen.

The Arts Council of Great Britain: What It Is and What It Does (1950), London: Arts Council.

The Arts in Wartime: A Report on the Work of CEMA, 1942 & 1943 (1944) London: CEMA.

Arts Council of Great Britain (1949) *Fourth Annual Report 1948–49*, London: Arts Council.

—— (1951) *Sixth Annual Report 1950–1951*, London: Arts Council.

—— (1952) *The Arts in Great Britain: Seventh Annual Report, 1951–1952*, London: Arts Council.

—— (1953) *The Public and the Arts: Eighth Annual Report, 1952–1953*, London: Arts Council.

—— (1954) *Public Responsibility for the Arts: Ninth Annual Report, 1953–1954*, London: Arts Council.

—— (1956) *The First Ten Years: Eleventh Annual Report, 1955–1956*, London: Arts Council.

—— (1957) *Art in the Red: Twelfth Annual Report, 1956–1957*, London: Arts Council.

—— (1958) *A New Pattern of Patronage: Thirteenth Annual Report, 1957–1958*, London: Arts Council.

Austin, J.L. (1980) *How to do Things with Words*, corrected 2nd edn, ed. J.O. Urmson and Marina Sbisà, Oxford: Oxford University Press.

Baer, Marc (1992) *Theatre and Disorder in Late Georgian London*, Oxford: Clarendon.

Bailey, Derrick Sherwin (ed.) (1956) *Sexual Offenders and Social Punishment*, London: Church Information Board.

Baker, Roger (1968) *Drag: A History of Female Impersonation on the Stage*, London: Triton.

Baldry, Harold (1981) *The Case for the Arts*, London: Secker & Warburg.

Barker, Clive (1966) 'Look Back in Anger – The Turning Point: An Assessment of the Importance of John Osborne's First Play in the Development of the British Theatre', *Zeitschrift für Anglistik und Amerikanistik* xiv, pp. 367–371.

Barker, Howard (1993) *Arguments for a Theatre*, 2nd edn, Austin: University of Texas Press.

Barnett, Corelli (1972) *The Collapse of British Power*, London: Methuen.

Barthes, Roland (1975) *The Pleasure of the Text*, trans. Richard Miller, New York: Hill and Wang.

Bartlett, Neil (1993) *Night After Night*, London: Methuen.

Beaton, Cecil (1965) *The Years Between: Diaries 1939–1944*, London: Weidenfeld & Nicolson.

Benjamin, Walter (1992) *Illuminations*, trans. Harry Zohn, London: Fontana.

Bennett, Alan *et al.* (1987) *The Complete Beyond the Fringe*, ed. Roger Wilmut, London: Methuen.

Bentham, Frederick (1950) *Stage Lighting*, London: Pitman.

—— (1970) *The Art of Stage Lighting*, revised edn, London: Pitman.

—— (1992) *Sixty Years of Light Work*, London: Strand Lighting.

Bentley, Eric (1948) 'Berthold Brecht as Thinker', in *Theatre Today: A Miscellany* (No. 1), London: Saturn, pp. 16–20.

Bernstein, Alec (1948) 'The Scene', *New Theatre* iv, 9 (March), pp. 10–11.

Bogdanor, Vernon (1970) 'The Labour Party in Opposition, 1951–1964', in Bogdanor and Skidelsky 1970, pp. 78–116.

Bogdanor, Vernon and Robert Skidelsky (eds) (1970) *The Age of Affluence 1951–1964*, London: Macmillan.

Boland, Bridget (1949) *Cockpit*, in *Plays of the Year: 1: 1948–49*, ed. J.C. Trewin, London: Elek, pp. 25–118.

Bolt, Robert (1958) 'English Theatre Today: I. The Importance of Shape', in Hobson 1958, pp. 140–145.

Bond, Edward (1980) 'The Romans and the Establishment's Figleaf', *The Guardian* (3 November).

Brecht, Bertolt (1993) *Journals 1934–1955*, trans. Hugh Rorrison, ed. John Willett, London: Methuen.

Brenton, Howard (1976) 'Ronald Hayman Talks to Howard Brenton About His Work', *New Review* iii, 29, pp. 4–20.

Bridie, James *et al.* (1944) 'The State and the Arts', *The Author* liv, 4 (Summer), pp. 48–54.

Brine, Adrian (1961) 'Mac Davies is no *Clochard*', *Drama*, New Series, 61 (Summer), pp. 35–37.

British Drama League (1945) *Exhibition: 'The British Playhouse from Fit-up to National Theatre'*, Catalogue, London: British Drama League.

British Medical Association (1955) *Homosexuality and Prostitution*, London: British Medical Association.

Brome, Vincent (1988) *J.B. Priestley*, London: Hamish Hamilton.

Brook, Peter (1950) 'The Contemporary Theatre: The Vitality of the English Stage'. *The Listener* (4 May), pp. 781–782.

—— (1955) 'The Influence of Gordon Craig in Theory and Practice', *Drama* New Series, 37 (Summer), pp. 33–36.

—— (1959) 'Oh For Empty Seats!' in Marowitz *et al.* 1981, pp. 68–74.

—— (1988) *The Shifting Point: Forty Years of Theatrical Exploration 1946–1987*, London: Methuen.

Brown, Ivor (1955) 'The Best of 1955', *Plays and Players* iii, 3 (December), pp. 10–11.

—— (ed.) (1956) *Theatre 1955–6*, London: Max Reinhardt.

—— (1960) 'Theatre, Press and Public', *Drama* New Series, 59 (Winter), pp. 28–30.

Brown, John Russell (1982) *A Short Guide to Modern British Drama*, London: Heinemann Educational.

Browne, Henzie and E. Martin Browne (1945) *The Pilgrim Story*, London: Frederick Muller.

Browne, Terry (1975) *Playwrights' Theatre: the English Stage Company at the Royal Court*, London: Pitman.

Burton, E.J. (ed.) (1959) *Theatre: Alive or Dead?*, London: Joint Council for Education Through Art.

Cannan, Denis (1951) *Captain Carvallo*, London: Rupert Hart-Davis.
—— (1956) *Misery Me*, London: Samuel French.
Caprio, Frank S. (1952) *Female Homosexuality: A Psychodynamic Study of Lesbianism*, London: Peter Owen.
Carr, W.I. (1958) 'Mr Osborne and an Indifferent Society', *Universities and Left Review* i, 4 (Spring), pp. 32–33.
Cary, Falkland L. (1945) *Practical Playwriting*, London: Simpkin Marshall.
Chambers, Colin (1989) *The Story of Unity Theatre*, London: Lawrence & Wishart.
Chambers, Colin and Mike Prior (1987) *Playwright's Progress: Patterns of Postwar Drama*, Oxford: Amber Lane.
Charques, R.D. (ed.) (1938) *Footnotes to the Theatre*, London: Peter Davies.
Cheshire, D.F. (1984) 'J.B. Priestley's *Johnson over Jordan* and the Work of Edward Carrick', *Theatrephile* i, 2 (March), pp. 15–20.
Chesser, Eustace (1958) *Live and Let Live: The Moral of the Wolfenden Report*, London: Heinemann.
—— (1959) *Odd Man Out: Homosexuality in Men and Women*, London: Gollancz.
Christie, Agatha (1954) *The Mousetrap*, London: Samuel French.
Christie, Dorothy and Campbell Christie (1951) *His Excellency*, London: Samuel French.
—— (1954) *Carrington, V.C.* London: Samuel French.
Church Information Board (1954) *The Problem of Homosexuality: An Interim Report by a group of Anglican clergy and doctors*, London: Church of England Moral Welfare Council.
Clum, John M. (1994) *Acting Gay: Male Homosexuality in Modern Drama*, revised edn, New York: Columbia University Press.
Collier, John W. (1947) 'Theatre Documentary', *Theatre Arts* xxxi, 7 (July), pp. 65–66.
Collins, Horace (1947a) 'Theatre Nationalisation', *Theatre Industry Journal* xxv, 102 (February), pp. 1–6.
—— (1947b) 'British Theatre Conference', *Theatre Industry Journal* xxv, 111 (November), pp. 1–5.
Cooper, D.E. (1970) 'Looking Back on Anger', in Bogdanor and Skidelsky 1970, pp. 254–287.
Cooper, Robert and Gibson Burrell (1988) 'Modernism, Postmodernism and Organizational Analysis: An Introduction', *Organization Studies* ix, 1, pp. 91–112.
Copeau, Jacques (1990) *Texts on Theatre*, ed. and trans. John Rudlin and Norman H. Paul, London: Routledge.
Corry, Percy (1954) *Lighting the Stage*, London: Pitman.
Cory, Donald Webster (1953) *The Homosexual Outlook: A Subjective Approach*, London: Peter Nevill.

Coward, Noël (1958) *Play Parade: V*, London: Heinemann.

—— (1962) 'These Old-Fashioned Revolutionaries', in *Encore: The Sunday Times Book*, London: Michael Joseph, pp. 176–180.

—— (1990) *Plays: Four*, revised edn, London: Methuen.

Craig, Sandy (ed.) (1980) *Dreams and Deconstructions: Alternative Theatre in Britain*, Ambergate: Amber Lane.

Crick, Malcolm (1985) ' "Tracing" the Anthropological Self: Quizzical Reflections on Field Work, Tourism and the Ludic', *Social Analysis* xvii (August), pp. 71–92.

Cripps, Stafford (1948) ' "—All the Signs of Vigorous Life" ', *New Theatre* iv, 9 (March), p. 9.

Crosland, C.A.R. (1956) *The Future of Socialism*, London: Jonathan Cape.

Cross, Beverley (1958) *One More River*, London: Rupert Hart-Davis.

Curtin, Kaier (1987) *'We Can Always Call Them Bulgarians': The Emergence of Lesbians and Gay Men on the American Stage*, Boston: Alyson Publications.

Darlington, W.A. (1954) 'Modern Acting', in Trewin 1954, pp. 111–130.

Darwin, John (1982) 'British Colonialism since 1945: a Pattern or a Puzzle?' *Journal of Imperial and Commonwealth History* xi, pp. 187–209.

—— (1986) 'The Fear of Falling: British Politics and Imperial Decline since 1900', *Transactions of the Royal Historical Society*, fifth series, 36, pp. 27–43.

—— (1988) *Britain and Decolonization: The Retreat From Empire in the Post-War World*, London: Macmillan.

—— (1991) *The End of the British Empire: The Historical Debate*, Oxford: Blackwell.

Davies, Alistair and Peter Saunders (1983) 'Literature, Politics and Society', in Sinfield 1983, pp. 13–50.

Davies, Andrew (1982) 'A Theatre for a People's Army: The Story of the ABCA Play Unit', *Red Letters* xiii (Spring), pp. 35–38.

—— (1984) 'Jack Lindsay and the Radical Culture of the 1940s', in *Jack Lindsay: The Thirties and the Forties*, ed. Robert Mackie, London: University of London Institute of Commonwealth Studies, Australian Studies Centre, pp. 74–80.

Davis, Joe (1949) 'A Trend of Modern Lighting', *Tabs* vii, 2 (September), pp. 5–9.

Davis, Porter (1950) *Sex Perversion and the Law* (2 vols), El Segundo: Banner.

Dean, Basil (1945) *The Theatre in Reconstruction*, Tonbridge: Tonbridge Printers.

—— (1948) 'The British Theatre Conference', in *Theatre Today: A Miscellany* (No. 1), London: Saturn, pp. 59–60.

de Jongh, Nicholas (1992) *Not in Front of the Audience: Homosexuality on Stage,* London: Routledge.

—— (1995) 'The Secret Gay Love of John Osborne', *Evening Standard* (24 January), pp. 12–13.

Delaney, Shelagh (1959) *A Taste of Honey*, London: Methuen.

Dent, Alan. (1951) 'English Reactions', *World Theatre* i, 3 (Autumn), pp. 28–31.

Derrida, Jacques (1976) *Of Grammatology*, trans. Gayatri Chakravorti Spivak, Baltimore: John Hopkins University Press.

—— (1987) *The Truth in Painting*, trans. Geoff Bennington and Ian McLeod, Chicago: University of Chicago Press.

—— (1988) *Limited Inc*, Evanston: Northwestern University Press.

Devine, George (1948a) 'Lighting and The Modern Theatre', *New Theatre* v, 1 (July), pp. 18–19.

—— (1948b) 'Interview: The Ideal Theatre Switchboard', *Tabs* vi, 2 (September), pp. 23–26.

—— (1950) 'Review: *Stage Lighting* by Frederick Bentham', *Tabs* viii, 3 (December), pp. 30–31.

—— (1953) 'Light, Shade and Balance', *Tabs* xi, 1 (April), pp. 6–7.

—— (1956) 'The Berliner Ensemble', in Marowitz *et al.* 1981, pp. 14–18.

—— (1957) 'The Royal Court Theatre: Phase One', in Hobson 1957, pp. 152–162.

—— (1960) 'How is it Done?', in *Royal Court Theatre 1958–1959*, London: English Stage Co., p. 26.

—— (1961) 'The Right to Fail', *Twentieth Century* clxix, 1008 (February), pp. 128–132.

Doty, Gresdna A. and Billy J. Harbin (eds) (1990) *Inside the Royal Court Theatre, 1956–1981: Artists Talk*, Baton Rouge: Louisiana State University Press.

Downs, Harold (1951) *Theatregoing: A Book For All Those Who Enjoy Seeing Plays And Also For Those Who Think They Might Enjoy Them More*, London: C.A. Watts.

Duff, Charles (1995) *The Lost Summer: The Heyday of the West End Theatre*, London: Heinemann – Nick Hern Books.

Dukes, Ashley (1942) *The Scene is Changed*, London: Macmillan.

Duncan, Ronald (1960) 'A Preface to the Sixties', *London Magazine* vii, 7 (July), pp. 15–19.

—— (1968) *How to Make Enemies*, London: Rupert Hart-Davis.

Edwards, Hilton (1946) ' "And the Lord Said..." Part One', *Tabs* iv, 1 (September), pp. 23–26.

Edwards, Sydney (1980) 'Anger and After', in *Celebration: Twenty Five Years of British Theatre*, London: W.H. Allen, pp. 10–26.

Eliot, T.S. (1951) *Selected Essays,* 3rd edn, London: Faber & Faber.

Ellison, Mike (1995) 'Osborne Lover Reveals Writer's Bisexuality', *The Guardian* (25 January), p. 20.

Elsom, John (1979) *Post-War British Theatre*, revised edn, London: Routledge.

—— (ed.) (1981) *Post-War British Theatre Criticism*, London: Routledge.

Ensor, Aubrey (1956) 'United Kingdom', in *Stage Design throughout the World since 1935*, ed. René Hainaux, Brussels: Elsevier, pp. 24–28.

Esslin, Martin (1970) *Brief Chronicles: Essays on Modern Theatre*, London: Methuen.

Farnham, Margot and Paul Marshall (eds) (1989) *Walking after Midnight: Gay Men's Life Stories*, London: Routledge.

Fawkes, Richard (1978) *Fighting for a Laugh: Entertaining the British and American Armed Forces, 1939–1945*, London: Macdonald and Jane's.

Federation of Theatre Unions (1953) *Theatre Ownership in Britain: A Report*, London: Federation of Theatre Unions.

Fernald, John (1956) 'Unfamiliar Method', *Adam International Review* xxiv, 254, pp. 13–14.

Findlater, Richard (1952) *The Unholy Trade*, London: Victor Gollancz.

—— (1953) 'The Autumnal Stage', *Twentieth Century* cliv, (December), pp. 460–468.

—— (1954a) 'The Producer', in Trewin 1954, pp. 159–177.

—— (1954b) 'Springtime in Shaftesbury Avenue', *Twentieth Century* clv, (April), pp. 364–374.

—— ed. (1981) *At the Royal Court: 25 Years of the English Stage Company*, Ambergate: Amber Lane.

Finney, Albert (1981) 'Recollections of a Lunch', in Findlater 1981, pp. 88–90.

Forman, Robert (1950) *Scene Painting*, London: Pitman.

Foucault, Michel (1977a) *Discipline and Punish: The Birth of the Prison*, trans. Alan Sheridan, Harmondsworth: Allen Lane.

—— (1977b) *Language, Counter-Memory, Practice: selected essays and interviews*, ed. with an intro. by Donald F. Bouchard, trans. Donald F. Bouchard and Sherry Simon, Ithaca: Cornell University Press.

—— (1979) *The History of Sexuality: An Introduction*, trans. Robert Hurley, Harmondsworth: Allen Lane.

—— (1980) *Power/Knowledge, Selected Interviews and Other Writings, 1972–1977*, ed. Colin Gordon, trans. Colin Gordon, Leo Marshall, John Mepham, Kate Soper, Hemel Hempstead: Harvester Wheatsheaf.

—— (1982) 'Afterword: The Subject and Power', in *Michel Foucault: Beyond Structuralism and Hermeneutics*, ed. Hubert L. Dreyfus and Paul Rabinow, Hemel Hempstead: Harvester Wheatsheaf, pp. 208–226.

Frayn, Michael (1963) 'Festival', in *Age of Austerity*, ed. Michael Sissons and Philip French, London: Hodder & Stoughton, pp. 317–338.

Freidson, Eliot (1970) *Profession of Medicine: A Study in the Sociology of Applied Knowledge*, New York: Dodd, Mead & Co.

Freud, Sigmund (1977) *On Sexuality – Three Essays on the Theory of Sexuality and Other Works*, Penguin Freud Library, vol. 7, ed. Angela Richards, trans. ed. James Strachey, Harmondsworth: Penguin.

—— (1979) *Case Histories II – 'Rat Man', Schreber, 'Wolf Man', Female Homosexuality*, Penguin Freud Library, vol. 9, ed. Angela Richards, trans, ed. James Strachey. Harmondsworth: Penguin.

Frow, John (1986) *Marxism and Literary History*, Oxford: Blackwell.

Fry, Christopher (1992) Personal Interview, 4 March.

Gale, Maggie B. (1996) *West End Women: Women and the London Stage 1918–1962*, Routledge: London.

Gallagher, John (1982) *The Decline, Revival and Fall of the British Empire: The Ford Lectures and Other Essays*, ed. Anil Seal, Cambridge: Cambridge University Press.

Gardiner, James (ed.) (1992) *A Class Apart: The Private Pictures of Montague Glover*, London: Serpent's Tail.

Garforth, John (1963) 'Arnold Wesker's Mission', in Marowitz *et al.* 1981, pp. 56–62.

Garland, Rodney (1953) *The Heart in Exile*, London: W.H. Allen.

Gascoigne, Bamber (1962) *Twentieth-Century Drama*, London: Hutchinson.

Gaskill, William (1981) 'My Apprenticeship', in Findlater 1981, pp. 57–61.

—— (1988) *A Sense of Direction: Life at the Royal Court*, London: Faber & Faber.

Gellert, Roger (1961) 'A Survey of the Treatment of the Homosexual in Some Plays', *Encore* viii, 1 (January–February), pp. 29–39.

—— (1985) *Quaint Honour*, in *Gay Plays: Volume Two*, ed. Michael Wilcox, London: Methuen, pp. 9–70.

Gilliatt, Penelope (1959) 'A Consideration of Critics', *Encore* vi, 5 (November–December), pp. 21–29.

Glasgow, Mary (1975) 'The Concept of the Arts Council', in *Essays on John Maynard Keynes*, ed. Milo Keynes, Cambridge: Cambridge University Press, pp. 260–271.

Goetz, Ruth and Augustus Goetz (1954) *The Immoralist*, based on the novel by André Gide, New York: Dramatists Play Service.

Goldsworthy, David (1994) *The Conservative Government and the End of Empire 1951–1957*, London: HMSO.

Goorney, Howard (1981) *The Theatre Workshop Story*, London: Methuen.

Gorelik, Mordecai (1947) *New Theatres For Old*, London: Dennis Dobson.

Graham-Campbell, Alison and Frank Lambe (1960) *Drama for Women*, London: G. Bell and Sons.

Granger, Derek (1958) 'Our Rising Stars', *Books and Art* i, 4 (January), pp. 6–7.

Green, Joyce Conyngham (1941) *Planning the Stage Wardrobe*, London: Thomas Nelson.

Greenwood, Ernest (1957) 'Attributes of a Profession', *Social Work* (New York) ii, 3 (July), pp. 45–55.

Grindea, Miron and Antony Ferry (1956) 'Presenting Brecht', *Adam International Review* xxiv, 254, pp. 2–3.

Groombridge, Brian and Paddy Whannel (1960) 'Something Rotten in Denmark Street', *New Left Review* 1 (January–February), pp. 52–54.

Guthrie, Tyrone. (1952) Interview, *Tabs* x, 1 (April), pp. 10–11.

Hailsham, Viscount (1955) 'Homosexuality and Society' in Rees and Usill 1955, pp. 21–35.

Hall, Peter (1983) *Peter Hall's Diaries: The Story of a Dramatic Battle*, ed. John Goodwin. London: Hamish Hamilton.

Hall, Stuart (1959) 'Something to Live For', in Marowitz *et al.* 1981, pp. 110–115.

—— (1960) '*Serjeant Musgrave's Dance*', *New Left Review* 1 (January–February), pp. 50–51.

—— (1961) 'Beyond Naturalism Pure: The First Five Years', in Marowitz *et al.* 1981, pp. 212–220.

Hall, Willis (1961) *The Long and the Short and the Tall*, in *New English Dramatists: 3*, ed. Tom Maschler, Harmondsworth: Penguin, pp. 11–92.

Hamilton, Iain (1956) 'Those Who Can't, Criticize', in Lumley 1956, pp. 113–128.

Handley, Graham (1990) *Look Back in Anger for GCSE*, Harmondsworth: Penguin.

Harding, James (1993) *Emlyn Williams: A Life*, London: Weidenfeld & Nicolson.

Hare, David (1997) *Platform Papers: David Hare*, London: Royal National Theatre.

Hartley, Anthony (1956) 'The London Stage: Drugs No Answer', in Lumley 1956, pp. 1–15.

Hartnoll, Phyllis (ed.) (1951) *The Oxford Companion to the Theatre*, London: Oxford University Press.

Harwood, Ronald (1984) *All the World's a Stage*, London: Secker & Warburg/BBC.

Hayman, Ronald (1979) *British Theatre Since 1955: A Reassessment*, Oxford: Oxford University Press.

Heather, Stanley (1972) *That Struts and Frets*, Ilfracombe: Arthur H. Stockwell.

Heinemann, Margot (1976) '1956 and the Communist Party', in Miliband and Saville 1976, pp. 43–57.

Hennessy, Peter (1993) *Never Again: Britain 1945–1951*, London: Vintage.

Hennessy, Peter and Mark Laity (1987) 'Suez – What the Papers Say', *Contemporary Record* i, 1 (Spring), pp. 2–8.

Henry, Joan (1960) *Look on Tempests* (2 parts), *Plays and Players* vii, 10 and 11 (July and August), pp. 25–31, and pp. 24–30.

Herbert, A.P. (1957) *'No Fine on Fun': The Comical History of the Entertainments Duty*, London: Methuen.

Herbert, Jocelyn (1981) 'Discoveries in Design', in Findlater 1981, pp. 83–87.

Hewison, Robert (1988) *In Anger: Culture in the Cold War 1945–60*, revised edn, London: Methuen.

Hinchliffe, Arnold P. (1974) *British Theatre, 1950–70*, Oxford: Blackwell.

Hobson, Harold (1954) 'The French Theatre in Britain', in Trewin 1954, pp. 231–245.

—— (ed.) (1957) *International Theatre Annual: No. 2*, London: John Calder.

—— (ed.) (1958) *International Theatre Annual: No. 3*, London: John Calder.

—— (ed.) (1959) *International Theatre Annual: No. 4*, London: John Calder.

—— (1984) *Theatre in Britain: A Personal View*, Oxford: Phaidon.

Hoggart, Richard (1957) *The Uses of Literacy*, Harmondsworth: Penguin/Chatto & Windus.

—— (1958) 'Speaking to Each Other', in Mackenzie 1958, pp. 121–138.

Hoggart, Williams and Raymond Williams (1960) 'Working Class Attitudes', *New Left Review* 1 (January–February), pp. 26–30.

Hollis, Christopher (1957) 'Keeping Up With the Rices', *Spectator* (18 October), pp. 504–505.

Home, William Douglas (1947) *Now Barabbas...*, London: Longmans.

Hooker, Evelyn (1956) 'A Preliminary Analysis of Group Behaviour of Homosexuals', *Journal of Psychology* xlii, pp. 217–225.

Hope-Wallace, Philip (1956) 'Atmosphere', in Lumley 1956, pp. 16–20.

Hopkins, Bill (1957) 'Ways Without a Precedent', in Maschler 1957, pp. 153–178.

—— (1959) 'John Osborne: From Anger to Elegance at £3,000 a week', *Lilliput* (April), pp. 21–29.

Howe, Stephen (1993) *Anticolonialism in British Politics: The Left and the End of Empire*, Oxford: Clarendon.

Hudd, Walter (1943) 'New Audience for Old', *Our Time* iii, 2 (September), pp. 15–18.

Huggett, Richard (1989) *Binkie Beaumont: Eminence Grise of the West End Theatre 1933–1973*, London: Hodder & Stoughton.

Hunt, Albert (1974) *Arden: a Study of His Plays*, London: Methuen.

Hunt, Hugh (1954) *The Director in the Theatre*, London: Routledge.

Hurren, Kenneth (1977) *Theatre Inside Out*, London: W.H. Allen.

Huxley, Aldous (1948) *The Gioconda Smile*, London: Chatto & Windus.

Hyde, H. Montgomery (1970) *The Other Love: An Historical and Contemporary Survey of Homosexuality in Britain*, London: Heinemann.

Innes, Christopher (1992) *Modern British Drama 1890–1990*, Cambridge: Cambridge University Press.

Institute for the Study and Treatment of Delinquency (1992) *The Problem of Homosexuality*, London: ISTD.

Ionesco, Eugene (1964) *Notes and Counter-Notes*, trans. Donald Watson, London: John Calder.

Jackson, Freda (1946) 'Theatre: A State Responsibility', *New Theatre* iii, 6 (November), pp. 12–13.

Jacobs, Nicholas and Prudence Ohlsen (eds) (1977) *Bertolt Brecht in Britain*, London: Irat-Theatre Quarterly.

Jellicoe, Ann (1958) 'Something of Sport', *Encore* v, 1 (May–June), pp. 25–27.

—— (1981) 'The Writer's Group', in Findlater 1981, pp. 52–56.

Johns, Eric (1945) 'Tomorrow's Theatre', *Theatre World* xli, 251 (December), pp. 27, 30.

Johnston, John (1990) *The Lord Chamberlain's Blue Pencil*, London: Hodder & Stoughton.

Jones, Mervyn (1976) 'Days of Tragedy and Farce', in Miliband and Saville 1976, pp. 67–88.

Joseph, Stephen (1957) 'No New Playwrights?' *Encore* iii, 5 (June-July), pp. 42–45.

Kahler, Miles (1984) *Decolonization in Britain and France: The Domestic Consequences of International Relations*, Princeton: Princeton University Press.

Kant, Immanuel (1987) *Critique of Judgement*, trans. with an intro. Werner S. Pluhar, Indianapolis: Hackett.

Kaye, Michael (1960) 'The New Drama', *New Left Review* 5 (September–October), pp. 64–66.

Kelsall, Glyn (1945) 'CEMA Marches On', *Theatre World* xli, 248 (September), pp. 27–28.

Kernodle, George and Portia Kernodle (1978) *Invitation to the Theatre*, 2nd edn, New York: Harcourt Brace Jovanovich.

Keynes, John Maynard (1945) 'The Arts Council: Its Policy and Hopes', *The Listener* xxxiv (12 July), pp. 31–34.

King, Philip (1956) *Serious Charge*, London: Samuel French.

King, Philip and Robin Maugham (1959) *The Lonesome Road*, London: Samuel French.

Kingston, Jeremy (1959) *No Concern of Mine*, London: Samuel French.

—— (1960) 'Are Heads Growing Tinier?' *London Magazine* vii, 7 (July), pp. 19–22.

Kinsey, Alfred C., Wardell B. Pomeroy and Clyde Martin (1948) *Sexual Behaviour in the Human Male*, Philadelphia: W.B. Saunders.

Kirk, Kris and Ed Heath (1984) *Men in Frocks*, London: Gay Men's Press.

Kisch, Eve (1943) 'Music in Wartime', *Our Time* ii, 13 (July), pp. 8–12.

Kitchin, Laurence (1962) *Mid-Century Drama*, revised edn, London: Faber & Faber.

Kitzinger, Celia (1987) *The Social Construction of Lesbianism*, London: Sage.

Kyle, Keith (1991) *Suez*, London: Weidenfeld & Nicolson.

Lacey, Stephen (1995) *British Realist Theatre: The New Wave in its Context 1956–1965*, London: Routledge.

Laing, Stuart (1986) *Representations of Working-Class Life 1957–1964*, London: Macmillan.

Lambert, J.W. (1956) 'The London Theatre Season', in Hobson 1956.

Landstone, Charles (1948) *You and the Theatre: A Pocket Guide*, London: Macdonald and Evans.

—— (1950) *Notes on Civic Theatres*, London: Arts Council of Great Britain.

—— (1952) 'The Public', *World Theatre* ii, 2 (Summer), pp. 3–12.

—— (1953) *Off-Stage: A Personal Record of the First Twelve Years of State-Sponsored Drama in Great Britain*, London: Elek.

—— (1954) 'The Provincial Picture', in Trewin 1954, pp. 73–90.

—— (1959) 'From John Osborne to Shelagh Delaney', *World Theatre* viii, 3 (Autumn), pp. 203–216.

Lane, Yoti (1959) *The Psychology of the Actor*, London: Secker & Warburg.

Leacroft, Richard (1949) *Civic Theatre Design*, London: Dennis Dobson.

Leavis, F.R. (1930) *Mass Civilisation and Minority Culture*, Cambridge: Minority Press.

—— (1936) *Revaluation: Tradition and Development in English Poetry*, London: Chatto & Windus.

—— (1962) *The Great Tradition*, Harmondsworth: Penguin, 1948.

Leavis, F.R. and Denys Thompson (1933) *Culture and Environment: The Training of Critical Awareness*, London: Chatto & Windus.

Leeming, Glenda (ed.) (1985) *Wesker on File*, London: Methuen.

Lessing, Doris (1957) 'The Small Personal Voice', in Maschler 1957, pp. 11–27.

—— (1959) *Each His Own Wilderness*, in *New English Dramatists*, ed. E. Martin Browne, Harmondsworth: Penguin, pp. 11–95.

Leventhal, F.M. (1990) ' "The Best for the Most": CEMA and State Sponsorship of the Arts in Wartime, 1939–1945', *20th Century British History* i, 3, pp. 289–317.

Lewenstein, Oscar (1994) *Kicking Against the Pricks: A Theatre Producer Looks Back*, London: Nick Hern Books.

Lewes, Kenneth (1988) *The Psychoanalytic Theory of Male Homosexuality*, New York: New American Library.

Lewis, Peter (1990) *The National: A Dream Made Concrete*, London: Methuen.

Littlewood, Joan (1959) 'Plays for the People', *World Theatre* viii, 4 (Winter), pp. 283–290.

—— (1994) *Joan's Book: Joan Littlewood's Peculiar History As She Tells It*, London: Methuen.

Lloyd Evans, Gareth and Barbara Lloyd Evans (eds) (1985) *Plays in Review 1956–1980: British Drama and the Critics*, London: Batsford.

Logue, Christopher (1958) 'To My Fellow Artists', *Universities and Left Review* i, 4 (Summer), p. 21.

Louis, Roger W. and Roger Owen (eds) (1989) *Suez 1956: The Crisis and its Consequences*, Oxford: Clarendon.

Lucas, Ian (1994) *Impertinent Decorum: Gay Theatrical Manoeuvres*, London: Cassell.

Lumley, Frederick (ed) (1956) *Theatre in Review*, Edinburgh: Richard Paterson.

—— (1972) *New Trends in 20th Century Drama: A Survey since Ibsen and Shaw*, 4th edn, London: Barrie and Jenkins.

Lyon, Peter (1989) 'The Commonwealth and the Suez Crisis', in Louis and Owen 1989, pp. 257–273.

MacIver, Peggy (1948) 'What the Conference Decided', *New Theatre* iv, 9 (March), pp. 6–8.

Mackenzie, Norman (ed.) (1958) *Conviction*, London: MacGibbon & Kee.

Macowan, Michael (1950) *Where is the Theatre?*, London: Bureau of Current Affairs.

Mander, John (1961) *The Writer and Commitment*, London: Secker & Warburg.

Mannheim, Karl (1960) *Ideology and Utopia: An Introduction to the Sociology of Knowledge*, London: Routledge.

Marowitz, Charles (1957) 'British Acting is Divorced from Reality', *Plays and Players* iv, 6 (March), p. 10.

—— (1958) 'The Art that went Astray', *Encore* iv, 3 (January–February), pp. 18–22.

—— (1959) 'Review: *The World of Paul Slickey*', in Marowitz *et al.* 1981, pp. 103–105.

—— (1960) 'Anti-Ionesco Theatre', in Marowitz *et al.* 1981, pp. 160–164.

—— (1962) 'Anger and the Absurd', *Plays and Players* ix, 11 (August), p. 57.

Marowitz, Charles, Tom Milne and Owen Hale (eds) (1981) *New Theatre Voices of the Fifties and Sixties: Selections from Encore Magazine 1956–1963*, revised edn, London: Methuen.

Marquand, David (1957) 'Lucky Jim and the Labour Party', *Universities and Left Review* i, 1 (Spring), pp. 57–60.

Marshall, Norman (1947) *The Other Theatre*, London: John Lehmann.

Martin, Kingsley (1953) 'The Abominable Crime', *New Statesman and Nation* xlvi, 1182 (31 October), p. 508.

Marwick, Arthur (1990) *British Society Since 1945*, Harmondsworth: Penguin.

Maschler, Tom (ed.) (1957) *Declaration*, London: MacGibbon & Kee.

McCullough, Christopher J. (1992) 'From Brecht to Brechtian: Estrangement and Appropriation', in *The Politics of Theatre and Drama*, ed. Graham Holderness, London: Macmillan, pp. 120–133.

Melville, Alan (1951) *Castle in the Air*, London: Samuel French.

—— (1970) *Merely Melville: An Autobiography*, London: Hodder & Stoughton.

Mendelssohn, Peter de (1950–1951) 'The Disillusioned Stage' (2 parts), *Theatre Newsletter* v, 107 and 113 (14 October and 6 January), pp. 1–2 and p. 5.

Methuen (1939) *A Complete Catalogue of Books Published by Methuen and Co. Ltd.*

—— (1959) *A List of Methuen Spring Books for 1959.*

—— (1960) *A List of Methuen Books for the Autumn and Winter 1960–61.*

Miliband, Ralph and John Saville (eds) (1976) *The Socialist Register 1976*, London: Merlin.

Miller, Sigmund (1957) 'On the Mid-Atlantic Point of View', in Hobson 1957, pp. 166–170.

Milne, Tom (1958) 'Art in Angel Lane', in Marowitz *et al.* 1981, pp. 80–86.

—— (1961) 'Luther and the Devils', *New Left Review* 12 (November–December), pp. 55–58.

Minihan, Janet (1977) *The Nationalization of Culture: The Development of State Subsidies to the Arts in Great Britain*, London: Hamish Hamilton.

Morris, Colin (1951) *Reluctant Heroes*, London: English Theatre Guild.

Morrison, Herbert (1949) 'Festival of Britain 1951', *Civic Entertainment* i, 2 (January–February), pp. 13–14.

Muller, Robert (1948) 'Stage Door', *Theatre Newsletter* iii, 61/62 (11 December), p. 3.

—— (1958) 'How I Write my Plays', *Books and Art* i, 6 (March), pp. 56–59.

Murphy, Philip (1995) *Party Politics and Decolonization: The Conservative Party and British Colonial Policy in Tropical Africa, 1951–1964*, Oxford: Clarendon.

Neu, Jerome (ed.) (1991) *The Cambridge Companion to Freud*, Cambridge: Cambridge University Press.

Neustatter, W. Lindesay (1955) 'Homosexuality: The Medical Aspect', in Rees and Usill 1955, pp. 67–139.

Nicoll, Allardyce (1938) 'Naturalism or Poetry', in Charques 1938, pp. 56–73.

—— (1976) *World Theatre: From Aeschylus to Anouilh*, 2nd edn, London: Harrap.

Noble, Peter (1948) *British Theatre*, London: British Yearbooks.

O'Connor, Sean (1998) *Straight Acting: Popular Gay Drama from Wilde to Rattigan*, Cassell: London.

Olivier, Laurence (1981) 'The Court and I', in Findlater 1981, pp. 37–41.

Osborne, John (1957a) 'They Call it Cricket', in Maschler 1957, pp. 61–84.

—— (1957b) 'Introduction', in Hobson 1957, pp. 9–10.

—— (1957c) 'You've Fallen For The Great Swindle', *News Chronicle* (27 February), p. 4.

—— (1968) 'On Critics and Criticism', in *Look Back in Anger: A Selection of Critical Essays*, ed. John Russell Taylor, London: Macmillan, pp. 69–71.

—— (1972) *A Subject of Scandal and Concern*, London: Faber & Faber.

—— (1981a) *A Better Class of Person: An Autobiography, vol. 1: 1929–1956*, London: Faber & Faber.

—— (1981b) 'On the Writer's Side', in Findlater 1981, pp. 19–26.

—— (1991a) *Almost a Gentleman: An Autobiography, Vol. 2: 1955–1966*, London: Faber & Faber.

—— (1991b) *Déjàvu*, London: Faber & Faber.

—— (1993) *Plays: One*, London: Faber & Faber.

—— (1994) *Damn You, England: Collected Prose*, London: Faber & Faber.

—— (1998) *Plays: Two*, London: Faber & Faber.

Osborne, John and Anthony Creighton (1955) *Personal Enemy*, Lord Chamberlain Plays Collection, Manuscript No. 1955/Box 14. (British Library.)

Otway, Travers (1948) *The Hidden Years*, London: Faber & Faber.

Ould, Hermon (1948) *The Art of the Play*, 2nd edn, London: Pitman.

Page, Malcolm (ed.) (1988) *File on Osborne*, London: Methuen.

Parker, Andrew (1991) 'Unthinking Sex: Marx, Engels and the Scene of Writing', *Social Text* ix, 4 (No. 29), pp. 28–45.

Parmentier, Guillaume (1980) 'The British Press in the Suez Crisis', *Historical Journal* xxiii, 2, pp. 435–448.

Parsons, Talcott (1968) 'Professions', in *International Encyclopedia of the Social Sciences: XII*, ed. David L. Sills, New York: Macmillan and the Free Press, pp. 536–546.

Pearce, Frank (1981) 'The British press and the "placing" of male homosexuality', in *The Manufacture of News: Social Problems, Deviance and the Mass Media*, revised edn, ed. Stanley Cohen and Jock Young. London: Constable, pp. 303–316.

Pick, John (1985) *The Theatre Industry: Profit, Subsidy and the Search for New Audiences*, London: Comedia.

Pilbrow, Richard (1979) *Stage Lighting*, 2nd edn, London: Cassell.

Plans for an Arts Centre (1945) London: Lund Humphries for the Arts Council of Great Britain.

Plowright, Joan (1981) 'A Special Place for Actors', in Findlater 1981, pp. 31–35.

Porter, A.N. and A.J. Stockwell (eds) (1989) *British Imperial Policy and Decolonization, 1938–64: Volume 2, 1951–64*, London: Macmillan.

Porter, Kevin and Jeffrey Weeks (eds) (1991) *Between the Acts: Lives of Homosexual Men 1885–1967*, London: Routledge.

Potter, John Deane (1959) 'Isn't it About Time Someone Said This...Plainly and Frankly', *Daily Express* (9 April), p. 8.

Priestley, J.B. (1939) *Johnson over Jordan: The Play and All About It*, London: Heinemann.

—— (1941) 'The Playwright's Problem', *The Listener* xxv, 637 (27 March), pp. 445–446.

—— (1947a) *Theatre Outlook*, London: Nicholson and Watson.

—— (1947b) *The Arts Under Socialism*, London: Turnstile.

—— (1948a) *The Plays of J.B. Priestley: Volume One*, London: Heinemann.

—— (1948b) 'Playwriting Q and A', *The Author* lviii, 3 (Spring), pp. 45–47.

—— (1953) 'Thoughts in the Wilderness: Block Thinking', *New Statesman and Nation* xlvi, 1182 (31 October), pp. 515–516.

—— (1962) *Margin Released: A Writer's Reminiscences and Reflections*, London: Heinemann.

Progressive League (1955) *Evidence Submitted by the Progressive League to the Home Office Committee on Homosexual Offences and Prostitution*. (Copy in British Library.)

Pullein-Thompson, Denis (1947) 'In Defence of Intervals', *Theatre Newsletter* i, 16 (15 February), pp. 6–7.

Quayle, Anthony (1990) *A Time To Speak*, London: Barrie and Jenkins.

Raffles, Gerry (1956) 'Theatre Workshop', *World Theatre* v, 3 (Summer), pp. 228–230.

Rattigan, Terence (1953) *Collected Plays* (4 vols), London: Hamish Hamilton.

—— (1995) *After the Dance*, intro. Dan Rebellato, London: Nick Hern Books.

Rattigan, Terence and Anthony Maurice (1939) *Follow My Leader*, Lord Chamberlain's Play Collection, Manuscript No. 1940/2, Box 2506. (British Library.)

Rees, J. Tudor (1955) 'Homosexuality and the Law', in Rees and Usill 1955, pp. 3–20.

Rees, J. Tudor and Harley V. Usill (eds) (1955) *They Stand Apart: A Critical Survey of the Problems of Homosexuality*, London: Heinemann.

Richardson, Tony (1993) *The Long-Distance Runner: An Autobiography*, London: Faber & Faber.

Ridler, Anne (1946) *The Shadow Factory: A Nativity Play*, London: Faber & Faber.

Ritchie, Harry (1988) *Success Stories: Literature and the Media in England, 1950–1959*, London: Faber & Faber.

Robinson, Ronald (1979) 'The Moral Disarmament of African Empire 1919–1947', *Journal of Imperial and Commonwealth History* viii, 1 (October), pp. 86–104.

Rosenthal, Andrew (1952) *Third Person*, in *Plays of the Year 1951*, ed. J.C. Trewin, London: Elek, pp. 345–441.

Ross, Alan (1960) 'A New English Theatre?', *London Magazine* vii, 7 (July), pp. 7–10.

Roud, Richard (1958) 'The Theatre on Trial', *Encounter* x, 7 (July), pp. 27–32.

Royal Court Theatre 1958–1959 (1960), London: English Stage Company.

Rusinko, Susan (1989) *British Drama, 1950 to the Present: a Critical History*, Boston: Twayne.

Samson, Anne (1992) *F.R. Leavis*, London: Harvester Wheatsheaf.

Sandiston, Gordon (1948) 'The Ownership of British Theatres', in *Theatre Today: A Miscellany* (No. 1), London: Saturn, pp. 57–58.

Sarron, Bernard (1945) 'The Decor By...', *New Theatre* i, 1 (December), p. 2.

Saville, John (1976) 'The Twentieth Congress and the British Communist Party', in Miliband and Saville 1976, pp. 1–23.

Savitsch, Eugene de (1958) *Homosexuality, Transvestism and Change of Sex*, London: Heinemann Medical.

Scruton, Roger (1985) *Thinkers of the New Left*, London: Claridge.

Sedgwick, Eve Kosofsky (1990) *Epistemology of the Closet*, Los Angeles: University of California Press.

—— (1992) *Between Men: English Literature and Homosocial Desire*, New York: Columbia University Press.

Segal, Zelda (1948) 'History of an Endeavour', *New Theatre* iv, 10 (April), p. 3.

Sequeira, Horace (1953) *Stage Make-up*, London: Herbert Jenkins.

Serjeant Musgrave at the Court (1990) A319 Literature in the Modern World, BBC Open University.

Seymour, Alan (1965) 'Too True, Not Good Enough', *London Magazine* v, 9 (December), pp. 60–64.

Shaffer, Peter (1958) *Five Finger Exercise*, London: Hamish Hamilton.

Shaw, Tony (1995) 'Eden and the BBC During the 1956 Suez Crisis: A Myth Re-examined', *20th Century British History* iv, 3, pp. 320–343.

Shepherd, Simon and Peter Womack (1996) *English Drama: A Cultural History*, Oxford: Blackwell.

Sierz, Aleks (1996) 'John Osborne and the Myth of Anger', *New Theatre Quarterly* xii, 46 (May), pp. 136–146.

Sinfield, Alan (ed.) (1983) *Society and Literature 1945–1970*, London: Methuen.

—— (1989) *Literature, Politics and Culture in Postwar Britain*, Oxford: Blackwell.

—— (1990) 'Closet Dramas: Homosexual Representation and Class in Postwar British Theatre', *Genders* 9 (Fall), pp. 112–131.

—— (1994) *The Wilde Century: Effeminacy, Oscar Wilde and the Queer Movement*, London: Cassell.

Smith, Richard (1994) 'What Are You Looking At?' *Gay Times* 190 (July), pp. 64–67.

Southern, Richard (1953) *The Open Stage and the Modern Theatre in Research and Practice*, London: Faber & Faber.

Speaight, Robert (1947) *Drama since 1939*, London: Longmans Green for the British Council.

Stafford-Clark, Max (1981) 'Under the Microscope', in Findlater 1981, pp. 195–98.

Steinbeck, John (1952) 'Your Audiences are Wonderful', *Sunday Times* (10 August).

Stevens, Thomas (1941) 'A New Model in Army Education', *Our Time* i, 7 (September 1941), pp. 8–15.

Strand Electric and Engineering Company (1961) *Lighting for Entertainment*, London: Strand Electric.

Summerfield, Penny (1986) 'Patriotism and Empire: Music Hall Entertainment, 1870–1914', in *Imperialism and Popular Culture*, ed. John M. MacKenzie, Manchester: Manchester University Press, pp. 17–48.

Taylor, George (1947) *Writing for the Stage*, London: Southern Editorial Syndicate.

Taylor, John Russell (1963) *Anger and After: a Guide to the New British Drama*, revised edn, Harmondsworth: Penguin.

—— (ed.) (1968) *Look Back In Anger: A Selection of Critical Essays*, London: Macmillan.

—— (1971) *The Second Wave: British Drama in the Seventies*, London: Methuen.

Temple, Joan (1946) *No Room at the Inn*, in *Embassy Successes: II*, ed. Anthony Hawtrey, London: Sampson Low, Marston, pp. 145–234.

Thomas, Charles (1951) *The Dramatic Student's Approach to his Make-up*, London: J. Garnett Miller.

Thomas, Hugh (1967) *The Suez Affair*, London: Weidenfeld & Nicolson.

Thompson, E.P. (1957a) 'Socialist Humanism: An Epistle to the Philistines', *New Reasoner* i, 1 (Summer), pp. 105–143.

—— (1957b) 'Socialism and the Intellectuals', *Universities and Left Review* i, 1 (Spring), pp. 31–36.

—— (ed.) (1960) *Out of Apathy*, London: New Left Books.

—— (1961) 'Review Essay: *The Long Revolution*' (2 parts), *New Left Review* 9 and 10 (May–June and July–August), pp. 24–33 and pp. 34–39.

Tolmie, A. W. (ed.) (1946) *'The Stage' Guide*, revised edn, London: Carson & Comerford.

Torstendahl, Rolf and Michael Burrage (eds) (1990) *The Formation of Professions: Knowledge, State and Strategy*, London: Sage.

Trewin, J.C. (ed.) (1949) *The Year's Work in the Theatre 1948–1949*, London: Longmans, Green, for the British Council.

—— (1951) *Drama 1945–50*, London: Longmans, Green, for the British Council.

—— (1953) *Dramatists of Today*, London: Staples Press.

—— (ed.) (1954) *Theatre Programme*, London: Frederick Muller.

—— (1957) 'The Best Plays and Players of 1956', *Plays and Players* iv, 4 (January), pp. 6–7.

—— (1965) *Drama in Britain 1951–1964*, London: Longmans for the British Council.

Trewin, Wendy (1954) 'A Woman's View', in Trewin 1954, pp. 215–230.

Trewin, Wendy and J.C. Trewin (1986) *The Arts Theatre, London 1927–1981*, London: Society for Theatre Research.

Tschudin, Marcus (1972) *A Writer's Theatre: George Devine and the English Stage Company at the Royal Court 1950–1965*, Bern: Herbert Lang.

Tynan, Kathleen (1988) *The Life of Kenneth Tynan*, 2nd edn, London: Methuen.

Tynan, Kenneth (1950) 'Where are the Playwrights?' *Theatre Newsletter* v, 105 (16 September), pp. 4–5.

—— (1957) 'Theatre and Living', in Maschler 1957, pp. 107–129.

—— (1958) 'Making Connections', in *Artist, Critic & Teacher*, ed. Alex Jacobs and Paddy Whannel, London: Joint Council for Education through Art, pp. 11–16.

—— (1964) *Tynan on Theatre*, Harmondsworth: Penguin.

—— (1967) *Tynan Left and Right: Plays, Films, People, Places and Events*, London: Longmans.

Union of Ethical Societies (1955) *Memorandum of Evidence to the Departmental Committee on Homosexuality and Offences Relative to Prostitution and Solicitation*. (Copy in British Library.)

Urry, John (1990) *The Tourist Gaze: Leisure and Travel in Contemporary Society*, London: Sage.

Ustinov, Peter (1948) 'Let us Take Stock', *New Theatre* iv, 8 (February), pp. 4–5.

—— (1950a) 'Is The Theatre Dead or Dying?', *Theatre Digest* 6, pp. 60–63.

—— (1950b) *Plays About People*, London: Jonathan Cape.

Vaïsse, Maurice (1989) 'France and the Suez Crisis', in Louis and Owen 1989, pp. 131–143.

Vargas, Luis (1960) *Guidebook to the Drama*, London: English Universities Press.

Wain, John (1957) 'Along the Tightrope', in Maschler 1957, pp. 85–106.

Walvin, James (1978) *Leisure and Society: 1830–1950*, London: Longman.

Wandor, Michelene (1987) *Look Back in Gender: Sexuality and the Family in Post-War British Drama*, London: Methuen.

Wansell, Geoffrey (1995) *Terence Rattigan: A Biography*, London: Fourth Estate.

Wardle, Irving (1978) *The Theatres of George Devine*, London: Jonathan Cape.

Warnke, Frank J. (1959) 'Poetic Drama on European Stages', *New Republic* cxli (24 August), pp. 30–31.

Warth, Douglas (1952) 'Evil Men' (2 of 3 parts), *Sunday Pictorial* (25 May, 1 June), pp. 6, 15, and p. 12.

Watt, David (1957) 'Class Report', in Marowitz *et al.* 1981, pp. 56–62.

Weeks, Jeffrey (1989) *Sex, Politics and Society: The Regulation of Sexuality Since 1800*, 2nd edn, London: Longman.

Wellwarth, George (1965) *The Theatre of Protest and Paradox: Developments in Avant-Garde Drama*, London: MacGibbon & Kee.

Wesker, Arnold (1958) 'Let Battle Commence', in Marowitz *et al.* 1981, pp. 96–103.

—— (1959) *Roots*, with an intro. by Bernard Levin, Harmondsworth: Penguin.

—— (1960) *The Kitchen*, in *New English Dramatists: 2*, ed. Tom Maschler, Harmondsworth: Penguin, pp. 11–61.

—— (1964) *The Wesker Trilogy*, Harmondsworth: Penguin.

—— (1994) *As Much As I Dare: An Autobiography (1932–1959)*, London: Century.

West, Donald J. (1955) *Homosexuality*, London: Duckworth.

Westwood, Gordon (1952) *Society and the Homosexual*, London: Gollancz.

—— (1960) *A Minority: A Report on the Life of the Male Homosexual in Great Britain*, London: Longmans.

White, Eric W. (1975) *The Arts Council of Great Britain*, London: Davis-Poynter.

Whiting, John (1956) 'The Toll of Talent in a Timid Theatre', *Encore* iii, 3 (Summer), pp. 5–6.

—— (1959) 'At Ease in a Bright Red Tie', in Marowitz, *et al.* 1981, pp. 105–110.

—— (1960) 'The Masses Is Too Stupid For Us', *London Magazine* vii, 7 (July), pp. 34–37.

—— (1966) *John Whiting on Theatre*, London: Magazine Editions.

Wickham, Glynne (1962) *Drama in a World of Science; and Three Other Lectures*, London: Routledge.

Wildeblood, Peter (1957) *Against the Law*, Harmondsworth: Penguin.

Wilensky, Harold L. (1964) 'The Professionalization of Everyone?' *American Journal of Sociology* lxx, 2 (September), pp. 137–158.

Willett, John (1984) *Brecht in Context*, London: Methuen.

Williams, Raymond (1952) *Drama from Ibsen to Eliot*, London: Chatto & Windus.

—— (1958) 'Culture is Ordinary', in Mackenzie 1958, pp. 74–92.

—— (1961) 'New English Drama', in *Modern British Dramatists: A Collection of Critical Essays*, ed. John Russell Brown, Englewood Cliffs: Prentice Hall, pp. 26–37.

—— (1964) *Drama from Ibsen to Eliot*, revised edn, Harmondsworth: Penguin/Chatto & Windus.

—— (1965) 'The British Left', *New Left Review* 30 (March–April), pp. 18–26.

—— (1968) *Drama from Ibsen to Brecht*, London: Chatto & Windus.

—— (1979) *Politics and Letters: Interviews with New Left Review*, London: New Left Books.

—— (1992) *The Long Revolution*, London: Hogarth.

—— (1993) *Culture and Society: Coleridge to Orwell*, London: Hogarth.

Williams, William Emrys (1971) 'The Pre-history of the Arts Council', in *Aims and Action in Adult Education*, ed. E.M. Hutchinson, London: National Institute of Adult Education, pp. 18–23.

Willis, Ted (1991) *Evening All: Fifty Years Over a Hot Typewriter*, London: Macmillan.

Wilson, A.E. (1949a) *Post-War Theatre*, London: Home and Van Thal.

—— (1949b) 'To Boo or not to Boo', *Theatre Digest* 4, pp. 158–161.

Wilson, Angus (1959) 'The Theatre Faces the World: Morality', in Hobson 1959, pp. 184–189.

Wilson, Sandy (1985) *Valmouth*, from the novel by Ronald Firbank, London: Samuel French.

'Wolfenden Report' (1957) *Report of the Committee on Homosexual Offences and Prostitution*, Cmnd 247, London: HMSO.

Wright, Ian (1979) 'F.R. Leavis, the *Scrutiny* Movement and the Crisis', in *Culture and Crisis in Britain in the Thirties*, ed. Jon Clark, Margot Heinemann, David Margolies and Carole Snee, London: Lawrence & Wishart.

Wright, Nicholas (1981) 'A Shared Aesthetic', in Findlater 1981, pp. 181–186.

Young, B.A. (1986) *The Rattigan Version: Sir Terence Rattigan and the Theatre of Character*, London: Hamish Hamilton.

INDEX

references to illustrations in bold

ABCA, *see* Army Bureau of
    Current Affairs
absurd drama 145–7
Ackland, Rodney 163, 225: *The
    Pink Room* (aka. *Absolute Hell*)
    157, 202–3
acting 73–4, 78–82
Albery, Bronson 50, 59
Albery, Donald 204
Allsop, Kenneth 146, 182, 212
amateur theatre 40–6
Amis, Kingsley 147, 217–18
Anderson, Lindsay 10, 20, 24, 66,
    68, 76, 81, 87, 89, 94, 98,
    110–11, 117, 119, 213, 215
Anderson, Maxwell: *The Bad
    Seed* 201
Anderson, Robert: *Tea and
    Sympathy* 159, 168, 175, 198,
    201, 204
anger 11–13, 31–2
'angry young man' 116–17, 231
Anouilh, Jean 81, 128, 151: *Ring
    Round the Moon* 95, **97**
Arden, John 5, 68, 150: *The
    Happy Haven* 119; *Serjeant
    Musgrave's Dance* 17, 22, 112,
    119
Army Bureau of Current Affairs
    62, 229
'Art for the People' 39, 44–5, 62,
    228
arts centres 49

Arts Council 38, 43, 45–46,
    48–50, 52, 55, 58–63, 65–69,
    83, 113, 130
Arts Theatre 208–10
audiences 94, 104–13, 182–5
'Aunt Edna' 107–8, 110
Austin, J. L. 9, 35, 36, 169

Bailey, James 96
Barker, Clive 73, 78
Barnett, Corelli 138–9, 141
Bates, Alan 81, 85
Beaton, Cecil 75, 95–6, 162–3
Beaumont, Hugh 'Binkie' 38, 53–6,
    148, 155, 162, 163
Beckett, Samuel 2, 145–7, 216:
    Waiting for Godot 6, 128
Benjamin, Walter 45
Bentham, Frederick 89–94, 230
Berliner Ensemble 93, 98, 148,
    149, 151, 153–4, 215
Betti, Ugo 129
Beyond the Fringe 168
body 29–30, 81
Boland, Bridget 62: *Cockpit* **132**,
    131–5
Bolt, Robert 119
Brecht, Bertolt 98, 111, 145,
    148–151, 232
Bristol Old Vic 44, 66
British Empire 13, 60, 130–1,
    135–142
British Theatre Conference 57–9
Britten, Benjamin 72, 162, 163
Brook, Peter 86, 87, 113, 128, 149

260